Double Your Money Every Three Years

Double Your Money Every Three Years

by Gerald Appel

Windsor Books, Brightwaters, N.Y.

Published by Windsor Books
P.O. Box 280
Brightwaters, N.Y. 11718

Manufactured in the United States of America

To Judy, Marvin and Marion
without whom no investment would really be worthwhile.

Contents

Introduction

This book is about how to make your money grow. And I do mean grow—not by five or six per cent a year—but by fifteen, twenty-five, up to thirty-five per cent. Enough to, perhaps, make you a millionaire while you're still young enough to pilot your own yacht. We'll get to the numbers in Chapter 2. What you have to consider at this point is your own attitude.

I'm frequently approached by acquaintances for investment ideas. Usually, I suggest something fairly conservative—deeply discounted convertible bonds, municipals, Treasury bills. None of these forms of investment are difficult to comprehend. Each will yield, over a lifetime, many thousands of dollars more than a savings account, and at virtually no greater risk. The response? Generally that the subject is too complicated, that the investor has no time to study the matter—don't I have a stock to double by next week? These are the same people who suffer decimation in the stock market, year in and year out, and for the same reasons—greed and a refusal to do their homework.

Habit, greed and fear are the bogeymen of investment success. What do I mean by habit? I mean placing your money in the stock market year after year, good market and bad, as though nothing else existed in the world. I mean heavy doses of the wrong kind of life insurance far beyond your needs. I mean savings accounts, filled like an overstuffed refrigerator, money kept lying idle for the event of the famine that never comes. I mean not learning, risking or investing–even when the odds are clearly in your favor.

Greed? That's impatience–looking for an immediate killing and assuming risks out of all proportion in order to hit the jackpot overnight. Money growing at 25% per year doubles in about three years. Is that too long to wait? Greed is not taking profits when it's time and refusing ever to take a loss.

And fear? That certainly goes without saying. Fear of loss or of new ideas. Fear of appearing ridiculous when you ask a broker some questions. Of your wife (or husband as the case may be). Of making a mistake. Of daring to join the select few that seize opportunity by the throat and squeeze profit out of it. Please put these fears aside. It's a lot better to have money than not to have it. Becoming rich through honest investment is no crime; if you feel guilty, donate a good piece of your winnings to your favorite charity or something. To be rich or not to be rich? It may really be your choice.

Investment success depends upon planning, systematic investment, setting realistic goals and sufficient study so that you become familiar with areas of investment that suit your particular needs and objectives. Willing to risk more to make more? Fine. There are opportunities galore–if you are willing to take the risk or if you are willing to put in some extra work. Satisfied just to beat the inflation game? Safety's your thing? There's plenty here for you too, sophisticated investment ploys that beat the bankbook by a mile.

In these pages you will learn:

How leverage can multiply the power of your money tenfold.
How convertible bonds can be used to play the stock market to bring an extra return with greater safety.
Which mutual funds really pay off.
How to clean up on precious metals.
How to pick up extra interest at your savings bank.
How fortunes can be made by you in real estate.
How to become a profitable lender.
What antiques are the current sleepers.
Dozens of ways to save on income taxes.
How to derive 25% income from reputable bonds.
How to multiply the cash value of your life insurance through a simple technique.
What is the most common investment error of them all.
How your daily newspaper can show you when it's time to move into an investment.
Which popular investments should now be avoided like the plague.

And, of course, much, much more.

The principles and basis of each investment are described. Potential returns, risks, liquidity and tax considerations are all evaluated and references are cited for those who wish to pursue their own investigations further.

Your end? I said it before and I'll say it again. Do your homework, investigate, study, ask questions–and when you feel ready, take the plunge.

You'll be glad you did.

Chapter 1

Frankly, It's A Matter Of Survival

Let's face it. The dollar's been going to the dogs. As if that's news. You've seen it yourself, I'm sure, much to both our regrets. One formal and one de facto devaluation, high prices almost daily—not simply for foreign exotica (now oil) alone but for the daily staples of living—gasoline, automobiles, food, almost anything you can name. Salaries have continued to rise—maybe if you're lucky you're coming out even—who knows, maybe even a little ahead.* But what about your retirement, your savings, your life insurance?

---

*Vis-a-vis salaries—*The Wall Street Journal* headlined on October 16, 1973, "Taking Home Less—Paycheck Buying Power Shrinks as Inflation Outruns Gain in Wages." The article went on to note that although the average paycheck had risen by $6.30 between October 1972 and August 1973, the actual purchasing power of a typical wage earner had declined by $3.15.

I do hate to be the purveyor of doom, but facts are facts. Your life insurance is buying you far less protection than you think. And the savings account? Well, if you're putting money aside for a rainy day, perhaps you'd better look again for holes in the umbrella.

THE SHRINKING POWER OF THE DOLLAR

I said it two paragraphs ago and I'll say it again. The dollar is going to the dogs. Measured in true purchasing power, the dollar at the end of 1972 was worth only 56.7¢ compared to the 1950 dollar and only 42¢ compared to the January 1945 dollar. I need not say that 1973 has made matters decidedly worse. In the five years from 1967-1972 alone, the dollar lost 21.4 percent in purchasing power. 1973 may add another 7 or 8 per cent. Nor does it appear that things will get any better. The dollar was under repeated attack throughout the early part of 1973, before firming on the international money markets in the latter half of the year. Faced with the prospect of a serious recession, the Federal Reserve Board may have to ease credit once again, further fueling the inflationary fires. Currencies throughout the world, unbacked increasingly by gold, are weakening. Prices are rising almost before our very eyes. There is no indication either that prices, with the possible exception of food, once up, will ever retreat. Nor can we count even on a decline in the price of food. For instance, *The Wall Street Journal* again, this time on August 6, 1973: "Export Rise Threatens to Empty Farm Bins, Push Food Even Higher. We're on the Verge of Panic . . . ."

Figures 1 and 2 show the sad story. Is relief in sight? As I said before, hardly. The rate of inflation overseas has been, if anything, worse than ours. Japanese labor costs are skyrocketing. Italy has been continuously in the throes of labor unrest. Hong Kong apartment rental rates are soaring. India still produces inexpensive goods—so do Taiwan and Korea—but worldwide sources of cheap labor are diminishing rapidly to the point where our labor is becoming relatively inexpensive on the world market. Couple the international labor shortage to the effects of devaluation and we end up with the result that Americans can no longer count upon the availability of inexpensive foreign goods to help our own cost of living. Example: The same Toyota Mark II sedan that went for $2,400 in 1969 had risen in price by early 1972 to $3,100, a 29% increase in less than three years. Not to mention what the Arabs plan to do with the prices of gasoline for that car. And by the way, have you traveled abroad recently? The American dollar is worth 30% less overseas nowadays. Traveling through Europe cost my family $100 per day in 1973. Three years ago, we took the same trip for $60 per day.

Just in case you have been planning to retire to a European chalet, here are recent inflation rates around the world.

Belgium	5.3%	Holland	7.5%	Ireland	18.2%
Austria	6.0	Mexico	16.0	Greece	11.0
W. Germany	7.2	Britain	9.0	Finland	10.7
France	6.7	Italy	12.7	Spain	10.0
Switzerland	10.9	Japan	16.4		

Cost of Living

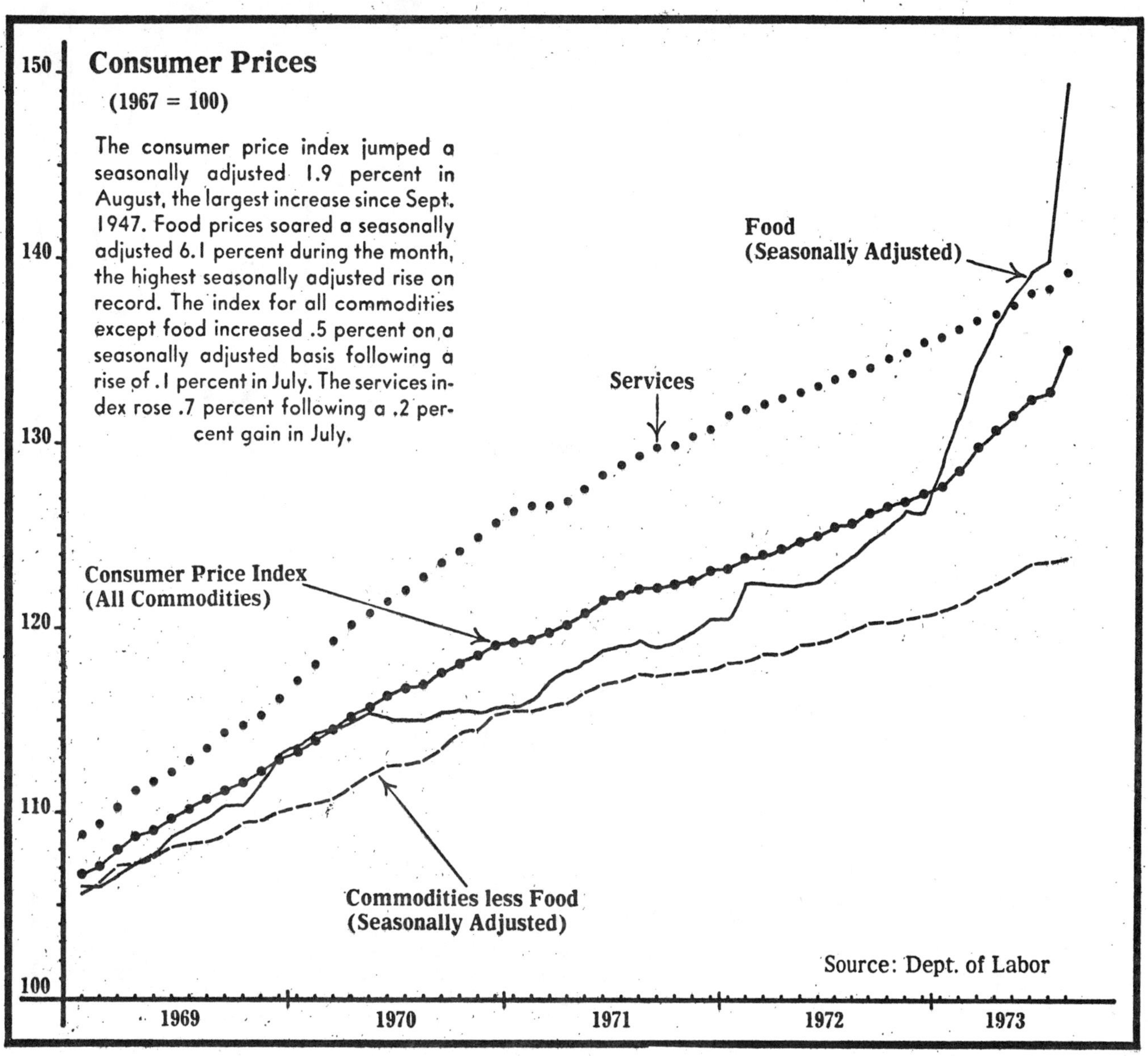

FIGURE 1
COST OF LIVING

Source: Media-General Financial Weekly, 113 N. Third St., Richmond, VA 23261

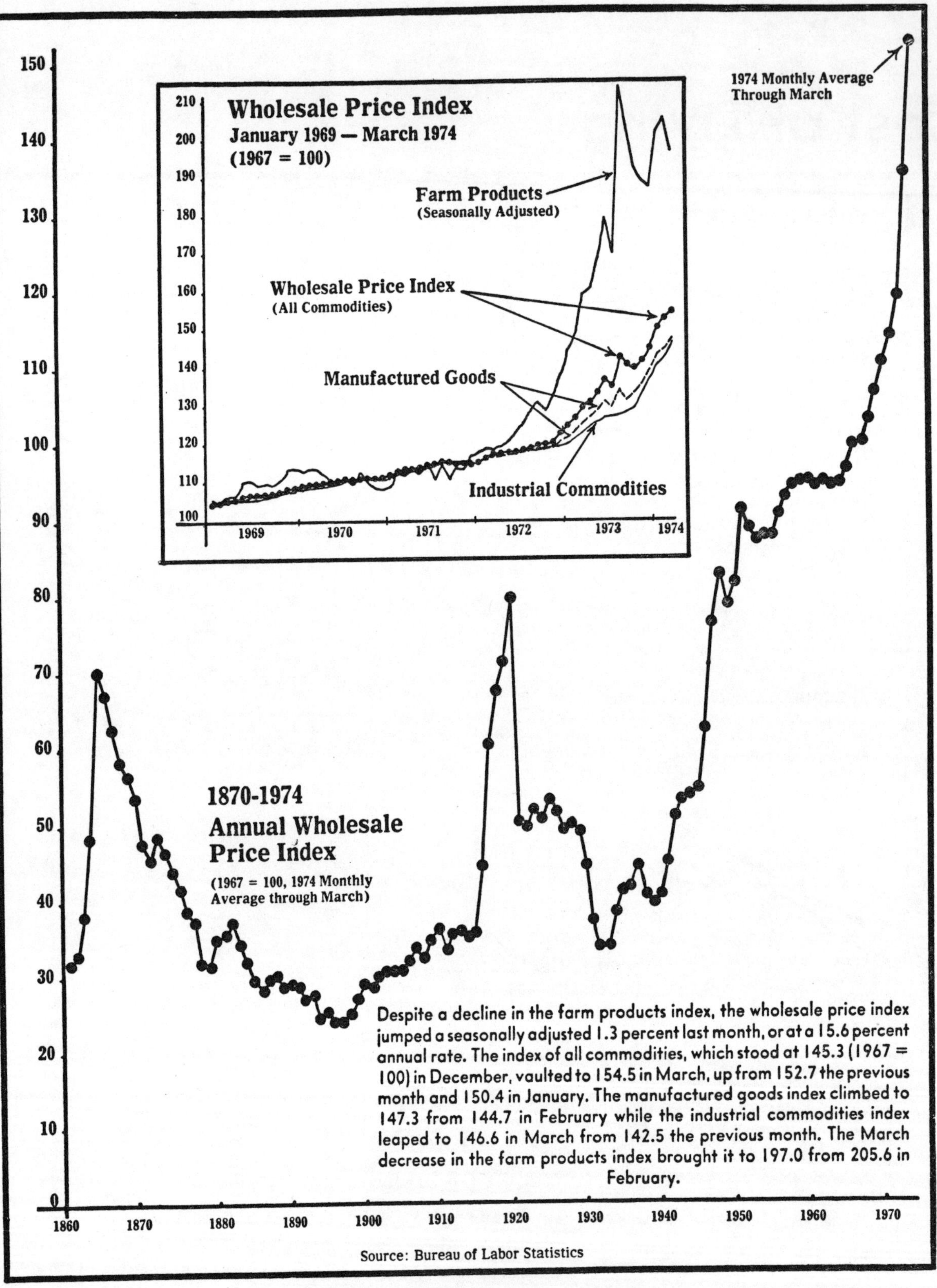

FIGURE 2: WHOLESALE PRICE INDEX

Source: Media-General Financial Weekly, 113 N. Third St., Richmond, VA 23261

During the week that this was written, two news items came across my desk. One pointed out that the rate of inflation in Japan the previous month had risen to over 27% on an annualized basis. The other was an announcement that West Germany was imposing a 10% tax surcharge on individuals and corporations to ease inflation, now up to a 7.5% annual rate, the highest since World War II. (*Wall Street Journal,* May 11, 1973). By the end of 1973, the inflation rate throughout the free world was approaching 10%.

Inflation as a way of life has been more common throughout the world in the past than in the United States. Wage earners usually seem to come through all right—usually—so long as wages keep apace with inflation. However, the savings and retirement funds that individuals accumulate over a lifetime become decimated.

More doom and gloom? How about the energy crisis—the shrinkage of our national petroleum, natural gas and coal supplies and the world's growing dependence upon the petroleum producing nations of the Middle East, whose own reserves do have limit. It has become a seller's market for oil, and prices for crude quadrupled in 1973. Experts are now predicting prices for gasoline of $1 per gallon and up within the next year or so, certainly by 1980, and a doubling of the costs of electricity. Add now to any product you purchase, potential increases based upon added production and delivery costs resulting from these factors. Not to mention shortages of other natural resources, silver and copper to name two. And by the way, have you seen what's happened to the price of paper lately? Is inflation here to stay? What do you think?*

Savings accounts are no real help either. Let's presume that the *true* rate of inflation in the United States stabilizes at five per cent (wishful thinking). I say true rate because, frankly, I doubt that official government statistics reflect what's really taking place. You know yourself what has been happening to your daily out of pocket costs for subway tokens, haircuts, cigarettes, movies and even the old nickel pack of gum. The U.S. Bureau of Labor Statistics can release all the soothing pap they want. You and I know better.**

Presuming, in any case, a five per cent rate of inflation, you might suppose that at five or six per cent interest, you're at least breaking even over the years on your bankbook.

But are you? What about the income taxes on that interest? Suppose you put $10,000 in

---

*If you think that I am pessimistic, you should see what the real prophets of doom are forecasting. I refer you to *America's Coming Bankruptcy* by Harvey W. Peters (Arlington House, 1973), *How You Can Profit From the Coming Devaluation* by Harry Browne (Arlington House, 1970—and he turned out to be right) and *Panics and Crashes And How You Can Make Money Out Of Them* by Harry Schultz (Arlington House, 1972). Also, we might note recent statements by Dr. Franz Pick who predicts an inflation rate of 20% in the United States within two years. Compared to these fellows, I'm a positive optimist when it comes to doomsday predictions.

**Similar thoughts have been expressed in *Barron's* ("Statistics Don't Lie" by Raymond F. DeVoe Jr., July 5, 1971) and in *New York Magazine* ("You're Right. The Inflation Is Worse Than They're Telling You." by Stanley H. Brown, May 14, 1973). Both articles cite the rise in the cost of items not included in Bureau of Labor Statistics compilations. For example, The *Barron's* article mentions increases in the cost of the *New York Times* (+50%), chewing gum (+60%), a slice of pizza (+40%) and a shoe shine (+100%). *New York Magazine* bemoans olive oil (+49% in one year), paprika (+40%) and fur coats (+100%). In the same vein, Sylvia Porter (*New York Post,* May 16, 1973) notes that the cost of dictating, writing and sending an average business letter has risen from $1.17 in 1953 to $3.31 twenty years later. These increases belie the "official" rate of inflation in the Northeastern United States of 36.5% since 1967 and 4.9% for the twelve months ending April 1973. (By early 1974 inflation in the United States was *officially* running into two digit numbers.)

a savings bank at six per cent interest, compounded annually. Interest return the first year, $600. If you're in the 32% tax bracket, $20-24,000 taxable income, your federal taxes *alone* on that interest amount to $192. Net interest then, after taxes, drops to $408. On the other hand, the true purchasing power of your original $10,000 will decline during that year by $500 (5% x $10,000). Net loss of purchasing power: $92 the first year alone.

The quagmire becomes even deeper the more we pursue the matter. Over the years, the total amount of your savings and interest will rise, even as its true purchasing power declines. If this results in your entering a higher income tax bracket, the federal government will take an even larger slice of your interest payments, leaving you with an even greater true loss. This applies to federal taxes only, now. It will be even more calamitous if you live in a state which levies a state income tax. I live in New York State. In addition to the federal tax of 32%, state residents would be clipped for an additional 8%, for a total tax on their bank interest of $240 and a resultant loss in true purchasing power, during the first year alone, of $140.

TABLE I

HOW SAVINGS BANKS COST YOU MONEY

(Presuming a taxpayer in the 32% federal income tax bracket, starting with $10,000, compounding his money at 6% annually, and a true inflation rate of 5%.)

End of Year	$10,000 becomes (after taxes on interest are deducted annually)	True Value of $10,000 at 5% Rate of Inflation
1.	$10,408.00	$9,500.00
2.	10,832.65	9,025.00
3.	11,274.62	8,573.75
4.	11,734.62	8,145.06
5.	12,213.39	7,737.81
6.	12,712.00	7,350.92
7.	13,230.65	6,983.37
8.	13,770.46	6,634.20
9	14,332.29	6,302.49
10.	14,917.05	5,987.37
11.	15,525.66	5,688.00
12.	16,159.11	5,403.60
13.	16,818.40	5,133.42
14.	17,504.59	4,876.75
15.	18,218.78	4,632.91
16.	18,962.11	4,401.27
17.	19,735.76	4,181.20
18.	20,540.98	3,972.14
19.	21,379.05	3,773.53
20.	22,251.31	3,584.86

The $10,000 has multiplied to $22,251.31 after income taxes on the interest have been deducted. However, the purchasing power of $10,000 has shrunk over the 20 year period to $3,584.86 or to approximately 36% of its original value. Based upon its original purchasing power, the $10,000 that you started with and have compounded up to $22,251.31 is now worth, actually, only $7,977.09, a loss over the 20 years of more than 20% insofar as *real* money is concerned! If you are in a higher tax bracket, the loss will be that much greater.

HOW MUCH SHOULD YOU KEEP IN SAVINGS ACCOUNTS?

I personally believe that many people squirrel their money away much too assiduously into savings accounts. Money should be set aside, of course, for vacations, household furnishings, down payments and such. But how much? Every surplus dollar? I think not. Many investments provide sufficiently limited downside risk and liquidity so that you can get to your money if need be—or use the investment as collateral for short term loans if you do have to raise some ready cash. It is true, of course, that you are not taking a gamble when you put your money into the savings bank. You are simply giving it away, drop by drop. Please understand. I am not recommending that you put money earmarked for special purposes anyplace but into the savings account. In other words, if you will be needing the cash within a few months for a down payment on a house, do not put it into the stock market, hoping for a quick killing. Such a move has to adversely affect your judgment and time runs against you on such transactions. But why keep big money in the bank towards retirement when there are investment vehicles available that provide a much greater return on your money with virtually as much security? We'll get to these later on; in the meantime, keep in mind that the government and inflation are hungry for your money, and that those "safe" savings accounts just serve it up to them on a silver platter.

I personally keep almost all my surplus capital working for me—distributed among bonds, stocks, real estate and a few other items that catch my interest from time to time. You, yourself, might feel more secure with a greater percentage of ready cash in plain sight, in a bankbook. If that suits you, it really will not hurt too much. But again, do not overdo it. Nobody ever became rich on 6% interest, free toasters notwithstanding.

INTRODUCING THE RATING SYSTEM

Just a brief digression here. The investments in this book are rated as to potential return, risk, liquidity and possible tax advantages. A is, of course, the highest rating; D the lowest.
Liquidity: The ease and rapidity with which an investor can dispose of his investment at fair, current market value for cash in hand. Pure cash is obviously the most liquid form of investment and merits an A or A+. Most listed stocks or bonds rate at least an A or A- since you can almost always sell at a reasonable market price, money in hand within a week. Real estate is obviously less liquid.

Potential Return: With six per cent in hand in the bank (8% now for longer term accounts), any investment has to do better to be worth the bother, and I will be recommending only those investments which do provide a good potential for outperforming the bank account. The amount of potential performance, based upon reasonable expectation, is what determines the rating. For example, it is possible for a stock to triple in a year, bringing in a 300% return (obviously an A). Still, the most astute market investors find 15-25% a more reasonable goal (still an A). Mutual funds have achieved returns closer to 9% on average (a B- or C+). Cash in the bank is D. The only form of investment with lower potential is cash in the mattress.
Risk: Precisely what it implies. Cash in the bank receives an A simply because you know what you are getting. If you take inflationary loss factors into account, however, you would have to rate it a D (sure loser). Triple A corporates and municipal bonds rate an A. Commodity speculation rates a D.
Tax Considerations: The extent to which an investment receives favorable tax treatment. Ordinary bank interest rates a D. Every penny has to be reported and is taxed at ordinary rates. Municipal bonds make A. Their interest is tax exempt.

The rating system shows you at a glance the type of investment under consideration. You, yourself, have to weigh the relative importance of the ratings in view of your own investment objectives and propensity to assume risk in exchange for potential reward.

For cash in savings accounts, the ratings then, are as follows:

Liquidity	A+
Risk	A
Tax Considerations	D
Return	D

THE GREAT INSURANCE HOAX

Whole life and endowment insurance are the great American rip-offs. Your friendly agent may pander "living benefits", "cash values", "how you get more out than you put in" but is unlikely to make much of a point about how the actual rate of appreciation of the cash value of the policy, the amount over and above what you would pay, say, for term insurance, amounts to less than 5%. Nor is he too likely to mention that, if you die and the beneficiary collects the face value of the policy, the cash value disappears. So for each year that you accumulate cash value (out of your premium dollars) your actual insurance over and above that cash value declines. Of course, you can add riders to increase the face value of your policy by the amount that the cash value increases, but that does involve extra premiums.

There is, no doubt, a place in family portfolios for whole life insurance (I myself carry such a policy) and in Chapter 2 we'll see how you can multiply the cash values therein considerably, at little risk. Some families prefer to have a regular system of savings forced upon them, and fixed rather than escalating premiums, which renewable term insurance does entail. (You can purchase level premium term insurance, however). Various pension and retirement plans are adapted particularly for insurance, and straight life, once established, does guarantee your continued insurability.

But can you really plan to retire on your endowment policy or the accumulated cash values of your straight life? Well, before you put your payment down on that Florida homestead, you might review Table II. This presumes, in Column A, a $25,000 cash value accruing in the policy and, in Column B, an endowment of $500 per month. What will these really be worth in the future based upon our hypothetical 5 per cent rate of inflation?

TABLE II

True Values of Cash Values and Endowments Based Upon a 5% Inflation Rate

End of Year	Column A True Purchasing Power of $25,000	Column B True Purchasing Power of a $500 Monthly Endowment
1.	$23,750.00	$475.00
2.	22,562.50	451.25
3.	21,434.38	428.69
4.	20,362.66	407.25
5.	19,344.52	386.89
6.	18,377.30	367.55
7.	17,458.43	349.17
8.	16,585.51	331.71
9.	15,756.23	315.12
10.	14,968.42	299.37
11.	14,220.00	284.40
12.	13,509.00	270.18
13.	12,833.55	256.67
14.	12,191.87	243.84
15.	11,582.28	231.65
16.	11,003.17	220.06
17.	10,453.01	209.06
18.	9,930.36	198.61
19.	9,433.84	188.68
20.	8,962.15	179.24
21.	8,514.04	170.28
22.	8,088.34	161.77
23.	7,683.92	153.68
24.	7,299.73	145.99
25.	6,934.74	138.69

There it is. You plan to retire on $500 per month and pay for that privilege with today's good dollars. Did you know that in terms of today's purchasing power, you will end up with less than $139 per month? Try that on your insurance agent for size. That $25,000 you were looking forward to? In real money, down to under $7,000. All the time, your friendly insurance company has been doing with your money what you should have been doing yourself over the years–investing for a halfway human return.

Don't kid yourself either that you'll live more cheaply once retired. We can concede that in many ways older couples spend less than younger–unfortunately usually not out of choice. Older couples do need less room in which to live, but conveniences of living loom all the larger when walk-ups become real trouble and when shopping simply must lie nearby. Then too, it is one thing for a pair of nineteen year olds to travel the youth hostel route. It is quite another thing later on in life. Medical bills assume an increasingly large role within the budget as life passes on, and medical costs have risen by 200%–that's right, 200%–since 1960. Even food, once a low inflation item, has joined the inflationary parade, and with a vengeance. And food is, I hardly need remind you, a necessity, not a luxury.

NEEDED: ALTERNATIVES TO THE STOCK MARKET

Remember the good old days when you could pick out a growth company, put it away and just let it grow? There are still some around, no doubt. McDonald's–before the energy crisis made everyone wonder how the motorists will reach the hamburger stands. Coca-Cola. Some drug companies. However, the public has been becoming increasingly disillusioned with the stock market. Commissions have been rising. The Dow stands below levels recorded 8 years ago. Yes, there are ways to beat the market, and I will be discussing some further along. However, bear moves have become increasingly violent, trading more difficult; the great 1945-1968 joyride appears to be over. The Dow made a new high during early 1973 while the majority of securities languished well below 1968 peaks. The latter part of the year was pure disaster. Is there a place for investment in common shares? Certainly, but do consider alternative forms of investment as well. You just cannot count on the stock market as an exclusive any longer. Top grade utilities, the group of stocks most accumulated for long term peace of mind, are a case in point. Most utility shares have been in the doldrums since 1964 or 1965. Their yields have remained firm; many have even risen. That's O.K. if current income is your thing–but most investors in utility stocks over the last eight or nine years have lost about as much via capital depreciation as they have picked up in dividends, and that is not even considering the effects of inflation over the past years. American Telephone, for example, sold for nearly $70 per share in 1964. It now sells for more than 30% less–nine years later. Counting the decline in the purchasing power of his money since 1964, an investor in Telephone would have lost 56% of the capital he started with.

THE SAD FACTS

That's it. Inflation has come to stay and the bank account, stock market and insurance policy alone cannot protect you from its ravages. Unless you are careful, you may find a life's financial preparation going down the inflationary drain. That's the bad news. Now for the good news. There are things that you can do about it—you can learn to diversify, to take advantage of investment opportunities as they develop—and perhaps even to become filthy rich as you go along. Even if you do not aim that high, or don't give a damn about making really big money, you really ought to familiarize yourself with some of the investment tactics within these pages.

Frankly, it's a matter of survival.

TAX TIP

Savings deposits can be a whole new ball game under the Keogh Tax Plan, a government sanctioned plan by which self-employed individuals or individuals working for certain non-profit organizations can set aside tax sheltered money for retirement. Although the plan is usually associated with professional persons, others can take advantage of its provisions also. If you are partly salaried and partly self-employed you can set aside a portion of your self-employed income in Keogh. This may be very suitable for free lance artists, writers, barbers, actors and so forth.

At the time of this writing, qualified taxpayers can set aside 10% of their self-employed income to a maximum of \$2,500. The administration is proposing an increase in this maximum to \$7,500 or 15% of income. You are taxed neither on that portion of your income diverted to these plans nor on income received by this tax sheltered money so long as it remains in the plan. Thus, for the man in the fifty percent tax bracket, the piddling six percent, taxable savings bank interest becomes, tax free, equivalent to 12%, since he has \$2,500 working for him (pre-tax dollars) rather than \$1,250 (post-tax dollars). Inasmuch as the interest received is likewise not taxed, the lowly bankbook more than matches the inflationary spiral. Income from the retirement fund so established is taxed in the years that it is drawn out by you, but presumably you are by then in a lower tax bracket. In the meantime, your money has been compounding tax-free.

Many savings banks have Keogh Plans available, contracts pre-prepared and government approved. If you believe that you may qualify, do make inquiry of your bank, tax lawyer or accountant.

SAVINGS BANKS UNDER THE KEOGH PLAN

Potential Reward	A- to B+	12% compounded, tax free is not bad. Actual real rate depends upon your tax bracket.
Risk	A	
Liquidity	D	Money may be withdrawn only with tax penalty.
Tax Considerations	A+	Without the tax shelter, forget it.

Incidentally, many insurance programs and mutual funds offer government approved Keogh

Plans for systematic retirement investment. Some brokerage houses also offer flexible Keogh investment plans in which a bank acts as trustee which allows you to invest in and even trade securities and other investments under Keogh. All the proceeds stay in the plan until retirement, and profits are not taxed until they are withdrawn. Merrill-Lynch, for one, has offered such a program at reasonable cost.

Chapter 2

A Little Positive Thinking Can Go A Long Way

Well, as I've been saying, the choice is up to you. You can lie down and roll over while inflation steals your life savings and robs you of your security, or you can move assertively, in fact taking advantage of those same forces that are creating chaos all around you. Plenty of opportunities exist for profitable investment and speculation, and there *are* vehicles available for profit to suit almost everyone. At your end, you need only to make up your mind to set your goals and to act accordingly.

The difference between passively hoping for the best and taking some sort of affirmative action can amount to thousands, even millions of dollars over the length of a decade—far more over the length of a lifetime. Did you know that if you can secure as little as a 7½ percent return on your money instead of 5 percent, for a period of twenty years, the difference over that period to you for each $10,000 you started with amounts to $15,946? All that's involved is moving your money from a savings bank to Triple A prime corporate bonds. The risk is virtually nil. If you can secure a 25 percent return (our goal in this book), you end up with a difference of $840,828! Risks? Obviously greater, but not so great as you might think.

Table I shows the amounts to which $10,000 will appreciate at differing annually compounded rates. Study the figures. The differences between passive hope and affirmative action practically hit you between the eyes. As I said before, it's up to you. Do you settle for the twenty-six grand? Or will you shoot for the million dollar column?

To secure the value of these amounts in term's of today's purchasing power, multiply the amounts your money will reach by the inflation factor on the right, e.g., at the end of the year 18, a 5% return, compounded, will bring your initial $10,000 to $24,066. If we multiply the $24,066 by .40 (the inflation factor), we see that your money will be worth, in terms of today's purchasing power, only $9,626.40.

SETTING YOUR GOALS

It's easy to want to be rich. It is harder to carefully think through, investigate, study and implement an investment program that suits your needs and is realistic in terms of your own financial position, and economic developments in general. This book offers plenty in the way of suggestion. You have, no doubt, heard of others. Take action at the appropriate time, but to quote Merrill-Lynch, do "investigate before you invest." Do investigate. And do invest.

How much to shoot for? I leave that to you.

SELECTING YOUR INVESTMENTS

Which investment vehicles should *you* choose? That depends upon a number of factors including your personal interests, temperament, the amount of money available to you when you initiate your program, age, time available to work at your investment and need for current as opposed to deferred income. Future earnings power has to be taken into account, and the whole program must be spiked with common sense.

PERSONAL INTERESTS

Preferably, your investments and personal interests should coincide. I know someone who is under the impression that a corporate bond is a unique form of glue and who suspects that General Motors is the only listed stock. Still, he is an avid stamp collector and has successfully invested over the years in collector postage stamps. The point is this. If you have some natural interest in the subject, your chances for successful investment are that much greater. You will maintain interest in significant current developments, the time you spend on your

TABLE I

The Amount That $10,000 Will Reach If Compounded Annually At The Given Rates (Rounded To Nearest Dollar, Taxes Not Included)

End of Year	5%	7½%	10%	12½%	15%	17½%	20%	22½%	25%	30%	Inflation Factor*
1	$10,500	$10,750	$11,000	$11,250	$11,500	$11,750	$12,000	$12,250	$12,500	$13,000	.95
2	11,025	11,556	12,100	12,656	13,225	13,806	14,400	15,006	15,625	16,900	.90
3	11,576	12,423	13,310	14,238	15,209	16,222	17,280	18,383	19,531	21,970	.86
4	12,155	13,355	14,641	16,018	17,490	19,061	20,736	22,519	24,414	28,561	.81
5	12,763	14,356	16,105	18,020	20,114	22,397	24,883	27,585	30,518	37,129	.77
6	13,400	15,433	17,716	20,273	23,131	26,316	29,860	33,792	38,147	48,268	.74
7	14,071	16,590	19,487	22,807	26,600	30,922	35,832	41,395	47,684	62,749	.70
8	14,775	17,835	21,436	25,658	30,590	36,333	42,998	50,709	59,605	81,574	.66
9	15,513	19,172	23,579	28,865	35,179	42,691	51,598	62,119	74,506	106,046	.63
10	16,289	20,610	25,937	32,473	40,456	50,162	61,917	76,096	93,132	137,860	.60
11	17,103	22,156	28,531	36,532	46,524	58,941	74,301	93,217	116,415	179,217	.57
12	17,959	23,818	31,384	41,099	53,502	69,256	89,161	114,190	145,519	232,983	.54
13	18,856	25,604	34,523	46,236	61,528	81,375	106,993	139,884	181,899	302,877	.51
14	19,799	27,524	37,975	52,016	70,757	95,616	128,392	171,358	227,374	393,741	.49
15	20,789	29,589	41,772	58,518	81,371	112,349	154,070	209,913	284,217	511,863	.46
16	21,829	31,808	45,950	65,833	93,576	132,010	184,884	257,144	355,271	665,422	.44
17	22,920	34,194	50,545	74,062	107,613	155,111	221,861	315,001	444,089	865,048	.42
18	24,066	36,758	55,599	83,319	123,755	182,256	266,233	385,877	555,111	1,124,563	.40
19	25,270	39,515	61,159	93,734	142,318	214,151	319,480	472,699	693,888	1,461,931	.38
20	26,533	42,479	67,275	105,451	163,665	251,627	383,376	579,056	867,361	1,900,511	.36

* Multiply by this factor to convert to today's purchasing power, assuming 5% inflation rate.

investments will not feel so onerous, and you will be able to fuse profit with intellectual play. Another example: someone who enjoys home repair may be a natural as an investor in small apartment houses. Doing his own repairs will save him considerable money and increase the returns on his investment. This principle is even more apt in antique and art investment.

TEMPERAMENT

Do you enjoy tracking your investments, worrying about them, making frequent decisions? Can you emotionally accept risk and occasional losses with an eye to the overall profit-loss picture? If the answer is yes, then the stock market may be for you. However, if ups and downs give you ulcers, consider bonds or some form of high yield note, concentrating on top quality. The returns may be less, but your diet will be more fun.

Your own temperament, as well as your financial position, should be taken into account in choosing investments. Many persons consider conservative investing a total bore and lose complete interest if there is no risk factor involved. These people are plungers—middle class gamblers graduated from Aqueduct. Sometimes they make it big, sometimes not at all. Other individuals simply cannot tolerate risk. Every fluctuation in their assets creates an emotional crisis. Again, such personalities should remain conservatively oriented.

Some investors prefer to captain their own ships, as it were. They insist upon making their own decisions and on no account will hand over to anyone else their investment fortunes. Others prefer not to be bothered at all. The former will purchase his own apartment house; the latter will join a realty syndicate.

TIME AVAILABLE

Some investments require more of the investor's time than others. Again, active stock market trading requires several hours per week. Dollar cost averaging in mutual funds requires less. Real estate can be time consuming if you operate your own deals. Scotch investment takes virtually no time.

Consider the time you have available and the value to you of that time. If you are a semi or full retiree, time may be a plentiful commodity. If, however, you are a busy physician, working 60 hours per week, time is both scarce and valuable. Every minute spent on investments could be profitably allocated to your own profession. Should you enjoy a change of pace, fine. But it may prove more economical to secure an investment advisor or a realty manager and to apply your own time to an area which produces consistent income for you.

Rule: Don't move into an area which requires more time than you can devote.

AGE

By and large, older persons should concentrate on investments which provide the maximum in *current* income and the minimum in risk. There is no point in speculating for your heirs, who will not be appreciative if you blow their inheritance in any case. Elderly persons do require current income to live on and since there is rarely a way in later life to re-establish ruined financial positions, they should concentrate on high quality, high yield investments such as Triple A corporate bonds, municipals, commercial paper, treasury notes, and high yield utilities. Option selling can be worthwhile too.

Younger people have the time to aim for longer term capital growth, to take risks and, in general, to subsume current income for the sake of the future. Use your judgment. There is a time to be conservative and a time to be more bold.

FUTURE EARNINGS POWER

Related to age are future earnings power and projected income needs. At what point will you need payoffs from current investments? When will you need to liquidate holdings? Is the investment meant for retirement, for college expenses or for vacationing? Will the income derived from investing be used to supplement other earnings at times or do you expect to consistently be able to add to your investments, while living off other sources of income?

Try to plan ahead. My own realty investments are timed to provide maximal returns during my children's college days. Although I may not have to draw upon the investment income at that time, those funds are mentally earmarked for educational purposes. If your future earnings promise to increase, you can probably afford to risk more and to enter more speculative investment areas. You may also be in a position to use leverage more actively. *Never risk more than you can afford to lose.*

DIVERSIFY BUT DON'T OVER-DIVERSIFY

From the mid 1940's to 1968, the bulk of American investors knew only one way. Buy into the stock market and wait. Sooner or later, everything will work out. This strategy did, indeed, prove successful for most—during the great bull market. Since 1968, nearly one million disillusioned investors have left the stock market, but many of them are unfamiliar with alternative forms of investment and do not know where to go.

MORAL

Don't put all your eggs in one basket. On the other hand, diversification can be carried too far. Invest only in as many areas as you can comfortably become proficient. Two or three major arenas should suffice, with some diversification within each. As fas as the stock market goes, much of my personal trading is concentrated into twenty odd convertible situations which I track closely. My realty operations are diversified geographically. You may prefer art, antiques or municipals as alternatives to the stock market. Leave yourself room for changing fashions and trends, but do not spread yourself so thin that you remain diletante investor, with fingers in simply too many pies.

THE SINGLE MOST IMPORTANT INVESTMENT STRATEGY

The January 1, 1973 issue of *Barron's Financial Weekly* carried the article, "Not A Bear Among Them", a compendium of high level market analysts unanimously predicting a market rise. The next week, the publication featured "1200 on the Dow", a bullish article in a similar vein. By May, the Dow Jones Industrial Averages had dropped nearly 200 points.

The rule is simple. Take investment positions only before the public has caught on and sell when your investment has achieved wide public popularity. The public, the media and your elevator operator are always the most bullish at market tops, and most bearish at bottoms. The time to buy stock is when the *New York Times* prints stories about 1929, mounting margin calls and an imminent depression. The time to sell is when the *Wall Street Journal* features articles pointing to Dow 1500, record auto sales and the best performing mutual funds. *Operate on contrary opinion,* against the vast majority vote.

This rule pertains to investments other than securities too. The big boom in low quality art took place in the late 1960's. At that time, every local art auction was billed as an art investment seminar, and young couples thoughout the country thought they were hanging IBM on their walls. Since then, low grade art prices have fallen, sometimes drastically. Co-ops in New York City were big news until 1969, when prices peaked. Now, you can hardly give them away. In recent years, fads have included stocks, mutual funds, art, gold, silver, palladium (a real bust when trading opened) and raw land. Some have continued to grow. Others have already fallen by the wayside. Even prime investments have their ups and downs. Try to take positions when investments are not in public view, and positively avoid competitive bidding with a speculative public market.

CURRENT INVESTMENTS IN AND OUT OF THE NEWS

The following investments are currently out of favor: stocks, mutual funds, old masters in art, Scotch whickey. *In favor:* wine (probably overplayed by now), bonds, land, antiques, coins, chinese art, gold, currency speculation, commodities. Income property never seems to attract much public attention one way or the other. To repeat: stay away from the crowd unless you're first or nearly first on line–take your profits when the public begins to crowd in on you. Remember, in the 17th century otherwise intelligent Dutchmen were mortgaging whole farms in order to buy single tulip bulbs.

HOW LEVERAGE CAN MULTIPLY YOUR FORTUNE

Leverage is one of the most powerful tools at the investor's disposal. It also happens to be a double edged sword. We'll get to that part later. What is it? Leverage is the technique of getting the maximum clout and appreciation potential from the least money. Usually, leverage involves borrowing, and using the combination of your own resources and borrowed money to gain more financial action than could be secured from your own capital alone.

Margin, for example, provides leverage to the stock market investor. Currently, margin requirements have been established at 50 per cent for most listed securities. That means that an investor can purchase securities by putting up, as a down payment, only 50 per cent of the security's value. The differential between your down payment and the total cost is lent to you by your broker, usually at interest of 1 to 1½ per cent above prime rate. How does this add to your profit potential? Let's presume that you have $6500 to invest and you want to put it into a $100 stock which subsequently rises to a selling price of $125 per share. Your $6500, unmargined or unleveraged, would have purchased for you 65 shares ($6500 ÷ $100 per share). These 65 shares would have appreciated to a total of $8125, resulting in a profit of $1625 or 25% of your original investment. Suppose, instead, you had employed leverage, purchasing 130 shares or $13,000 worth on margin. Your down payment is still your $6500, but now you have borrowed $6500 from your broker on the strength of your own ability to put up 50%. The 130 shares, as per the previous example, increase from $100 to $125 or to a total value of $16,250. Net profit, $3,250. This represents a 25% gain still in the price of the securities, but a *50% gain now* on the amount of money with which you actually started. You have profited by borrowing. (Commissions and interest charges not included). When you close out the transaction, you simply repay the broker what you owe him and pocket the extra $1625 profit.

I said leverage was a double edged sword. Suppose the stock fell from $100 to $75 instead of rising? Loss, leveraged, $3250 or 50% of your capital against $1625, or 25% unleveraged. 1929 was caused in part by heavily margined accounts going under and early 1973 brought many calls from brokers to overly-margined customers for extra collateral. Many businesses are highly leveraged; that is, they operate heavily on borrowed funds. When things go well, the returns on the original capital can be excellent. If business falls off! Well, notes and interest charges still have to be met. At those times, leverage is a distinct disadvantage.

Table II shows the effects of leverage on the return of investments. Notice that the higher the leverage employed, the greater are both the risk and potential reward.

We can see that if you are 90% leveraged in an investment, you will double your money if the investment rises by only 10%, but that you will lose 100% of your original outlay if the investment declines by only 10%. And that's exactly what happened in 1929 when stocks could be purchased at 10% margin.

A COMMON SENSE APPROACH TO LEVERAGE

In one popular book relating to investments, the tale is told of a businessman who borrowed money to improve his business. According to the author, the businessman decided to place the borrowed funds into a commodity play instead, ultimately walking off with a huge profit.

TABLE II

Percentage Gains And Losses Of An Investment Leveraged To Various Degrees Based Upon The Profit And Loss If The Investment Were Unleveraged

Percentage Of Your Investment	Leverage Factor	Unleveraged Percentage Change of the Investment -50%	-40%	-30%	-20%	-10%	0	+10%	+20%	+30%	+40%	+50%
100%	0%	-50	-40	-30	-20	-10	0	+10	+20	+30	+40	+50
90	10	-55.6	-44.4	-33.3	-22.2	-11.1	0	+11.1	+22.2	+33.3	+44.4	+55.5
80	20	-62.5	-50.0	-37.5	-25.0	-12.5	0	+12.5	+25.0	+37.5	+50.0	+62.5
70	30	-71.4	-57.1	-42.9	-28.6	-14.3	0	+14.3	+28.6	+42.9	+57.1	+71.4
60	40	-83.3	-66.7	-50.0	-33.3	-16.7	0	+16.7	+33.3	+50.0	+66.7	+83.3
50	50	-100.0	-80.0	-60.0	-40.0	-20.0	0	+20.0	+40.0	+60.0	+80.0	+100.0
40	60	-125.0	-100.0	-75.0	-50.0	-25.0	0	+25.0	+50.0	+75.0	+100.0	+125.0
30	70	-166.7	-133.3	-100.0	-66.7	-33.3	0	+33.3	+66.7	+100.0	+133.3	+166.7
20	80	-250.0	-200.0	-150.0	-100.0	-50.0	0	+50.0	+100.0	+150.0	+200.0	+250.0
10	90	-500.0	-400.0	-300.0	-200.0	-100.0	0	+100.0	+200.0	+300.0	+400.0	+500.0

The author's moral, I think, had to do with using business loans to finance successful gambling operations. I am still a little surprised that the author did not recommend selling the business altogether to put the proceeds into a 500–1 shot at the track. You can really get rich fast that way–if the horse comes in.

The point I want to make is that investors should apply some common sense in applying leverage to investments. I do not recommend wanton speculation. I do recommend that you compute the odds on a leverage play; if they are in your favor, go right ahead and borrow. Credit can sometimes be quite conservative. We'll examine a virtually guaranteed leverage play later in this chapter. In the meantime, I suggest that you consider the following operating rules:

1) Do not borrow if the projected return on your borrowed money is slightly more than your interest charges, unless the risk is absolutely minimal. Example: Do not borrow money at 12-18% to play the stock market, for instance, by opening a revolving credit account in order to secure money to start margin accounts. In effect, this is operating on 100% leverage. Too few people make above 18% annually in the market to justify the work, interest liability, and considerable risk involved.

2) Do not borrow if, financially and temperamentally, you cannot afford the risk.

3) Do borrow to finance safe and well-secured investments, e.g., realty property, high quality bonds, discounted high quality convertible bonds.

4) Consider borrowing if you can put the money into safe, current income-producing plays in which the current income exceeds your interest charges.

5) Borrow only as much as you need for the purpose at hand. Do not over-extend your credit and ability to repay. You may become locked into your investment and have to repay from other sources of income.

6) Keep track of interest charges. These can add up. If you borrow at 12% to finance an investment, and the investment breaks even, you've *lost* 12% (the interest charges). It can take several years to extricate yourself from a debt cycle.

Do stay ready to borrow from any and all sources (at reasonable rates) for solid deals which offer excellent odds for favorable return. Leverage can and should be employed at times. Just so long as you use some common sense and do not get carried away. *Good leverage bets* include income real estate, corporate and municipal bonds, common stocks (only at the right time and only in moderation), option selling, mortgage purchases, raw land (for speculation only) and gold and silver coins. *Poor leverage bets:* common shares (bought at wrong time), mutual funds (unless you're conservative), commodities (unless you are a master trader and then think twice), art, Scotch and wine, low quality bonds. *In any case, borrow only as much as you can readily handle.*

HOW TO USE LEVERAGE TO INCREASE THE CASH VALUE OF YOUR LIFE INSURANCE POLICY BY 24%

As I said before, insurance has been the great American rip-off. Insurance buyers have been receiving, via their policies, investment returns in the area of 3-5%, while John Hancock and the others do with your money what you should be doing yourself, investing for a decent return. Still, there are points in favor of whole life insurance and there is one tactic that you can employ to make something better of your policy.

The key lies in a simple leverage procedure, based upon the fact that most older policies allow you to borrow out the cash value of the policy at 5% interest (in New York State), usually 6% elsewhere. This is true 5 or 6% interest, not the inflated type that really amounts to 9-10%. The loan stipulation makes it feasible to profitably collateralize your policy. Instead of paying your full premium, you pay only the difference between the total premium and the cash value of the policy. The amount of the cash value is borrowed by you from the insurance company as a loan on which you pay annual interest. Since this is such an inexpensive loan, the money is readily invested elsewhere at a higher rate of return. Your profit: the difference between your rate of return on the borrowed money and the interest charges you pay to carry the loan.

During the halycon days of 1967-1968, insurance salesmen were promoting collateralization plans to finance mutual fund purchases. Many investors were badly burnt, since the loan

TABLE III

Twenty-Five Year Results of Collateralizing a Typical $25,000 Whole Life Policy at 5% Interest and Investing the Funds Secured at a 7½% Return

Year	Cash Value	Amount Borrowed	Annual Interest Paid On Loan at 5%	Uncompounded Income At 7½% Annually from the Borrowed Money
1	$375	$375	$18.75	$28.13
2	750	750	37.50	56.25
3	1,125	1,125	56.25	84.38
4	1,525	1,125	56.25	84.38
5	1,900	1,125	56.25	84.38
6	2,325	1,125	56.25	84.38
7	2,725	1,125	56.25	84.38
8	3,150	1,550	77.50	116.25
9	3,575	1,975	98.75	148.13
10	4,025	2,425	121.25	181.88
11	4,475	2,875	143.75	208.88
12	4,925	3,325	166.25	249.38
13	5,375	3,775	188.75	283.13
14	5,850	4,250	212.50	318.75
15	6,300	4,700	235.00	352.50
16	6,775	5,175	258.75	388.13
17	7,275	5,675	283.75	425.63
18	7,750	6,150	307.50	461.25
19	8,250	6,650	332.50	498.75
20	8,750	7,150	357.50	536.25
21	9,200	7,600	380.00	570.00
22	9,675	8,075	403.75	605.63
23	10,125	8,525	426.25	639.38
24	10,600	9,000	450.00	675.00
25	11,050	9,450	472.50	708.75

Total Interest Paid to Insurance Company:	$5,253.75
Total Income Received at 7½%:	7,873.95
Net Profit by Exercise of Leverage:	2,620.20

had to be repaid someday and many of the popular funds have since suffered heavy declines. Life insurance should be treated conservatively, and the loan of the cashvalues should be placed only into safe investment areas. Even with this caveat, you can do quite nicely for yourself at minimum risk by investing in high grade bonds, now yielding in the area of 7½%, and compounding the additional returns.

As an example, let's consider a typical $25,000 whole life policy providing cash value from inception. We will presume that you borrow from the company at a 5 per cent rate of interest and invest in 7½% Triple A corporate bonds. Yields of 10-12% can now be secured in B rated bonds, but we will stress safety in this play. Table III shows the results you would achieve, excluding taxes paid by you on your investment income and the tax deduction you receive for the interest you pay the insurance company. *Tax Tip:* To maintain your right to deduct the interest you pay on the loan, you must not borrow out the cash value in more than three of the first seven years that you hold the policy. Therefore, the chart shows no additional borrowing for the years 4-7.

Your Cash Value has, in effect, been increased from $11,050 to $13,670.20 for a percentage gain of 23.7%. This presumes that you pay the interest due on the loan each year from the proceeds of your investments and that you *have not* reinvested the accumulated differentials between the income you receive and the interest you pay. If you had compounded the differentials as they accumulated, the results would be even better. I chose not to do that as an offset against bond commission costs and income taxes, also not included. The differential between outlay and income expands each year, as you can see by a study of Table III. Had we added another five years, the profit differential would become approximately 50% larger.

And this is simply a straightforward, conservative leverage play that can be employed by anyone. It all just goes to show you; a little positive thinking can go a long way.

Chapter 3

"In Twenty Years You Might Just Become A Millionaire."

Investing In Income Properties

Potential Return,	A (our target is 25% compounded annually)
Risk,	B+
Liquidity,	C
Tax Considerations,	A–

Ten thousand dollars becomes:

In five years,	*$ 30,518*
In ten years,	*93,132*
In twenty years,	*867,361*

ABOUT REAL ESTATE

Before we get into the landlord business, a few words about investing in real estate. *I personally do not know a single person who has lost money on realty investment.* I do know several though who have built small amounts of capital into veritable fortunes. Now, I am obviously not saying that money cannot be lost on real estate investment. If you try hard enough, you can do almost anything. And I am aware that there *are* plenty of sheep around town who have gotten fleeced by buying, sight unseen, a piece of desert, or who have otherwise fallen for some hard promoter's sales pitch. In fact, I do know of at least one couple who had to threaten to sue to reclaim their purchase price on a piece of raw land. And, additionally, it is possible to buy blindfolded into an emerging slum. Hence, the B+ rating for safety instead of an A.

Among the success stories, I know a number of couples who have entered income real estate as mere neophytes, coming out with fantastic returns, at least several more who have cleaned up on raw land, and others who are thriving on syndicate deals. For every couple I know personally who have profited in these ways, I have hard information regarding twice as many who have parlayed small money into big on realty operation. We'll get to the actual numbers later. In the meantime, keep this in mind. Only about one per cent of real estate mortgages result in foreclosure. That puts the odds at about 99-1 in your favor. As we get into the various real estate ploys in this section, you'll see why.

THE EXCEPTIONS

There are only two exceptions to the rosy outlook presented above. Investors in big city co-operatives have, in recent years, been frequently disappointed. Co-op prices in New York City, for example, peaked along with the stock market in 1968-1969. Since then, deterioration of the city's inner core, coupled with the paucity of stock investment profits, has caused price declines in New York City co-ops of up to fifty per cent—and this in the face of four year's inflation. Buildings you couldn't bribe your way into in the past have been going a-begging. *Moral:* If you buy a co-op, study its location and the demographic development of its surroundings. Co-ops, however, outside of inner cities have appreciated in value and, in many cases, investors have done quite well. Location, of course, is the key.

The second exception lies in over-priced summer and vacationland communities. Many of these do not appreciate a la the glorified ads, and many developers do not create the Shangri-Las promised to their customers. More about that in Chapter 4.

THE PROFIT MAGIC OF REAL ESTATE LEVERAGE

For starters, let's ignore the landlord lobby. Levitt did not get to buy his gold-fauceted yacht on a 6% return and Lefrak didn't get to own half of New York City on 5% either. The realty boys are entitled to their display of public poverty as an argument against rent control but *we* do not have to take them seriously. Sure, if you count the total purchase price of the investment, returns may run to about 6%. But review Chapter 2, Leverage, and see where the ball game's really at.

When you consider that apartment buildings can frequently be purchased with only a 20-25% down payment, you can readily see that the 6-8% the landlords claim as profit really represents a profit in the area of 25-40% on their invested capital, and that's not always including the tax shelters involved. For example, let's use the following rough figures:

Cost of Building, $100,000.
Profit on Building, $8,000 annually.
Landlord's Claimed Rate of Return, 8%.

Not much, considering his labor. However, let's do it again:

Cost of Building, $100,000.
Cash Out of Pocket to Buy It ($20,000 including down payment and expenses).
Profit on Building, $8,000 annually.
Real Rate of Return, 40%!

And that's what the realty men *do not* talk about. Most real estate investments benefit from these leverage possibilities, some largely in terms of income, and some in terms of capital gains. Chapter 4 illustrates the leverage possibilities in capital investment.

FACT OR FANCY?

Fact. I know of a couple, for example, that owns two apartment houses which are run just about as inefficiently as possible. All repairs, even the most minor, are farmed out. Hired labor does all the lawn mowing, snow cleaning, painting and garbage removal. The husband and wife are absentee landlords, 95%. Despite this, one house brings in 30% a year and the other, 27%. They are in the market for a third now. Almost all the income is currently tax sheltered, which means that the couple is receiving, in effect, current returns of approximately 50% and 45% on their money. In their tax bracket, that's the rate of *non-sheltered* return they would need to match the *tax-sheltered* profit.

PYRAMIDING – THE KEY TO ULTIMATE FORTUNE

Pyramiding is to real estate what compounding is to savings deposits—the re-investment of investment income to constantly expand the amount of return of the original investment. If you need the current income from your realty operation, fine. Thirty per cent is nothing to sneeze at—not even twenty per cent, for that matter. You can use the current money as retirement income, for the kids' college expenses or for an annual splurge abroad if you want. But real estate fortunes are not made that way. They are made by reinvesting all current cash income and by refinancing your mortgages every eight years or so to raise new purchase capital, so that as much of your money as possible is working for you at all times.

Go back to the very beginning of this chapter. We will presume that your rental income, expenses and the values of your property do not change with the years. If you put $10,000 down on your first house, make a 25% profit annually, and reinvest this profit regularly in new property at a 25% return, you will end up with $867,361 at the end of twenty years! (Taxes not included).

At that point, if the rate of amortization return is 15% and cash flow, 10%, your holdings will be bringing you in about $130,104 in amortization and about $86,736 each year in cash income. Even allowing for dollar shrinkage at 5% per year, your original $10,000 has increased, in terms of today's purchasing power, to $312,250 and your cash retirement income, again in terms of current purchasing power, will amount to $31,225 per year. (If you hold to 25 years, the $10,000 down becomes $2,646,976, annual cash income–$264,698!). And that, I think, is sailing off into the sunset in style. If you start young enough, you can practically retire at high noon.

REAL ESTATE – THE GREAT INFLATION HEDGE

The above figures are based upon the premise that the only income you will derive from your holdings is rental income, and that rents vis-a-vis expenses will remain constant. This is most conservatively estimated. Your returns, in actuality, should be much higher. Why? Rental property values are based largely upon the amount of rental income derived from a property. We'll go into pricing in more detail below. Rents, like everything else, rise with inflation–and the rise in the rentals you charge has to be accompanied by a rise in the resale value of your investment. Hence, your properties should show a capital increase, as well as increased rental profits over the years. Typical properties have increased in value 10% this year alone based upon rental increases. Investors who purchased last year at 25% down and sell now would realize a 10% gain (less sales costs) over their purchase price, but a 40% gain in the last year alone based upon the actual cash originally put into the deal.

Costs of running the property–fuel, taxes, maintenance–do increase along with rent as a result of inflation. However, your mortgage payments remain constant, and your rate of amortization versus the interest you pay on the mortgage increases as the mortgage is repaid. And yes, buildings do wear down over the years, requiring repair. But what about the costs of replacement of real estate? Has your own dwelling lost value over the years, or have the increasing costs of lumber, labor, land, masonry and other materials increased the value of your home even as it has aged? In Great Neck, New York, for example, homes selling for $50,000 only seven years ago, now sell for $85,000.

The point is this. The total value–gross net income and resale price–of your investment should more than offset any inflationary declines in the value of the dollars you put into income property. And you should be able to produce returns far in excess of what I am estimating. Even as your buildings age, the land upon which they sit increases in value each year. In 1946, land represented only about 12 per cent of the total value of a single family home; by 1973 this proportion rose to over 22 per cent.

SELECTING YOUR PROPERTY

Income properties may be divided into three classes: (1) residential, (2) residential-commercial and (3) commercial. The first are properties rented exclusively for residential purposes. The second class includes properties which are partly residential, partly commercial—for instance a small taxpayer apartment house with stores beneath the apartments. The third class is purely commercial: shopping centers, professional buildings, office space etc. I suggest that you confine your investment to purely residential property. Rents are simpler to calculate, there is less need for renovation to suit tenants, and you are protected against changes in commercial fashion, business bankruptcy and the gradual deterioration to which many commercial neighborhoods are subject. However, plenty of entrepreneurs have enjoyed excellent returns on commercial property. I personally believe that residential property is simpler to handle, but if you want to own the Empire State Building or Yankee Stadium, be my guest.

SIZE

A good rule of thumb to follow is that the more apartments you can get for your down payment, the better. In the area surrounding New York City (steer clear of inner core properties, no matter how attractive the price), \$10,000 down gets you a three or four family deal; \$5,000 can swing a two family. In other sections of the country, you may do better or worse. Professionals frequently advise against the purchase of any apartment house under four families. I do not agree. I have known people to do very well, even with single family dwellings, because they adhered to the buying formulae cited later on.

Small apartment houses offer the following advantages:

1) You can start with relatively little money.

2) You can scatter locations, by diversification lessening the risk of neighborhood deterioration.

3) You are more likely to be able to select an ideal location; prospective properties are more likely to be surrounded by single family private homes.

4) The tenants will provide many of their own services: hall cleaning, policing of outdoor areas, etc.

5) You are less likely to be harassed by rent controls, tenant associations, etc.

6) The tenants are more likely to develop a proprietory interest in the property—to maintain it well.

7) You do not need to hire help: superintendent, porters, doorman, etc.

Larger apartment houses offer the following advantages:

1) Your investment is concentrated in fewer places. Hence, less travel on your part.

2) It becomes more economically feasible to hire a resident manager or superintendent to run the building for you.

3) You can often secure quantity discounts on items such as fuel.

4) You may feel a greater pride of ownership.

5) Accounting and legal services may be cheaper if concentrated in one property.

6) If you go the syndicate route, potential investors will probably prefer a larger property.

I personally opt for a larger collection of smaller as opposed to a smaller selection of larger properties. My own experience indicates to me that it is feasible to operate smaller properties with a minimum of personal activity and involvement. Since the landlord transacts directly with his tenants, relationships develop which have usually resulted in the tenant's reliable maintenance of their apartments. Owners have also been able to elicit co-operation in that, when repairs are needed, the tenants themselves often make the preliminary arrangements—subsequently confirmed by the landlord. Hair-raising business tactics? Yes. But they work. Many tenants have proven quite assiduous in saving the landlord's money, if a good relationship exists.

But again, this is a ball game that can be played several ways. If you prefer large amounts of cement in one place, start as large as you like. Sooner or later, investors in income property do tend to move up from smaller to larger buildings—often because the leverage is better and the travel less.

LOCATION

All right, we've decided on residential property, large or small. What now? We go looking. In practice, before you do anything, secure some preliminary numbers from your broker over the telephone. Let's assume that the figures are in the 25% return ball park. *There is no single factor so important to the success of a real estate investment as its location.* It is for that reason that I favor smaller units. Often, these exist as rental pockets within neighborhoods of privately owned homes—premium areas for renters, who are usually willing to pay premium rents for relative privacy, use of lawn, and middle class association. *Do* check the proximity of schools, shopping, commutation, medical and dental services, and general transportation. *Do* verify the trend of population, urban or suburban blight, commercial encroachment, and possible highway construction—you do not want an expressway on your front lawn. Drive around. Approach the proposed purchase from all directions. *The best sign:* new single family residential construction in your area. It is far better if your property is the worst on the block than the best. A little paint, and your building won't make you so self-conscious. To repeat: well-located buildings practically rent themselves.

ABOUT THE BUILDING

Brick and stucco are better than wood (termite fodder and requires painting). Shingle is

O.K., but not as good as brick. Check the roof, heating plant, basement, plumbing and for the presence of termites. If you're not expert, hire a professional building inspector. However, make certain that he does a thorough job as some are quite careless.

The availability of garages is a plus, as are shade trees, some lawn, and a generally attractive exterior. *Do not* expect homes or apartments necessarily similar to your own. Evaluate the apartments not by your needs, but in terms of the local rental market. Are the apartments equal in quality to similarly priced units in the area? If so, they meet your criteria as an investment. Large grounds and manicured lawns may be your own thing as a homeowner, but do you really want the expense of providing such goodies to your tenants? I think not. Some lawn or grounds for picnicking, cook-outs and play, yes. A formal lawn for appearance, no.

If you offer a clean, well-maintained and well-located premises, you should rarely see a vacant day.

HOW MUCH SHOULD YOU PAY?

The majority of properties are offered at inflated prices and are not worthwhile investments. Oh, sure, they'll bring in 10-15%. However, we're shooting for at least 25%, and, if you're patient, you'll get it. *First rule:* No matter how anxious you are to begin, wait for the right location at the right price. When you get it, don't haggle. Tie up the property for yourself one way or another. Expect to take six months to locate your first deal and three months for the second. In between, you will reject dozens. Is it worth it? Well, again, how does a 25% return strike you?

Here's a quick rule of thumb to have ready when the broker calls. *Shoot for a property priced at about five times annual rental, and go no higher than six.* Such properties, if otherwise acceptable, almost always fit our investment goals. Presuming that the property does meet the 5 times rent rule, and you like it otherwise, then subject it to the following further tests.

1) Compute the total annual rental. Figure the rents that currently exist, including occupied apartments only. Any vacancy should be treated as a warning signal, no matter how plausible the seller's story. Be certain that the rentals are legitimate, properly leased, and do not involve any special deals between the present owner and his tenants. Ignore the usual claims that the units are underpriced and that rents can be raised tomorrow. If that does turn out to be true, it's an extra. The only thing that counts is the rent in hand. Presume that the previous owner is just as smart and no more philanthropic in nature than yourself.

2) From the rent, deduct known property taxes. These taxes should be verified by you or your representative at the county or local government office. Also deduct known costs of utilities and heating.

3) Multiply the difference between rental received and the total of taxes and utilities paid out by 6.7. The result is the price you should aim for in purchase. Where the location is truly excellent, you can exceed this figure by 10% or so.

Example:

Gross Rental of Property	$8,000
Taxes on Property	1,100
Other expenses: (heat, utilities)	800 (estimate)
Net difference	6,100
Price You Should Pay	40,870 (6100 x 6.7)

If we add 10% leeway, you can pay $44,957. Pay no more!

A Third Test:

If you are really eager to get going and find the above requirements too stringent in your area, you can make use of a third formula, which will generally prove profitable if you can secure the property with a low down payment.

If your cash flow, excluding repairs, equals 10-15% of your initial investment, you can make the purchase. But do not exceed formula #2 by more than 15% in any case. Cash flow is the profit you see in actual dollars, not amortization.

Example A (an actual case)

Proposed Price of Building.		$25,500
Initial Investment (Down payment + legal and closing costs)		6,000
Gross Rental.	$5,280	
Mortgage payments and taxes		3,080
Fuel		600
Insurance		150
Utilities and services		225
Miscellaneous		100
		4,155

Cash flow: (excluding repairs) ($5,280 minus $4,155.00) . . . $1,125

Cash flow as a per cent of initial investment 18%

This 18% return meets the criteria very well, allowing ample room for ongoing repair costs and vacancies. Notice also that the cost of the property amounted to less than five times annual rental. With repairs averaging about $400 per year, cash profit annually amounts to 12% and amortization now approximately 15%, for a total return of 27%. The rate of amortization will increase over the years as interest charges decline. This house was secured for a down payment of 10% of the purchase price. The purchasers were able to take over an existing bank mortgage and the sellers provided a favorable second mortgage. Therefore, the expenses at closing–title insurance, legal fees, payment for existing fuel and so forth–amounted to only about $900. Does the deal seem small? Over the next 20 years, this $6,000 investment figures to bring in $14,000 cash profits, plus better than $22,000 in amortization for a total profit of $30,000–not compounded. That same $6,000 compounded in a savings bank at 5% would bring in only $9,918 in interest. And that doesn't include rent raises.

Incidentally, by formula #2 this property was worth only about $22,500 (or $24,725 if we add 10% leeway). However, the low down payment and favorable mortgage terms (one at

5¾%, one at 6¾%) made the deal worthwhile. Sometimes, in negotiation, you can swap off favorable terms for a price concession to the seller.

A HELPFUL TOOL

You will require a book of mortgage payment tables on hand when you figure your deals, so that you can estimate the monthly payments required to carry your mortgage. An excellent book of charts of monthly mortgage payments has been available from Realforms, P. O. Box 1, Brookline, Mass. 02146. The cost is low, in the area of a few dollars, depending upon the type of book you order and its binding. Send for the catalogue.

For the moment, however, the following table can give you some idea as to what to expect:

TABLE I

Amount of Monthly Payment Needed to Amortize Each $1,000 Unit of Mortgage

Term	At 6%	At 7%	At 8%	At 9%	At 10%
5 years	$19.33	$19.80	$20.28	$20.76	$21.25
10 years	11.10	11.61	12.13	12.67	13.22
15 years	8.44	8.99	9.56	10.14	10.75
20 years	7.16	7.75	8.36	9.00	9.65
25 years	6.44	7.07	7.72	8.39	9.09
30 years	6.00	6.65	7.34	8.05	8.78

To pay off a $1,000 mortgage in 15 years at 7% interest would require 180 monthly payments of $8.99. For a $6,500 mortgage this would be $58.43 monthly (6.5 times $8.99).

NEGOTIATING PLOYS

Presuming that a property does appear financially viable, is in an excellent area and suits you otherwise, you will want to put up a "binder" to hold your right to the deal pending further investigation and negotiation. Be certain that your binder stipulates your right to withdraw your bid should your lawyer so advise. "Subject to lawyer's approval", written on the check usually suffices. It is very difficult to enforce a realty deal based upon the binder alone. However, your offering and the owner accepting the binder does imply at least some seriousness on both sides. Your aim is to encourage the seller to withdraw a promising property from the market. Your next steps will involve verification of the stated taxes (believe no one), rents (speak to the tenants—you could learn a lot), zoning ordinances, needed repairs and any violations on the property. When you sign the actual purchase contract, your lawyer will secure from the previous owner the necessary representations to cover these and other items.

Your actual negotiation should begin from your end with a fixed notion of your maximum price, the rate of return you expect, and certain conditions, if necessary, e.g., that the seller see to major repairs. Try to buy in with as small a down payment as possible; 20% should be your goal. Realty mortgages are a cheap form of borrowing. Frequently, you will have to arrange for a second mortgage provided by the seller. Pay no more than the prevailing rates. Try to negotiate a lower rate, if possible. Even in a reasonably priced deal, there is some room for negotiation. However, on a deal that meets all the pricing criteria, do not let the house get away from you on a minor matter of principle.

At contract and closing, read the contract carefully yourself and be certain that you understand and agree with all provisions. We have heard of several instances in which lawyers failed to insert or inserted incorrectly important stipulations. By the closing, your lawyer should have seen to all necessary documentation–title reports, surveys, etc.

If possible, let your lawyer do the heavy arguing. If you take a second mortgage from the seller, you will be in some sort of relationship with him for many years to come.

HOW THE REAL ESTATE TAX SHELTER ADDS TO YOUR PYRAMID

Real estate is one of the supreme tax shelters and under the Tax Reform Act of 1969, residential real estate retained a favored tax sheltered status. A property qualifies as residential if 80% of gross rental income during the year is derived from dwelling units. However, these units must not be rented on a transient basis, e.g., motels. See your accountant for details and exact specifications–these amount to a book in themselves.

The residential owner has a choice of various depreciation methods, which is significant since more rapid depreciation can put greater *current* cash in your pocket. However, the typical straight line method *keeps* the most cash for you in the long run. We'll get back to this a little later. First, a definition or two.

Depreciation is an allowance for the deterioration of property on the premise that a building ages and each year loses some of its remaining usable life. This allowance is carried on the books as an *expense item,* even though no actual cash expense is involved. As a result, the actual cash flow and profit shown each year by a building can be reduced for tax purposes at *no immediate cost* to the owner. The building must be held for at least one year to qualify.

Let's see what this means in practice. Returning to example A, we have our building, which cost \$25,500, bringing in a net income *before* depreciation of \$1,625. The balance sheet appears like this:

Income:	Gross Rental:	\$5,280.00
Expenses:	Taxes:	\$1,100
	Interest:	1,080
	Repairs:	400
	Fuel:	600
	Insurance:	150
	Utilities:	225
	Miscellaneous	100
Total Expenses:		\$3,655.00

Net Profit: Cash flow, $725 or 12.1% of the $6,000 down payment.
Amortization, $900 or 15.0%

Total Profit: $1,625 or 27.1%

If you own this property and are in the 40% tax bracket, your income taxes due would amount to $650 (40% x $1,625), or nearly all your cash flow. Remember, for tax purposes *amortization counts as profit. Caution:* In computing purchase terms for any property, be certain that the investment provides sufficient cash flow on hand to meet income tax requirements which are based upon total profits. Otherwise, your investment will require you to pay the taxes due out of other income sources.

Now, let's add depreciation to the computation. Land is not depreciable, but we can presume that of the purchase price, $25,500, $23,000 is allocated for the building itself, only $2,500 for the land. This proportion varies, of course, by location and property. Since the building was purchased used, we can also presume, for tax purposes, that it has a remaining useful life of 20 years and has no salvage value thereafter. Therefore, we will depreciate it at 1/20 of its remaining life span, or 5% per annum, and add $1,150 (5% x $23,000) to the expense side of our annual ledger. Result, only a $475 annual profit, against which income taxes must be paid ($1,625 profit - $1,150 depreciation allowance). Tax liability, in the 40% bracket, now only $190 instead of $650.

This tax saving is not free and clear, however. Upon resale, you deduct from your purchase price, in computing your capital gain and loss statement, the total amount of depreciation claimed over the years. Suppose you sell this building in ten years for $25,500, the same price you paid for it. Normally, you would be obligated for no capital gains taxes. However, you have depreciated the building by $11,500 over the ten years. Your cost is thus computed for tax purposes at $14,000 ($25,500 minus $11,500 claimed depreciation). You are subject to capital gains tax at the rate of one-half your normal tax rate, presumptively in our example, 20% (½ x 40% tax bracket). Total capital gains tax due, *only upon sale.* $2,300, or one-half the $4,600 taxes on these profits which you would have paid over the years if not for the magic of the depreciation allowance! If you hold the building until retirement, your effective tax rate at the time may be even lower since you will be in a lower tax bracket. And, until resale, you have the use of the money yourself instead of having to hand it over to Uncle Sam.

There are methods of depreciation, other than straight line, which allow for more rapid depreciation and increased shelter against current income. However, if you elect these, the Internal Revenue Service recaptures upon sale all your tax savings at normal tax rates, not as capital gains. Therefore, your long term gain is less than if you depreciate by the straight line method. Discuss the various possibilities with your accountant. Many realty professionals suggest the sale of realty property after the depreciation is exhausted, since the tax shelter vanishes at that point.

OTHER TAX PLOYS

If you expand your holdings from small to large properties, attempt to trade in your property as part of the deal rather than selling it for cash. If you can manage this (a creative broker can help you), you pay no capital gains taxes on your profits until your new holdings are liquidated for cash.

Still another ploy is possible at selling time. Presume that at sale you show a capital gains profit of $11,500; tax due as per previous computation, $2,300. You may elect to receive a large part of your money in mortgage payments, in effect, as an annuity. If you accept no more than 30% of the sale price in any one year, you do not pay the capital gains taxes in the year of sale. You pay taxes each year following the sale only in the proportion that you receive the money. This stretches out your tax liability and retains for you maximum use of the proceeds of the sale. If you receive more than 30% of the purchase price as a down or complete payment, you must pay at once the complete capital gains tax due on the transaction.

This should be kept in mind when selling, and as an argument in your purchase negotiations, since the seller will benefit in the same way from accepting a small down payment from you. As your holdings expand, the ability to delay tax payment becomes increasingly significant.

In computing the profit and loss statement on your property, do not ignore expenses such as telephone calls, travel relating to your investment, postage, stationary, etc. These small items add up over the course of a year and a well-kept diary of these expenses can save considerable tax money over the years.

Various tax rulings and changes in law have occurred in recent years and are occurring right now. Consult with your tax lawyer and accountant to determine the latest regulations and to arrive at the best tax handling for your individual situation. But do remember, the higher your tax bracket, the more the value to you of any tax shelter or delay in your tax obligation.

OPERATING THE PROPERTY

All right. The deal is made, contracts signed and closing executed. What about running your real estate empire?

You might, perhaps, have settled on one of two choices. If the property was previously well-maintained, rents are probably near current maximum and increases, depending largely upon inflation, will remain moderate. If the property has been poorly-maintained, you may have hit upon a real find–since you now have the opportunity to upgrade and increase your rentals, perhaps sharply. Since value depends upon rental income, this provides the chance to multiply both current income and resale value at relatively small expense to yourself.

Put the property in shape. Repair defective plumbing, doors, roofs, and hardware. If necessary, have exterior trim repainted and halls and interiors panelled. Potential rent increases arising from such steps are considerable. For every $240 per year you increase rental, a modest $20 per month, you increase the value of the property by $1,200 or so. If you prefer to keep the present tenants, propose to them a more moderate rent increase on the condition that they repaint their own apartments—offer to supply materials. More often than not, your tenants will appreciate the improvement and will more than cooperate. Make reasonable repairs and alterations—but only if potential rent increases justify the expense.

Sooner or later vacancies occur. If your buildings are well-located, these vacancies will fill quickly. Insist upon at least one month's security and one month's rent in advance. Do not be taken in by sad stories and promises. The tenant who cannot raise the security at the outset is a poor risk, and even if you win a judgment some day, there are probably plenty of creditors on line ahead of you. If possible, secure two month's security. Such a procedure is more feasible if you rent yourself, rather than through an agent, since the tenant owes the rental agent a commission in addition to the money you get; but my own experience has been that it is worth having less security in hand to avoid the bother of showing apartments. You can have tenants sign leases if you prefer, but in most cases you're probably as well off without them, so long as you have written agreement of 30 days notice for vacating. In most instances, you will be better off *without* an unhappy tenant. Insist that rents be paid promptly and be ready with eviction forms and procedures just in case. Familiarize yourself with local proceedings.

In the event that you want to avoid any and all of the bother of administrating your properties, many realty brokers will assume the complete management of your properties for a management fee of five or six per cent of gross rental. If you opt in that direction, expect a return of 12-15% on your investment instead of 25%.

After initial improvement of the property (possibly financed), there is relatively little to do besides collecting rent checks, paying bills and arranging for occasional repairs. Have someone on hand, however, to respond to emergencies should you go on vacation. Every eight years or so, consider refinancing your mortgage, so that you can reinvest your amortization profits in new properties.

PITFALLS

1) Disreputable sellers who lie regarding expenses, taxes, violations, rental income and neighborhood. Check yourself. Drive around. Pay particular attention to nearby deterioration on the one hand and nearby overconstruction of apartment units on the other. New buildings, offering rent concessions, can be tough competition.

2) Your multiple family dwelling may be illegal. Your lawyer should secure legal representations as to the legality of your property. Do not buy an illegal property just because the law has turned the other way for years. Suburban communities are tightening up in zoning enforcement.

3) Major repairs may be required, unexpectedly. That is a risk. Do them. It averages out over the years and if you purchased by the formulae, there is plenty of margin for error.

4) Vacancies may indeed occur. Location, however, usually saves the day. Stick to excellent areas relative to your class of tenant.

5) The government may kill the tax shelter. This *is* a possibility. So is rent control. How-

ever, again, if you purchased carefully, the investment should be sound even without the tax shelter and with limits to rent increases. Mortgage costs remain fixed and you are paying off in inflated dollars.

6) You can't always sell on a moment's notice if you need money fast, true. Real estate rates only a C for liquidity. You can, though, frequently secure a second mortgage if you need ready cash. You'd be surprised how property ownership ups your general credit rating.

SELLING

You should consider selling for any one or more of the following reasons:

1) You've made your million and want to relax and enjoy it.

2) You want to upgrade to larger units.

3) Your tax shelter has run out; no more depreciation can be taken.

4) The neighborhood is beginning to deteriorate.

5) You personally wish to relocate.

6) There is a drastic change for the worst in the rental market.

7) Conversely, there has been a sudden upsurge in property value and according to the laws of contrary opinion, you decide it's time to take profits.

Consider getting the very best price for your properties by accepting small down payments in return for high total price and maximum interest on the mortgage which you can offer yourself. This will provide you with an almost lifelong income at capital gain taxation. If you are adept mathematically, you can conjure up a deal which provides a very high current return to your buyer while providing you with an excellent price for your resale. Suppose you sell that $25,500 house for your purchase price, taking only $3,000 down and the rest over twenty-five years at 8%. You will receive over the twenty-five years, $55,110 for that property, counting amortization, this time to you, plus interest.

It all sounds too good to be true? Don't take my word for it. Look around, compute the numbers. Ask people who are in the business. When you're satisfied, take the plunge.

Who knows? In twenty years you might just become a millionaire.

Chapter 4

"In The Meantime You Can Always Camp Out On Your Investment"

Investing In Raw Land

Potential Return,	A–
Safety,	B–
Liquidity,	C–
Tax Considerations,	C

One thing's for certain. The country isn't getting any larger. The slowdown in population growth notwithstanding, Americans are pursuing land acquisition with a fervor unseen since the old homestead days. Couple an increasing demand with a supply diminishing because of highway construction, development of suburban and retirement communities, new exploitation of natural resources and the modern day fad of summer as well as winter home ownership and you have an investment bonanza. Nor do you have to worry about overproduction a la the electronic calculator; the supply of land is fixed, once and for all.

For example, the area surrounding New York City. Summer home or old farm purchasers are having to move further and further away from the metropolitan area to find property priced at all within reason. Old farms, priced at a few thousand dollars during the late sixties, now sell for $25,000, $30,000 and higher. Sample listings: 177 acres, $66,000; 105 acres, $24,500; 30 acres, $28,000. Prices in some cases have reached over $1,000 per acre–for land you could have secured for $60 or $70 an acre only seven or eight years ago.

However, there are still cheaper parcels available, outside the populous states. In Montana, you can secure 1650 acres of raw, undeveloped farmland for $329,800 or about $200 per acre. In Wadena County, Minnesota, a 240 acre farm was recently put up for sale, complete with farmhouse and equipment, for $22,000. Less than $100 per acre and only 150 miles outside of Minneapolis (looks like good potential in this one). Florida homesites, though, have really escalated in recent years–the result of retirees seeking warmer climates and land development operations burgeoning to facilitate the quest. One recent study showed homesite costs in Florida up 10% in just four months.

The potential is there all right–if you pick your location well. Risks abound, of course, but these can be minimized with some judgment.

All told, the average price of land has grown at a compound rate of 7 per cent over the past fifteen years, nearly triple the average rate of increase in the consumer price index–and the rate of growth has continued to exceed the cost of living. The U.S. Department of Agriculture reports that farm realty values rose 13 per cent during 1972 alone. Building plots in fine urban and suburban areas have matched this rate of growth, and are excellent alternatives to large vacation acreage.

A reasonable goal then, appears to be a 10-15% price appreciation on your land parcel per year. However, you can do much better if you leverage your play, and even better than that if you combine leverage with wholesale purchase, retail resale operations.

Risks? Certainly. Land values were decimated during the depression. But so was everything else. The recession of 1970 hurt land speculators only slightly, in contrast to the stock, art, condominium and certain antique markets. Can you think of a better inflation hedge?

THE POWER OF LEVERAGE IN RAW LAND OPERATION

Unlike rental properties, which provide steady income to their owners, raw land offers the larger prospect of rapid capital gain, but provides limited potential for income during holding periods. This is a disadvantage. However, the capital gain prospects are enormous. Presume a parcel purchased for $100,000 and sold for $115,000 one year later. A 15% return is not at all bad at capital gain tax rates, but nothing to really rave about. But consider this. To swing the deal, you may require only $25,000 down–the rest is mortgage. Even allowing for interest charges of say $5,625 (7½% of $75,000 for one year), your net profit may lie in the area of eight or nine thousand dollars easily, a rate of return of about 34% (based upon $8,500 net profit per $25,000 investment). The more you can leverage the deal, the better your potential return. Land deals have been leveraged up to 90%, and occasionally you can do even better than that. The deal cited above, leveraged at 90%, brings in about an 80% return per year. As always, leverage works both ways, but land doesn't usually collapse in value a la Equity Funding, so maximal use of leverage usually makes good business sense.

HOW TO MAKE A REAL KILLING

Buy wholesale, sell retail! That's all there is to it. Land purchased in large quantities costs less per acre than the same or equal quality land subdivided into smaller divisions. For example, a 600 acre unit may sell, as a total unit, for $60,000 or $100 per acre. Subdivided into homesite sized one acre parcels, the same land could easily retail at $350 per acre, a 250% markup. That's where the real profit lies.

What accounts for this? It's simple enough. Just consider the psychology and economics of land purchase. The majority of people are neither interested nor foresighted enough to properly invest in land. They simply want a vacation site for $300, for example, or $2,000-$4,000 in popular areas, seems a reasonable amount to pay. Nor are they willing to arrange for a one hundred thousand or quarter of a million dollar deal. Therefore, large scale buyers are fewer and further between than small scale purchasers, and sellers have to make price concessions in order to swing wholesale deals. Land, after all, is simply a commodity, and in almost every form of business, it is cheaper to buy wholesale. Why doesn't the original landowner subdivide and retail himself? Some do. For the others, well, why doesn't Hershey run its own candy counters?

The basic tactic is simply this. Purchase the largest quantity of *fully acceptable* land you can secure for your money, and try to secure the maximum markup possible through intelligent subdivision and marketing. Near major cities, look for and expect at least a 200% markup on wholesale purchases. Further out, where risks are somewhat greater, expect at least a *700-900%* price markup through subdivision. Now multiply *that* by the leverage factors and see the potential returns involved, even after the deduction of advertising and other expenses.

WHAT TO LOOK FOR

To repeat, in real estate the key to success lies in the selection of proper and profitable locations. Invest where the demand lies. What does this mean in terms of raw land? Your buyers will want to be located within driving range of their homes so that weekend trips become feasible. For most families, that means vacation properties located no more than 200 miles from home, or approximately a four hour drive. Gasoline shortages may, in the future, restrict this range. Therefore, an investor in raw land should confine his investigation to properties located no more than 200 miles from major metropolitan centers. This rule can be violated if you have delineated the direction of metropolitan growth, upsurges in population in nearby medium sized cities, and if you have the financial resources and patience to carry the property while you are waiting for the population to arrive. This means a potentially longer holding period before resale, but greater ultimate profit since your initial purchase should come at low prices.

Second, your land should be nicely situated near natural attractions. National and state parks and large bodies of water are desirable. Lake George in New York State is one example. Modern vacationers are strongly sttracted to water—boating, water skiing, snorkling, scuba diving are now "in" sports. Best is actual waterfront property with lake frontage. This is followed by property adjoining water, offering water use rights. And finally, water view property has appeal. It is not absolutely essential for property to involve water to attract purchasers, but water in some form is a very major plus (brooks and streams count also). Examine local tour books. Are there natural and man-made attractions nearby—caves, waterfalls, animal farms, amusement parks, zoos, museums, athletic areas, public swimming? Each of these adds to the value of surrounding property.

Do not ignore the availability or lack of availability of winter sports. America has become a nation of skiers, snow-mobiles and bobsleds. A favorite plaything for the modern generation is the winter vacation home, in areas adjoining ski centers. These are purchased for personal and personal-rental use, and are becoming increasingly popular. Property offering a combination of summer-winter recreation is, of course, the most desirable.

Do select investment sites within reasonable proximity to necessary shopping, churches, medical facilities, movie houses and other town facilities and services. City folks may talk about wanting to get away from it all to the great outdoors, but most families prefer to be within at least easy driving distance of civilization's amenities. As an example, the Berkshire vacationland developed around the Tanglewood Music Festival in the areas of Springfield and Lenox, Massachusetts. Nearby towns naturally offer diversity in amusements, dining, shopping—and simply a change of pace to summer home owners. Tourist trails also offer antique shopping, another recent fad, and the ever-present summer auctions, now becoming increasingly popular.

And finally, check out the major transportation arteries to the area you are considering. Is transportation feasible during rainy periods, snow? Are new highway connections to the vicinity of your proposed holding being contemplated or, better yet, in the beginning phase of construction? New highways almost always presage the development of a resort area; get in before the development matures. The building of a highway interchange can affect land values dramatically. *The New York Times* (June 11, 1973) reported a jump in one parcel of Wyoming land from \$100 to \$3500 an acre upon the proximate location of an interchange of the Interstate Highway.

HOW DO YOU KNOW YOU'VE PICKED RIGHT

Once you have decided upon the general vicinity—and do take into account the travel to and fro necessary on your part to handle the operation—the next step is to verify your conclusions. First, contact local real estate brokers. Discuss with them the pricing history of surrounding land. Do not buy into any area that has not shown at least a 15% annualized rate of growth in value in recent years. Do not take anyone's word. Ask to see records of transactions, changes of deed, past and present advertisements. Then, evaluate the prevailing markups in the area. By how much is subdivided land marked up locally as opposed to larger parcels? If the locale meets these two criteria, the 15% appreciation history and at least a 200% markup history, you can proceed further into selecting your individual site.

SELECTING THE INDIVIDUAL SITE

Your first decision lies with whether you plan to develop a completely raw piece of property, whether you plan to buy and sell completely raw land, or whether you plan to transact in both ways in at least partially developed land.

Completely raw land may have no, or only partial, road access to its component areas. Road frontage or access will, of course, become ultimately essential to homesite owners. To the extent that this exists, the more the land is worth. Every improvement you provide for the land increases its value. However, you must ascertain, *before you become involved,* the going rates for developed as opposed to undeveloped land. Concurrently, you have to secure *firm* estimates for your proposed improvements and then compute whether the whole procedure pays for you. Improvements may include road building, beach construction, dock provision, leveling, planting, tree removal, and the provision of electricity and wells.

I personally recommend that all but professional land developers stay with the purchase and sale of land that is, at the least, virtually fit for building, as is. Some road construction, unpaved, may be feasible but further improvements become highly complex and time consuming.

Your purchase should meet the location criteria, specified above, appear attractive and, if possible, have some connection—no matter how remote—with bodies of water. Before purchase, conceive of possible subdivisions. How will you lay out the property to minimize road construction to all parts (if provided), to comply with local zoning ordinances (verify these personally), and to still be able to offer attractive homesites?

It usually pays, in subdividing, to offer advantages to compensate for the liabilities of any particular section. For example, sites at the water can be smaller than sites some distance away, so the purchaser has some compensation for the lack of actual water frontage. Waterfront sites, of course, are more expensive than others. Try to visualize views from the total property and from each individual homesite. Subdivision is something of a creative art mixed with business judgment; however, careful planning involving a map of your property should work out quite well. Subdivide in lots sized consistent to the area and general quality of neighboring construction. Economic levels tend to group together.

Do check your proposed purchase for water level, accessibility of electricity, underlying terrain, drainage, tree and plant disease, and danger of flooding. Hard rock undersoil will result in excessively high drilling costs, presuming that well construction is possible at all. The rest is self-explanatory. In many states, the state Department of Agriculture will help you to identify symptoms of leaf and tree disease, a bane of forest or shade property.

CHECKLIST FOR WHOLESALE PURCHASES OF VACATION LAND

1) The location should lie within four hour's drive of a major metropolitan center.
2) New highway construction is headed towards your site.
3) There are natural and man made attractions nearby.
4) The site is not too isolated from nearby towns, but provides some sense of privacy.
5) Comparable real estate in the area has been appreciating at a 15% annual rate.
6) Comparable land, subdivided, has been providing at least a 200% markup.
7) The land does not require overly expensive development.
8) Local taxes and zoning regulations are not too prohibitive.
9) The land lends itself to attractive subdivision.
10) There will be no undue problems in securing water, electricity or telephone services.

ANOTHER PROFITABLE PLOY

Developed raw land can frequently be secured at a discount early in the life of a vacation development, either with or without the necessity of your purchasing more than one site. However, it may be advantageous for you to purchase several sites as investments, even if you require just one for yourself. Your bargaining power is highest early in the game. The developer may be short of ready cash since he has outlayed money with few returns as yet. He may also be just a little anxious as to the fate of his venture—money in hand is always inviting. The development corporation, in addition, frequently provides commitments to improve the land. These improvements usually are undertaken even while the land is being parceled out. Once this is accomplished, the whole area becomes more attractive, and early customers often have to pay lower prices than latecomers. By buying a few extra parcels early and selling later, you can often end up with a virtually free homesite for yourself, and as an investor you do save, at the cost of lesser profits, the trouble of locating, financing and investigating larger deals. Just make certain that your developer is reliable.

FINANCING

Mortgage money is not as readily available for unimproved land as it is for improved land, which includes homes. However, 5-10 year mortgages may be available. The Federal Housing Administration may lend up to 50% of the value of undeveloped land plus 90% of the estimated cost of development for periods of up to 10 years. You may also be able to secure shorter term commercial loans from your bank if you can present a logical and reasonable plan of action. The seller may be willing to provide a mortgage in order to clinch a deal, but do try to secure an arrangement whereby you receive clear title to partial segments of the land should you prepay part of the mortgage. This facilitates your ability to sell off portions as you go along, and to develop model homesites. It may be possible for you to secure a mortgage indirectly by refinancing your own home mortgage and using the proceeds for land investment. This is probably the cheapest form of money you can secure. Syndication (Chapter 6) may help too. Finally, farmland, including a farmhouse, does qualify for regular mortgage loans.

Keep one thing in mind, however. Raw land does not provide income until resale. You have to finance taxes, interest and mortgage payments, assessments, development and advertising from other income sources. This is a basic disadvantage to investment in raw land. Income properties do provide current income sufficient to more than offset expenses, and there is rarely a rush to sell off a profitable apartment house. (Occasionally, however, raw land can bring in income in the form of timber sales or grazing fees. Some people rent out to campers.)

WHAT TO AVOID

Never, but never, buy land sight unseen. The March 1972 issue of *The Capitalist Reporter* carried a story, "Watch Out For New Mexico Land Promoters." In essence, one tale related how clever operators "gave away" ¼ acre pieces of land as raffle prizes for only $49.30 "closing fees". Original cost to the developer, $20 per acre. Another tale in the article dealt with subdivided desert wasteland, sold to out of state buyers via shrewd mail promotion. Remember, clever photography can go a long way.

I personally know at least one couple bilked by promise of lakes to come, who invested thousands of dollars in ¼ acre of swamp. They even saw the land, and a huge excavation that was earmarked, "the future trout-stocked lake". Be certain that any contracts you sign are specific as to the type of timing of promised improvements, and that you are clearly entitled to a refund should the developer default.

Take nothing for granted. Urban lawyers are more likely to stick to the letter of legal procedure than rural lawyers. The latter generally mean well and trust the personal relationships built up in small communities. However, rural surveys are often vague and more than one investor has found that he had for one reason or another no clear title insurance, and full representations. Check all taxes or zoning regulations personally. If your land is near a municipality, it may fall within town jurisdiction. Become aware of any local plans to upgrade zoning ordinances.

"Contracts for deed" are bad news for land purchasers, and should be avoided, if at all possible. The majority of land companies sell on an installment loan basis, through contract for deed contracts. The developer retains possession of the deed until the buyer fully completes payments. Should you default on a payment, he can cancel the contract and you have forfeited your payments to date–just as a furniture company can repossess furniture for non-payment. Even more odious, the developer continues to own the land, against which he may have liens. Other creditors may claim the land right from under you, should he go bankrupt. Remedies: If you must sign such contracts insist upon your payments being held in escrow, the deed held by a trustee and have the contract recorded at the local land office. Better yet, try to secure a mortgage and not borrow from the developer.

OTHER RAW LAND OPERATIONS

Most of the above pertains to raw land ultimately earmarked for vacation site resale. However, suburban land can prove quite profitable, purchased in building lot sized parcels. Cities such as Tucson and Sante Fe have been growing rapidly. The Eastern section of the United States is developing into a huge megapolis. Every major city appears to be spawning satellite living centers, as the more prosperous move out of the cities within which they work. Secure maps and see if you can trace the flow of population, buying land in the path of population movement, on the outskirts or within the boundaries of growing towns. In New York State, such areas include Rockland, Nassau and Suffolk counties. Georgetown, outside of Washington, D. C. is another example. What does your state offer?

Economic and social developments can have strong effects upon the value of land. A New York City Teacher's strike in the late sixties resulted in an immediate 40% jump in land value in Great Neck, a nearby suburb. Prices settled down after the strike, only to rise again as violence escalated within the New York City public schools. Need I comment as to the impact of Disney World on Florida real estate, or the realty collapse created near Cape Kennedy by the closing of the rocket program. The development of new universities almost always increases nearby property value. Highway construction has already been mentioned.

INSIDE TIP

I hear from sources in the know that realty speculators are quietly accumulating land along the proposed route of the Trans-Alaska pipeline. Imagine, if you will, the towns that may develop to house construction crews, railroad stations, and supply depots. Be alert to such opportunities.

WHERE THE ACTION IS

Growth Stock Outlook (P.O. Box 9911, Chevy Chase, Maryland, 20014) published, on May 15, 1973, an article relating to population trends. The report noted that moving companies such as Allied Van Lines and Aero Mayflower Transit maintain statistics which count the number of families moving into and out of a particular state. Obviously, net migration into a state will add a potential land premium while net migration out of a state reduces population growth to the limits of net births over deaths minus outflow of families. With the national population apparently stabilizing, this movement of families may become a major determinant of land values. (Keep your eye on per capita income also).

At this time, the following states are attracting new migrant families:

Arizona	Delaware	Nevada	Oregon
Arkansas	Florida	New Hampshire	South Carolina
California	Georgia	New Mexico	Vermont
Colorado	Hawaii	North Carolina	

The following states appear to be in a migration balance:

Alabama	Kentucky	Mississippi	Tennessee
Alaska	Louisiana	Missouri	Texas
Connecticut	Maine	Montana	Virginia
Idaho	Maryland	Nebraska	Washington
Indiana	Massachusetts	Oklahoma	West Virginia
Kansas	Minnesota	Rhode Island	

The following states show a net outflow of families:

Illinois	New Jersey	Ohio	Utah
Iowa	New York	Pennsylvania	Wisconsin
Michigan	North Dakota	South Dakota	Wyoming

However, although Wisconsin is a net outflow state, prices for its land have grown by 21 per cent, the highest of all the states. The Real Estate Investors Report (August 1973) reports that the lowest increases have been recently recorded in California, Utah, Arizona and Louisiana.

TAX CONSIDERATIONS

Raw land does not offer any particular tax advantage; in fact, there is a possibility that the Internal Revenue Service will decide that you are in the land development business as a dealer if you subdivide and improve, therefore charging you tax at normal instead of capital gains rates. If you can establish yourself as an investor, you may sell at capital gains and if you take no more than 30% of the sales price in one year, you can pay the taxes as the money comes in to you. You are more likely to be able to establish yourself as an investor rather than a dealer if you let a broker completely handle and control all your operations. Also, if you swap some other property directly for your land investment, you are not liable for any immediate taxes if the property you disposed of shows a profit. Do consult a realty accountant.

HOW TO SAVE ON TAXES FOR YOUR VACATION HOME

The Tax Reform Act of 1969 limited the amount of tax deduction on vacation homes in various ways. If you occupy the home part time, and rent part time, you can now deduct, as rental expenses, only an amount equivalent to the income you receive from the property. Formerly, you could deduct all expenses related to rental even where they exceeded the amount of income you derived from the property.

Nor can you legally get around this, say, by purchasing the summer home outright with funds borrowed from other sources. This ploy has been employed with the idea that the interest on such loans would be deductible elsewhere and not applied to the deduction ceiling on the summer home. The IRS has ruled, however, that interest on a loan taken to finance a summer home must be counted towards the expense ceiling. However, the burden of proof rests with the IRS.

There is one legal out for the summer home purchaser. If you can establish that your purchase was made primarily for investment rather than personal use, all expenses are deductible, even if they exceed the gross rental income from the property. Tax laws presume an activity is engaged in for profit if it shows a profit in two out of five consecutive years. Therefore, you may be able to build in a long term tax deduction by fully renting your vacation property during your first years of ownership, securing the necessary profit documentation, and then changing to part-rental, part-personal usage.

Do check this out with your lawyer and accountant.

SUMMING UP

Raw land is obviously not for the very passive investor. It's more work than the stock market, and for a while the poison ivy will grow faster than your money. However, investing in raw land has paid off very handsomely over the years to speculators willing to do the necessary investigation and to wait the requisite time to cash in.

You too may have to wait a bit for the grand payoff. In the meantime, you can always camp out on your investment.

Chapter 5

"If You Can't Make It Alone, There's Really Nothing Wrong With Getting A Little Help"

Investing In Syndicates, Condominiums And Real Estate Investment Trusts

Potential Returns,	A to C+, depending upon the tactic
Risk,	B
Liquidity,	A to C–, depending upon the tactic
Tax Considerations,	A– to D, depending upon the tactic

Up to this point, our realty ploys have required, as a minimum, the flair of the entrepreneur. Investing in both income property and raw land require that you do something besides making a simple purchase. Syndication maneuvers offer various options. You can either passively deposit your money and let the returns come in, or you can become the investor supreme–organizing, operating and profiting from running your own show.

Potential returns vary according to the strategy you select. Your own operation can be established at virtually 100% leverage–potential returns therefore almost infinite in exchange for greater amounts of work. Investment in someone else's syndicate, which requires virtually no labor, should bring in 12-20% for most deals, with variations on the theme possible to suit the needs of very high income investors. Real Estate Investment Trusts offer basically, on the one hand, an opportunity to enter the real estate game indirectly through the purchase of high yield securities and, on the other, a source of financing your own development deal. As dividend payers, Real Estate Investment Trust Companies (REITs) are excellent. You can expect dividends in the area of at least 8-11% annually. More on all this below.

REAL ESTATE SYNDICATES

A real estate syndicate is a group of persons who join together to carry through a real estate venture too large financially, and/or too complex for any of its members to handle alone. For example, presume that you plan to invest in income property, but prefer to concentrate on larger units. You might do one of two things. The first option involves your rounding up investment money or prospective partners for your venture–the total group forming the syndicate. The combined financial resources of the members should be sufficient to swing a deal that none of the members can or wish to handle alone. As the organizer, you probably will have to take an active role in forming the group, explaining terms, concluding the deal, and then possibly in directing the management of the property. A second alternative involves the investment of your money in a syndicate formed by someone else. Your returns are less, but your investment in time and labor is minimal. Both are viable options; the second will probably have the broader appeal.

STRUCTURE OF SYNDICATES

Syndicates can take the form of corporations, general partnerships or limited partnerships. The corporate structure is usually not recommended for income property syndicates because depreciation tax shelters cannot be passed along from a corporation to its stockholders as an offset against their ordinary income. Depreciation allowances, as we have seen, constitute a major plus for realty investors.

A general partnership is one viable structure for syndicates. The general partnership requires a partnership agreement, specifically drawn up to distinguish the structure from a corporation. For example, in a corporation stockholders enjoy limited personal liability in the case of any claims against the corporation. In a partnership, partners can be held personally liable for claims against the partnership. This is a disadvantage, but usually outweighed, in real estate, by the tax shelter benefits.

As an investor you might simply join or create a partnership. As a syndicator, a general partnership is the simplest legal entity for you to organize. Round up a few rich aunts, set up a partnership, and you're in business. But keep these disadvantages in mind:

1) any partner can obligate other partners by his acts,
2) the partnership may have to be dissolved in the event of the death of one of its members,
3) all partners have full personal liability and,
4) there are no rights built-in for any partner to sell his share of the partnership.

Certain structures can be created to minimize some of the working relationship problems inherent in any partnership, e.g., an outside manager can be hired and empowered to make all decisions regarding management of held properties. If you are starting your first syndicate and are securing money from friends and relatives, do consider the simple partnership. I have had offers of investment money from several sources since I began operations in rental property, and everyone expects to put in something extra over my contributions to compensate for my time and trouble.

The majority of syndicates are organized along the lines of *limited partnerships.* A limited partnership involves two classes of partners, the *general partner* and the *limited partner.* The general partners (usually the organizers) actually run the show, forming the syndicate, locating and operating the properties and so forth. Limited partners receive a share in the profits and benefit from the tax shelter, but usually have no voice in actual management. Limited partners *are not personally liable* for the operations of the partnership, their liability limited to the amount of their investment. In this manner, they enjoy the protection enjoyed by corporate stockholders while still retaining the benefits of the tax shelter–in effect, the best of both worlds. Therein lies the secret of the popularity of this form of syndicate structure.

If you are considering investment in an existing syndicate do be certain that the syndicate under consideration is structured to provide both the tax shelter and limited liability. If you are structuring your own, bear in mind that the formation of a limited partnership is somewhat complex legally (but by no means impossible) and you will need expert legal assistance. If you do plan to start your own syndicate along these lines, yourself the general partner, keep in mind also that you bear more comprehensive liability than the limited partners.

WHY DO IT?

There is plenty of money to be made. The organizer can often secure a virtually free ride for his efforts, through the medium of the syndicate fee. The *syndicate fee* is the amount other partners pay to the organizers of the syndicate. It frequently involves a management fee for running the property, generally in the area of 4-6% of gross rentals. As often as not, the syndicator receives, in addition, a piece of the property free or in the case of raw land syndications, a free share of the profits. Not all syndications involve a syndicate fee. As an investor, try to avoid it. However, don't blacklist a deal just because there is a syndicate fee. If the deal's otherwise worthwhile, you just might want to give the man his extra piece.

Caution: If you are paying a syndicate fee to the organizer in the form of a percentage of the property, be certain that there is a clause in the agreement which precludes his selling the property and taking his cut until and unless you are guaranteed at least your original investment as your share of the proceeds. The organizer's share should be subordinate to the investors' return of original capital. Unless this clause exists, there is nothing to prevent the organizer from, say, taking 20% of the $100,000 property as a fee, selling it immediately, pocketing $20,000 and returning only $80,000 to the investors.

PROFIT POTENTIAL

I've already said it. As a syndicator you get practically a free ride on very little outlay. Investors seek different *types* of returns, depending upon their income level. Most investors seek some combination of cash flow (current income in cash), amortization profit (as the syndicate pays off its mortgage) and tax shelter. In many cases, profits are almost completely tax sheltered. Well heeled investors, however, may have little interest in current income. Tax shelter's their thing. There are syndicates which show no profit at all but are very desirable to investors in high tax brackets, because of large depreciation allowances built into the deals. For example, I am familiar with one syndicate in which the limited partners put up $50,000 apiece. The syndicate shows no profit but it does provide $30,000 in tax shelter for each $50,000 invested. To investors in the 70% tax bracket, that means a $21,000 current tax savings or a 42% current return via tax relief on their money. You will probably opt for some cash flow return. Expect to receive perhaps 8-10% in cash, another 8-10% in amortization. Settle for no less that 12% total; preferably, shoot for 20%. These returns fall somewhat below our goal of a 25% payoff on our investments, but considering the tax shelter involved, you'll be doing better than O.K.

SELECTING YOUR SYNDICATE

First off, try to deal with a management that has a proven track record, a long standing reputation in the community, and several properties in operation which are open to your fiscal and personal examination. Request references and check them out. Contact the Better Business Bureau in the locality. Profitable syndicators rarely have to advertise; there are waiting lists of investors. If they do advertise, the ad should be low key, and all terms should be evaluated by both your lawyer and accountant. Beware of those hard sell telephone solicitations and mail ad campaigns which have sprung up from time to time. Many syndicators are either realty brokers or lawyers; you can initiate activity by contacting such professionals in your area.

Evaluate your own financial needs. If you require current income, accept only deals that offer a satisfactory current return. The prospectus submitted to you should be exact and specific in terms of the properties involved, projected income, tax shelter, expenses, risks, the extent of your liability and the various forms of renumeration paid to the sponsors. Many investors never examine the actual properties involved, but you should do so. You may be living with yours for a long time.

Check the possible avenues of liquidation open to you should you need to pull out your money. Many partnerships do not offer provision by which you can sell your share. Some syndicates allow no sellout, others a sale of shares only to existing partners, and still others allow you to sell outside the partnership, but only with the partnership's approval.

If you are organizing your own, draft a proposal that is specific in all these areas, clearly delineating the advantages and disadvantages involved in the proposed operation. A hard sell only makes your investors suspicious and leaves you open to legal assault.

SELECTING THE INVESTMENT

Real estate syndicates can be formed for investment in any one of a variety of realty properties. Apartment developments are among the most popular because of the income flow, stability, simplicity in management and tax shelters involved. If you are first starting your own, I recommend the residential income property route. Commercial properties–shopping centers, office buildings and professional centers–are also popular, but they are more difficult to operate, and more complex fiscally.

Raw land is less popular but not necessarily less profitable. The disadvantage lies with the need for investors to continue to add capital for taxes, mortgage payments and interest, after the initial investment, until the land is sold. There are no tax shelters available to speak of. The aim is for large capital gain rather than ongoing income.

The New York Times, June 3, 1973, featured an article, "A Money Machine Attracts Investors". The money machine is condominiums–recently a very hot item in many locations. Condominium construction can be heavily leveraged and construction money borrowed from Real Estate Investment Trusts. The profit magic of condominiums lies in the fact that the total value of the units individually sold to buyers is greater than the value of the same amount of units combined and rented out by one owner were the property to be maintained as a rental development. Also, the builder receives profits relatively quickly, as soon as the units are sold, unlike rental income which is drawn out over many years. And, of course, there are fewer landlord headaches. Potential returns? *The Real Estate Investors Report,* July 1973, reported a study in Boston which showed condominium apartments up 14% in a single year, up 32% in five years. Since these purchases are leveraged via mortgages, returns on capital are much greater.

Disadvantages? No tax shelter. Profits are taxed as ordinary income, in contrast to which the ultimate sale of a rental property is treated as a capital gain. Recently, the profit potential of condominiums has been fantastic, even in areas where rental markets have been soft. Beware, however, of inner city luxury condominiums; their pricing has not held up as well. So long as building costs keep rising, in many cases putting single family and rental units out of range, the general condominium market should stay firm. *Caveat:* If you are buying a condominium apartment more for resale than for occupancy, try to establish how many other investors are doing the same. If everyone tries to get out at the same time, a glut on the market may develop, with a resultant squeeze on the prices you can secure.

GETTING STARTED

As an investor, you won't need much preparation. Have ten to twenty-five thousand ready for starters, your legal and accounting people ready, and go shopping. Expect to have at least 5-6 partners. Check your real estate section, local realty organizations and preferably your real estate lawyer for leads. Investigate until you are satisfied, and then invest. Syndications in income property have been quite successful, by and large. Nonetheless, keep the following disadvantages in mind:

1) You are probably going to be a non-voting member in a limited partnership and, once in, you have limited control of your destiny.

2) Your investment is not particularly liquid; your money, once committed, doesn't come out readily. Make sure the promotors don't get too big a piece, free.

3) Your personal interests may become lost in the interests of the partnership.

4) The syndicate tax shelter is a prime target for potential tax reform. If they eliminate the tax shelter, the deal loses an amount of its appeal. Keep posted on the regulations and happenings in Congress.

5) *Not* every syndicate is successful. There have been a number of well-publicized failures, and from time to time syndication fads sweep the country, attracting marginal and/or shady operators. Many syndicate flops arise from investment in realty exotica, rather than from bread and butter enterprises. Properties should be well capitalized, not highly leveraged.

Check the past performance of the syndicator. If he has been in business for a number of years in stable properties, he's probably all right.

Lest this discourage you, keep the advantages going in your head also—the steady returns, no work, limited liability and, so far at least, the tax shelter.

Getting started as a syndicator is more complicated, particularly if you plan to advertise publicly. Consult your lawyer for the necessary procedures which are complex and must conform to regulation.

If you are new to the real estate game altogether, you might start, if possible, with a duplex or three family of your own—just to get the feel of property management and to establish your credentials. From there on, the size of your operation need be limited only by your imagination and access to investment funds. There is really not all that much difference between operating a small apartment house and a large unit.

REAL ESTATE INVESTMENT TRUSTS

Real Estate Investment Trusts, virtually created by acts of Congress in the 1960's, receive federal tax exemption if they meet certain criteria. These include the maintenance of 75% of assets in real estate, mortgages, cash, or government securities. Seventy-five per cent of gross income must be derived from real estate. Most important to the investor, 90% of taxable income has to be distributed to shareholders, of which there must be at least 100. This produces excellent dividend yields, often in excess of 10% per annum.

REITs operate by investing in high yield, short term mortgages, their profit derived from the difference between what they must pay to borrow money and the amount of money they receive when lending, generally for new construction. Should you decide to build your own condominium, you might very possibly turn to a REIT for construction money. Problems have arisen in the industry relating to national credit conditions, the rate of new construction, and the problem of loan defaults, necessitating foreclosure. Still, investors over the years have been rewarded with consistently rising dividend payouts, and at late-1973 levels, REITs offered investors a fine return for their money. Incidentally, since you invest in REITs by purchasing shares in the companies usually listed on the major exchanges, you can leverage the operation for an even higher return by purchasing the securities at 50% margin. You get, on 50% of your holdings, as extra income, the difference between the high rate of dividend payout and the interest you pay to carry the margin loan. A REIT paying 11% unmargined, actually yields almost 13½% purchased at 50% margin, at 8½% interest rates paid by margin accounts to the brokerage houses. 1973 saw margin costs rise to 11% and more; however, in many years, 8½% rates pertain. A good occasion to employ leverage.

Investment in shares of REITs are, naturally, subject to the whims of the stock market. REITs have periodically come into investor popularity. They were hot items during the late 1968, early 1969 period, and again in late 1970 and late 1971 in anticipation of housing booms. These securities are interest sensitive and usually rise during periods of easy money. Like bonds, they are good purchases as interest rates peak. If ups and downs give you ulcers, stay away. If you can tolerate the swings, and instant liquidity has appeal, you may consider investment in any or some of the REITs listed here. Check with your brokerage house for up to date information on price and current yield. This data is also carried in many financial newspapers, such as the *Wall Street Journal.* All told, REITs offer an exceptionally high dividend payout, excellent liquidity, and a chance at capital gain in addition to income. Risk is high in view of the possibility that the security shares may drop in value subject to market conditions. However, the market fluctuations of REITs tend to be slightly less in magnitude than most stocks and, because of their high yields, they enjoy a basic price support.

There are at least two REIT mutual funds in existence, the CNA-Larwin Investment Company and the REIT Income Fund. These are closed end funds; their shares are not redeemable at net asset value, but trade on the open market, usually at a discount from the true value of the shares. These funds, in mid-1973, were providing yields in the area of 10 per cent, and offer the advantage of diversification since they invest in a variety of REITs.

The following REITs have shown either constant or rising dividend payouts over the years. Check with the research wing of your brokerage house before taking positions.

Company	Rising Dividends Since	Yields (Autumn, 1973)
Atico Mortgage Inv.	1970	11.7%
Chase Manhattan Mtge.	1971	8.5
Continental Ill. Realty	1969	11.3
First Penn. Mtge.	1971	10.5
Tri-South Mtge. Inv.	1970	10.0
Wachovia Realty Inv.	1970	9.8
Wells Fargo Mtge.	1971	9.5
Connecticut General Mtge.	1970	9.8
Continental Mtge. Investors	1962	10.0
Diversified Mtge. Investors	1970	14.3
Equitable Life Mtge.	1971	9.8
First Mtge. Investors	1962	10.8
Hubbard Real Estate	1970	8.7
Mass Mutual Mtge.	1971	9.8
Money Mtge. Investors	1971	8.6

CAVEATS

Some question has been raised regarding the ability of the REITs to continue to grow and expand. For example, in a dull housing market to whom can they lend money? Adverse conditions for REITs include periods of tight money and periods of limited construction activity. Essentially, this is a cyclical rather than a growth industry. It should be pointed out again, however, that REITs have not been as volatile as most securities and have maintained their fine dividend payout over the years.

A shakeout appears to be developing in the industry at this time, (1974), the result of tight money, and a run of failures on the part of debtors to REITs. As a result, the industry has come heavily into investor disfavor, with shares selling at historic lows. Very possibly, we may see the failure of some firms, forced mergers, and even some dividend cuts. Still, odds are that the industry and most of its members will survive the upheaval, and eventually recover lost popularity. As I said above, this is a cyclical industry.

There they are. Three devices for teaming up with others to make your realty dollars grow. Form your own syndicate–using other people's money. Join a syndicate–using other people's know-how. Or, reap the rewards of lending indirectly via the REIT.

Consider any or all of the three. After all, if you can't make it alone, there's really nothing wrong with getting a little help.

Chapter 6

"Neither A Borrower Nor A Lender Be, But If You Do Have To Lend, 12-20% Really Isn't Such A Bad Return"

Investing In Discount Mortgages

Potential Return,	B
Risk,	B+
Liquidity,	C–
Tax Considerations,	D

This is the last of our realty ploys, the tactic for the man who has everything and who simply wants to put it to work for him to produce nice regular monthly income checks. Ideal for the retired and not quite retired, and not at all bad for compounding in the 14% column.

Fourteen per cent does not reach our goal of a 25% return, but the investment technique is quite safe and requires relatively little effort. You will double your money in less than six years and $10,000 will become over $100,000 within eighteen years, so the rate of return is nothing to sneeze at.

The risk is small—if you play your cards carefully. Investment in mortgages should involve no greater risk than owning your own property, less than investing in raw land.

Liquidity is poor. To dispose of your holdings, you will almost certainly have to offer a discount on the mortgages you are holding, although buyers should be plentiful if you do come down in price a bit.

Too bad about the taxes. There are no shelters on interest income, and Uncle Sam gets to claim his full share of the proceeds—every penny of it.

THE BASIC TECHNIQUE

Investing in mortgages can take two forms. You can act as the provider of an original mortgage, usually a second, to an individual or a corporation. State usury laws prohibit your charging more than the statutory limit, ranging from 7½-10% depending upon the state, if the loans are to individuals. Loans to corporations can be based upon higher rates and you can receive up to 25% interest, for example, in New York State, if you are willing to stay awake nights. Count on perhaps 12% if you are lending to corporations of some credibility.

These returns are at best fair, considering your trouble and the fact that, at present, triple A corporate bonds yield near 7½% and B bonds over 10%. It's the second hand mortgage strategy that brings in the goodies.

DISCOUNTED MORTGAGES

Here is how it works. Mortgage money is tight and becoming tighter, particularly for income property, unsubsidized by government backed programs. Sellers of income property are finding it difficult to sell unless they are willing to accept a second mortgage to supplement whatever first mortgage the buyer can maneuver from his friendly banker. Suppose, for simplicity's sake, that the seller accepts a second mortgage of $10,000, of a one year duration, at 7½%. He needs or wants the cash in a hurry so he offers the mortgage, usually through a mortgage broker, at a discount, say, for $9500.

Mortgages are computed at true interest. The actual interest payments each month drop as the note outstanding is reduced, but the money you have lent out, cash out of your pocket, drops in proportion also. We will presume that the $10,000 mortgage is due in one installment at the end of one year.

Income to Original Lender:

Loan Provided:	$10,000
Interest Received:	750
Rate of Return:	7½%

Income to Discount Purchaser:

Investment to Purchase one $10,000 Note at 5% Discount:	$9500
Interest Received:	750
Profit On Note (You paid $9500 for the note. The original borrower now owes *you* $10,000).	500
Total Profit on $9500 Investment:	1250
Rate of Return	13.2%

Your purchase of a 7½% note at a 5% discount for one year holding period results in a return of 13.2%. Not bad for all concerned. The buyer of the property gets his mortgage. The seller gets his cash in hand, less $500, and *you* make 13% on your money. Usury laws, incidentally, apply only to the face interest on the note, not to the return you make by discount purchase. A five per cent discount is typical for a one year note. Longer duration mortgages usually sell in the area of a 20% discount, the amount of discount varying with the length of the mortgage—the longer the mortgage period, the larger the discount. Why? Suppose the above note and terms were for two years, interest due annually and principal due at the end of a two year period.

You would receive after two years:

Interest:	$1500 ($750 per year)
Profit on Principal:	500
Total Profit:	2000 or an average of $1000 per year profit
Rate of Return:	10.5% annually

It is actually even less than this since a factor has to be allowed for the delayed return of your $500 profit on principal. Yield tables should be consulted for the actual rate of return on mortgages, but 10.5% in the example is approximately correct.

You can see, though, why longer term mortgages sell at greater discounts than short term. They have to in order to provide the rate of return necessary to attract mortgage investors. To compute the profitability of a deal, you must secure and learn to use yield tables. Consult your mortgage broker, bank, accountant or lawyer.

THE BASIC TACTIC

The basic tactic then is clear. For maximum return on discounted mortgages, the mortgage investor purchases existing mortgages at discounts commensurate with the rate of interest signified by the note and the length of the note's maturity. When prevailing yields from competitive income investments are high, investors will demand and receive higher discounts on the mortgages they purchase. When competitive income rates drop, lower discounts will be available. Currently, no investor should accept any but a very short term mortgage which yields under 10-12% to maturity. Lower rates of return for longer term notes are not competitive with alternate forms of investment.

THE BASIC STEPS

If this form of investment has some appeal to you, your first step is the determination of the amount of money you have available for this purpose. This is a safe investment technique which brings in income each month. Your risk on each investment is ever-declining since each repayment represents partial return to you of the money you laid out for starters. Therefore, leverage can be used to get you started, so long as the return you secure is sufficiently higher than the interest you pay to justify the trouble. Suggestion: consider refinancing your own home mortgage. If you can do that, say, at 8% and secure 14% on discounted seconds, you will make, in twenty years on a $10,000 starter, more than $27,000 in profit That's pure extra cash on a fully leveraged position. No point in your bank getting it all. Try becoming your own bank.

The second decision involves the type of mortgage in which you plan to invest. As we noted before, investors can offer original mortgages or purchase existing notes. You can pick up a mortgage originally written on a property transaction, or you can put up a "hard money" mortgage–lending cash outright to some property owner, the note secured by a second mortgage on his property. Do you wish to lend to private homeowners, income property investors, commercial builders or a combination of all of these? There are good possibilities inherent in all variations. The safest operation is probably investment in discounted second mortgages that are secured by private homeowner property. The shorter the remaining life of the mortgage, the safer the investment. More about this below.

The third step involves the securing of offers so that you can select the deal most favorable to you. Any of the following should bring in plenty of investment opportunities: (1) Advertise in your local newspaper (real estate section) that you have mortgage money available. (2) Contact local realty brokers and let them know. Many deals that would otherwise fall through can be saved by the presence of a third party willing to accept an extra mortgage or (3) seek out mortgage brokers who themselves advertise, and who list mortgages for sale. In some communities, this requires a bit of detective work; in others, the brokers make themselves quite well known. Once you have made the contact, your broker should keep you regularly posted as to offerings. He may call you directly as something comes up or periodically send listings to you.

EVALUATING THE DEAL

To restate the obvious, you are going into the money lending business. You want to receive the optimum combination of high return, safety and limited headache. For safety, expect to sacrifice some return. *To Establish Safety:*

1) Determine the amount of collateral backing the loan. For example, let's suppose that you are offered a mortgage of $10,000 on an income property. Your first step is to appraise the market value of the property. If it has recently changed hands, you can presume that the price at last sale represented fair market value. If not, employ one of the formulae in

Chapter 3 to determine the market value of the property, based upon the rental income it derives and the expenses it involves. We will assume that you determine the value of the property to be $35,000. *Do this yourself.* Trust neither the seller of the mortgage nor the mortgage broker—both interested parties. In the event of foreclosure, you may have to digest that property. We will presume that the property is worth $35,000; your proposed loan is $10,000. How much of the other $35,000 is already committed ahead of you? Upon inquiry, you establish that there is an existing first mortgage outstanding of $18,000 which takes precedence over your claim, should foreclosure develop. There are no other liens on the property. Therefore, should you have to foreclose, your loan is secured by $17,000 worth of property. You will be obligated, should you foreclose, for the payments due to the holder of the first mortgage; $18,000 of the $35,000 value belongs to that party in priority to your interests. Would you be able to sell the property, if need be, for $28,000, so that you can settle the first mortgage and recapture your loan? If you have correctly appraised the property's value, yes, readily, and probably at some additional profit to you.

Your risk is highest early in the investment. As your loan becomes repaid, the ratio of loan outstanding to property value declines and you are increasingly protected.

First mortgages offer more safety than seconds since the first holder has prior claim. If you do invest in a second, establish contact with the holder of the first. In the event he forecloses and puts the property up for auction, you will want to take action to protect your interests—possibly involving the purchase of the property yourself. This is *not* a "consummation devoutly to be wished", unless you want to enter the real estate business, but is a real risk of the game. Do not be put off by this caveat, however. Ninety-nine per cent of all mortgages *are* paid off in full.

2) Do a check on the owner of the property. He probably will not care at all whether the mortgage holder sells his paper to you or not, and he may or may not be co-operative. Still, a little snooping and looking go a long way. If the property is income producing, what is the current rate of vacancy? Is the property, private or income, well maintained? Check the books of the mortgage holder. Have mortgage payments been made on time by the mortgagee in the past? What is the owner's equity in the property? If the owner has already made $20,000 worth of mortgage payments on a $35,000 property, he will try as hard as possible to avoid foreclosure. Properties that are highly leveraged may produce fine profits for the owner, but are riskier for the lenders since the owner may not have ready cash on hand to meet large mortgage and other loan payments, in the event that vacancies develop.

3) "Seasoned" mortgages are safer than fresh ones. A "seasoned" mortgage is a mortgage that has already been partially repaid. Seasoning represents increased owner equity, a history of repayment, shorter maturity. Expect, however, lesser discounts on seasoned mortgages. They are desirable and do look for them.

4) The shorter the maturity period the better. A short maturity involves less time for neighborhood change and property deterioration. During these inflationary times, it also means that you secure your repayment of principal at closer to today's purchasing power.

5) Be certain that the terms of the mortgage include a fairly rapid return of principal. Some notes include monthly payments, primarily of interest charges, with a balloon payment

due at the end for principal repayment. These notes are relatively unsafe since your investment remains tied up while the owner of the property is not developing an increasing equity himself. The amortization plan of the note, therefore, should provide for constant and rapid repayment of principal. Generally, the shorter the original maturity of the mortgage, the more rapid the principal repayment since longer term notes involve greater interest charges each installment.

6) Establish the amount of liens, tax liabilities and so forth against the property. Be certain that the title to the property is clear. You may wish to require a new title insurance policy as part of the deal, if the existing policy is not recent. Have your lawyer insist upon the necessary representations for you. In the event of foreclosure, you are liable for existing liens.

7) Private homes are usually safer than income properties, unless the latter are running at a solid profit. Investors in income property are liable to default on taxes, mortgage payments, and other bills if their properties are running at a loss–skimming off as much current income cream as possible before letting the creditors have the property.

DO NEGOTIATE

If investigation satisfies the safety requirements, you are now ready for some negotiating. The seller of the mortgage will, of course, attempt to sell for as little discount as possible. As a buyer, you are looking for the best discount you can get. The rest is negotiation. Decide beforehand the minimum return you will accept for that particular deal on your investment and stay within your limits. You do have to live with a mortgage deal, usually for several years. Sometimes you can trade off one item against the other, e.g., if you insist that the mortgage seller provide title insurance, you may have to pay for that via a lesser discount.

MANAGEMENT

Your accountant will help you set up the necessary bookkeeping operations for keeping track of your accounts and for reporting income to the Internal Revenue Service.

Like rent, your mortgage payments should be *in your hands* by the due date. And like renters, payees tend to be late by a few days at least. Ten days is an acceptable grace period, but be firm in not allowing your debtors to go beyond that. Foreclosure is a last resort. It is time consuming, involved, and puts you in the position of being responsible for property you may not wish to own. Therefore, from time to time you may have to consider refinancing notes to help debtors who have come upon hard times. In the worst of cases, you may even end up advancing cash to them for tax payments, as an example, to forestall foreclosure from other sources. By and large, however, you will receive payments regularly—nothing more required than a nasty letter or two to late payers.

Tax Tip: Do not forget to deduct your travel, telephone calls, letters and use of home office space from your mortgage investing income. These are legitimate deductions.

SUMMING UP

Mortgage investment provides steady income and repayment of principal, your loans backed by fine collateral–sound property and the underlying land. Look for deals that provide a minimum 12% return, but shoot for 14-20%. The investment program involves a minimum of risk and trouble and can be fully leveraged.

Disadvantages lie in the fact that your money is tied up, often for years, and once in, it costs to get out again. You also have to deal with people, handle late payments and maintain accurate bookkeeping.

On balance, investment in mortgages is a sound and solid, if stolid, way to have your money make money. The old adage, "neither a borrower nor a lender be" may be true, but if you do have to lend, 12-20% really isn't such a bad return.

Chapter 7

"When You Come Right Down To It, Buying Mutual Funds Is, Essentially, Buying The Stock Market."

Investing In Mutual Funds

Potential Reward,	B–
Risk,	C
Liquidity,	A
Tax Considerations,	B–

The bloom is certainly off the rose. After two decades of glory, which saw some 8.7 million Americans become mutual shareholders, the mutual fund industry is hurting, and hurting badly. The denouement began during 1971, when investors first began to take their marbles out of the mutual fund circle to roll them elsewhere. 1972 was the first year in the

Mutual Fund Net Subscriptions

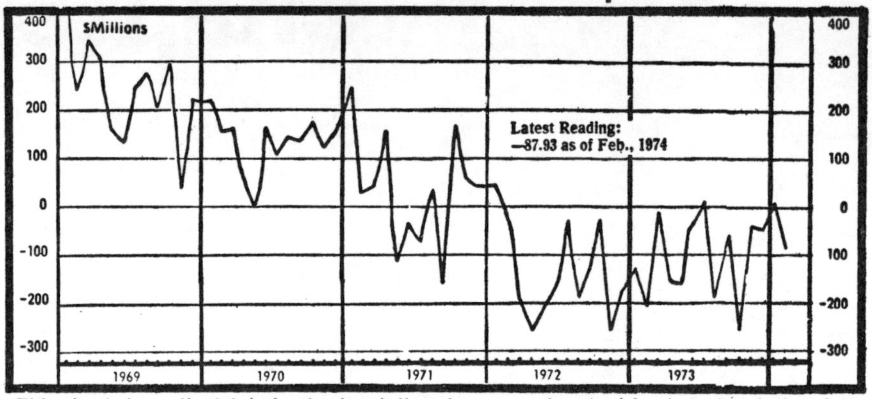

This chart shows the total of net subscriptions to open end mutual funds (subscriptions less redemptions). The trend toward more or less net buying generally has paralleled the movement of the odd lot purchase to sale ratio.

FIGURE 1

MUTUAL FUND NET SUBSCRIPTIONS

Source: Media-General Financial Weekly, 113 N. Third St., Richmond, VA 23261

49 year history of the industry in which investor purchases of mutual shares were exceeded by liquidations, a trend which has continued into 1974. Suddenly, the funds are on the defensive. What Watergate was to the White House, so the bear markets of 1969-1970 and 1973 were to Enterprise and the Manhattan Fund. Clearly, the gunslingers of the middle sixties are no longer the folk heroes of the American Financial scene. See Figure 1 above.

In all fairness, however, recent criticism of the mutual fund industry is not all that warranted. While it is true that in recent years the funds have occasionally underperformed the major market averages, it is also true, as Mr. John C. Bogle, president of Wellington Management Company, pointed out, May 1973, in a speech to the Investment Company Institute, that the major market indices are weighted to favor the more heavily capitalized companies, and that the funds, on balance, did outperform by far the average security during 1972. The Standard and Poor's 500, a weighted average, gained 15½% during 1972. The average of Lipper's 530 funds showed a 9½% gain. However, the total mutual fund industry, weighting each fund's performance by its total assets, gained 13% (The Lipper Averages are unweighted by fund size). By comparison, the average NYSE issue showed a gain of only ½%. There is, therefore, some case to be made for the concept that professional fund management does provide something for investors, and that investments in mutuals will outperform random or uninformed individual security selection–in any case, at least some of the time. (Other studies have pointed in the opposite direction–to wit, that randomly selected portfolios equal the performance of managed portfolios.)

The funds, however, have no one to blame for the current disillusionment and criticism but themselves. Mr. Bogle obviously decries the criticism of fund performance as unfair and unwarranted, claiming that the speculative smaller funds are given too much weight in the public reporting of the industry's performance and that during 1972, at least, comparison to the Standard and Poor's 500 is inequitable. But what of the mutual industry's contributions to the current crisis of expectations? Was the industry complaining during the fifties and early sixties when it was precisely these smaller funds that hypoed up the fund performance averages, thereby drawing the sheep into the fold? Did the industry contribute nothing to public expectations of 25-30% annual appreciation? What about those graphs that used to be so popular, showing how fund investments far outperformed the dowdy Dow?

If 1971 was the beginning of the end, and 1972 the year that the funds really took it on the chin, then 1973 was the year of repentence. Suddenly, income funds came into vogue and suddenly funds and investment managers were talking about *matching* the Dow and the S & P. With the performance cult dead, new investment gimmicks began to proliferate, a recent ploy involving the computerized selection of portfolios which would simulate the performance of the Standard and Poor's Index. A far cry from the days when funds locked themselves into lettered securities.

WHAT CAN THE INVESTOR EXPECT FROM INVESTMENT IN MUTUAL FUNDS?

A study by William A. Dreher of *Pensions Magazine* showed that from 1965-1971, equity mutual funds achieved a compound return of 6.8% compared to 6.4% for bank managed funds and 6.2% for insurance managed pension funds. During this time, the Standard and Poor's 500 gained 6.1%. Another study revealed that in the decade 1963-1971, including dividend returns compounded, mutual funds achieved a compounded growth rate of 10.7% compared to 10.0% for the S & P. By comparison, from January 1954 through mid-June 1973, the Dow Jones Industrial Averages gained slightly less than 6% compounded. Figuring an average dividend rate of about 4% on the Dow, we can conclude that investments in mutuals have somewhat outperformed both the Dow and the Standard and Poor's indices and may well be a viable alternative to individual self-stock selection for many investors. However, the advantage is slight, less than a one percent improvement over random selection.

As an investor, is it worth shooting for a 10-11% return? Clearly, these returns fall far short of our 25% goal. Clearly too, bonds, for example, offer tough competition, Triple A's now yielding better than 7½% and B's going to 12% and up—all at far less risk than mutuals. More important are basic questions involving the stock market and the future of equity investment in its broadest sense. The Dow rose by more than 230% in the twelve years from 1954-1966. It has gained nothing at all over the past seven years; in fact, it has declined in the interim by as much as 37% from early 1966 levels. The net redemptions which have plagued the mutual fund industry since 1971 are only reflective of the public disenchantment with common share securities in general, which has been reflective too in the recent closing of nearly one million private investor accounts. Should the market embark on another major

TABLE I

An Average $10,000 Fund Investment 1950-1971

YEAR	$10,000	% CHANGE	GAIN	LOSS	Compared with 5% interest compounded annually $10,000
1950	$11,089	+10.89	$1,089		$10,500
1951	12,734	+14 .84	1,645		11,025
1952	14,166	+11.24	1,432		11,576
1953	14,150	– .11		$ 16	12,155
1954	20,233	+42.99	6,083		12,763
1955	23,805	+17.65	3,572		13,401
1956	25,604	+ 7.56	1,799		14,071
1957	23,023	–10.08		2,581	14,775
1958	32,088	+39.37	9,065		15,514
1959	36,198	+12.81	4,110		16,290
1960	37,403	+ 3.33	1,205		17,105
1961	46,911	+25.42	9,508		17,960
1962	41,484	–11.57		5,427	18,858
1963	48,519	+16.96	7,035		19,801
1964	54,866	+13.08	6,347		20,791
1965	66,256	+20.76	11,390		21,831
1966	62,785	– 5.24		3,471	22,923
1967	84,294	+34.26	21,509		24,069
1968	99,138	+17.61	14,844		25,272
1969	85,100	–14.16		14,038	26,536
1970	78,616	– 7.62		6,484	27,863
1971	94,008	+19.58	15,392		29,256

Figures in this table are based on annual performance averages of funds listed in the Management Results section of Wiesenberger's *Investment Companies,* except for the categories of bond and preferred stock funds, tax-free exchange funds and international funds. Annual average performance was derived by adding each fund's performance and dividing by the number of funds. New funds were added as they appeared in the Wiesenberger volumes which were used. In 1950, 1961 and 1970, for example, the number of funds was 40, 145 and 307, respectively. Investment results assume initial investment of $9,150 following deduction of sales charges of 8½ percent and subsequent reinvestment of dividends and capital gains.

Source: Mutual Fund Almanac, 1973 by Yale Hirsch, The Hirsch Organization, 6 Deer Trail, Old Tappan, N.J. 07675

upleg, then investments in mutuals may pay off big. Certainly, mutual investors who know when to buy in and when to sell out do far better than long term holders. However, should the market, long term, repeat the performance of the thirties and forties, fund investment will produce, at best, only a moderate return. Should, heaven forbid, 1929 strike once more . . .? You get the idea.

However, lest I leave you with visions of selling apples on streetcorners, keep this in mind. According to the *Mutual Funds Almanac,* 1973, $10,000 invested in the average mutual grew to over $102,750 by the end of 1972. This compared most favorably to the returns from a 5% compounded investment of $30,715 for the same period. *Suggestion:* Some investment should be placed into equity situations. However, do diversify your capital by spreading investments elsewhere as well.

RISKS

High. From 1942-1968, long term holding of common equities almost always paid off. In recent years, it has become a new ball game. Mutual funds *do not* rise during bear markets. During the 1969-1970 bear market, for example, stocks on average, and mutuals, both lost about 36% in value. During early 1973, only a handful of funds managed to eke out even modest gains, and for the most part these were funds heavily invested in gold shares, hedged, or in international situations.

LIQUIDITY

Excellent. Load funds, of course, penalize investors who have paid 8½% commissions to buy in, should they wish to sell. However, no-load funds, which offer far better value, charge at worst only a slight redemption fee and no purchase commissions. You can get your current market value in cash in your hands within a few days, and you can sell out at any time. Incidentally, it is probably preferable to leave your mutual shares on deposit with the fund. Otherwise, you run the risk of theft, have to provide storage, and become involved in a somewhat more cumbersome redemption process.

TAX CONSIDERATIONS

Fund holdings upon sale are charged or credited as a capital gain or loss, long or short term depending upon the length of the holding period. Holding periods of less than six months are considered short term, and gains or losses are charged or credited as ordinary income, subject to the limitations for deductions of losses on equity investments. Dividends are charged to income, subject to the limitations of dividend exclusion. Should you participate in an automatic dividend reinvestment plan, each such transaction represents a fresh purchase.

Many mutual funds do offer Keogh Plan participation which is very advantageous to long term holders, raising, in that case, the rating of *Tax Considerations* to A. A number of funds also offer automatic withdrawal plans for those who wish to draw income from their fund investments on a regular basis. Such plans enjoyed considerable appeal during the fifties and sixties when mutuals were appreciating at better than 10% per year. Investors were able to draw out their gains as income, leaving the original principal untouched. However, during declining periods, monthly withdrawals do eat into the principal of your assets, thereby reducing your chances of recovering any losses since there is a reduction in the amount of capital left to do the work.

TAX HINT

Try to avoid purchasing funds just prior to the dates of capital gains and dividend distributions. When a fund makes a distribution to shareholders, the net asset value per share of the fund declines by the extent of the distribution since it is the investors' money that is being returned to them. However, although new shareholders have gained nothing via the distribution, they are required to report it nonetheless. The distribution, capital gain or dividend, is considered taxable income, and the investor just prior to such distributions incurs a tax liability even though he has really not seen any appreciation in his investment. Do check with your load fund salesman or the no-load prospectus, and, if possible, defer your purchase until just after the fund goes ex-distribution.

LOAD OR NO-LOAD?

No contest. No-loads win hands down. The load fund sector of the industry has attempted to propagandize the virtues of an 8½% commission charge, aided and abetted by their stockbroker allies who pocket commissions when the selling is done via the brokerage offices.

Edward E. Duke (*Selecting Your Mutual Fund: A Professional Program for Producing Perpetual Profits,* Exposition Press, 1972) argues that load funds should outperform the no-loads because their sales force ensures a constant flow of money into their coffers. Ralph Kingsbury attempts to dilute the issue (*Bulls, Bears and the Gadfly,* Carlton Press, 1971), claiming that it is the fund's performance that counts in the long run, not the commission. He concedes, however, that the sales charge does put the load funds under a distinct handicap. Alan S. Feinstein, (*Making Your Money Grow,* Selby Publishing Co., 1972) comes to a conclusion favoring no-loads, but based, I think, on spurious logic. The no-load, reasons Feinstein, has to work harder to achieve excellent performance because of the lack of a sales force and because of limited advertising. The only selling device such funds have is their performance record. It would appear to me that every fund hopes to achieve outstanding performance and that excellence is no less desired by load than by no-load funds.

A most telling blow in favor of no-loads was administered by Yale Hirsch, (*No-Loads Have a Helluva Head Start,* The Hirsch Organization, 1972). Summing up investor experience, 1951-1970, Mr. Hirsch demonstrated that over that twenty year period, a $10,000 original investment in load funds would have appreciated to $53,051 while the same 10 grand put into no-loads would have grown to $68,010 or 28.2% more. Incidentally, had the no-loads been burdened with an 8½% sales charge, as a group they would still have outperformed the load funds, in this case by 15.7%. Clearly, the load adds nothing to a fund's performance. The average annual appreciation for no-loads during this time was 11.5%. For load funds, the average appreciation was 10%.

To appreciate the handicap incurred by purchasing a load fund, consider the following table:

TABLE II

Performance Required of Load Funds to Catch-Up to No-Load Funds

Assuming a no-load fund is starting out with $10,000, while a load fund–after an 8½% sales charge–is starting out with $9,150:

- A load fund appreciating 10% more per year than a no-load, will catch up in about 10 years.
- A load fund appreciating 20% more per year than a no-load, will catch up in about 5 years.
- A load fund appreciating 30% more per year than a no-load, will catch up in about 3½ years.
- A load fund appreciating 40% more per year than a no-load, will catch up in about 2½ years.
- A load fund appreciating 50% more per year than a no-load, will catch up in about 2 years.

Source: *No-Loads Have a Helluva Head Start,* Yale Hirsch, The Hirsch Organization, 1972.

SIZE

Smaller funds have generally made the headlines, but larger funds tend to be steadier performers.

We will define small funds as funds having less than $50 million in total assets. Of the top 25 performers of the 563 funds monitored by the *Mutual Funds Scoreboard* during the first quarter of 1973, eighteen were funds with under $50 million and, in fact, seventeen had under $25 million in assets. Similar results pertained during 1971 and 1972. The smaller funds led the parade in both those years. The explanation is simple enough. Small funds can be more flexible, acquiring and dispensing of share assets in keeping with market developments. A good selection of a hot stock, or two, exercises greater proportionate influence within the total portfolio of smaller funds. New cash inflow during strong markets, spurred by good fund performance, often adds a high proportion to the cash base of smaller funds, fueling additional profitable investment as the market rises.

In fact, both Edward E. Duke and Alan S. Feinstein urge investors to concentrate their capital in small funds featuring a large inflow of fresh cash. The flexibility of smaller funds was illustrated by Janus (assets, $32 million), which was able to get into an over 85% cash position early in 1973, and by Cambridge Appreciation (assets, $.4 million), which achieved a nicely hedged position early in the year· Dreyfus cannot swing billions of dollars of assets in that manner.

On the other hand, adversity hits the small funds the hardest. Nicholas Strong ($65.5 million) lost over 35% asset value in the twelve months ending May, 1973 and Redmond Growth ($5.7 million) lost 30%. If the smaller funds dominated the winner's circle in 1971 and 1972, it was the larger funds which placed and showed. *The Mutual Fund Scoreboard* reports that, on average, in both years, the larger funds outperformed the smaller. In 1971, funds with over $100 million in assets outperformed funds with under $100 million by one or two percentage points. In 1972, funds with over $25 million in assets averaged an 11.8% gain; smaller funds gained only 7.1%. In general, larger funds fill their portfolios with less speculative vehicles than smaller mutuals. 1972 was the year for blue chips; 1967 was another matter altogether. Performance in the end apparently depends more upon how a fund's style matches the prevailing market climate than upon anything else. In total then, when small funds are right, they often turn out to be very, very right. When they are wrong, they are frequently wrong with a vengeance. You have to decide for yourself the extent to which you want to speculate. I do suggest that you divide your assets among at least a few funds; it rarely pays to put all your eggs in one basket.

TABLE III

How Mutual Funds Performed — 1967-1972
(Funds of $100 Million or Over in Assets in 1968)

	Total Funds In Group	Fund Group	Average % Gain or Loss in Net Asset Value* 1967	1968	1969	1970	1971	1972	What $10,000 Grew to:
	44	Growth	+46.2%	+12.0%	-13.6%	-10.7%	+20.3%	+11.5%	$17,136
	29	Growth & Income	+25.4	+15.4	-11.1	+0.8	+14.8	+13.6	16,912
	9	Income	+20.1	+17.3	-14.7	+4.1	+14.5	+8.7	15,570
	12	Balanced	+17.3	+12.5	-11.1	+2.8	+15.0	+10.9	15,381
Totals	**94**	**Averages**	**+33.6%**	**+13.6%**	**-12.6%**	**-4.0%**	**+17.4%**	**+11.8%**	**$16,714**
Dow Jones industrials:		Actual	+15.2	+4.3	-15.2	+4.8	+6.1	+14.6	12,983
Adjusted for cash and stock dividends			+19.0	+7.7	-11.6	+8.8	+9.6	+18.3	15,982

*Performance includes the year to year increase in net asset value per share, plus all capital gain distributions, and income dividends received during the year. Sales charges and taxes have not been taken into account.

Source: Mutual Fund Almanac, 1973, by Yale Hirsch, The Hirsch Organization, 6 Deer Trail, Old Tappan, N.J. 07675

ONE SIDELIGHT

Small funds do not stay small if they are successful. If you are seeking maximum performance via the small fund route, keep in mind that success will continue to attract fresh money into the fund, ultimately resulting in growth to a size which can no longer sustain the performance level which attracted the buyers in the first place. It is an interesting paradox—success breeds failure in a sense. The story of the Enterprise Fund is an excellent example of this paradox.

TYPES OF FUNDS

The variety of funds available can present a confusing morass to the potential investor who is attempting to make a choice of investment vehicle—all the more (since fads change) depending upon the market climate. Once upon a time, when the bull was snorting loudly, growth funds were the rage, and performance the cult. Now, income is no longer a dirty word and bond funds are becoming popular. Next year? Who knows? In any case, herein are listed some broad categories of funds and their more or less common objectives. Do look over the prospectus of any fund before buying, to determine the objectives for that particular fund.

Growth Funds: These are the guys who shoot for the big killing via the capital gains route, the fellows who stock up on Polaroid, Avon, IBM, McDonald's and Equity Funding. During the sweet sixties, these funds provided glamour to the industry and this group still comprises the majority of all funds. Do not expect too much in the way of dividends if you play on this table, but during good times the gains can be spectacular. Until very recently, growth funds achieved, on average, considerably more in the way of capital appreciation than other classes of funds. They have continued to maintain some advantage over the past six or seven years, but their relative performance has been declining. *Performance funds* are the go-go funds of the growth group, their portfolios marked by frequent turnovers and trading.

Hedge Funds: Hedge funds *theoretically* protect shareholders against market declines because their prospectii and policies allow short selling during bear markets to offset long positions held. Many private hedge partnerships have succeeded greatly in this manner; however, public mutuals have not done quite as well. One stellar performer during early 1973, Cambridge Appreciation, is a small hedge fund.

Growth Income Funds: Somewhat more conservative than growth funds, these funds do seek some dividend payout for investors—averaging about 4% during 1972 versus about 1% for growth funds.

Income Funds: You guessed it. High payout and price stability are their hallmark. In 1972, their average dividend yield was 5%. Income funds are more stable than other classes of funds and have averaged about a 7½% return, all told, over the years, including dividends. Frankly, I see no real point in putting money into these situations when prime bonds are yielding 7½%.

Bond Funds: A recent "concept" in the industry. Variations are based upon the type of bond the fund rides (e.g., municipal, conservative, convertible, speculative). Lately, the idea has caught on that bonds can be traded, with the funds selling off rising bonds to position themselves into higher yielding "underpriced" notes, thereby keeping the yield of the fund's assets at a level of 7½% or better. Sort of a performance ride for the rocking chair set. Big danger: this new breed of go-go performer may just accumulate one speculative bond too many in order to push their yield from 7½ to 8%.

Convertible bond funds specialize in convertible bonds, in my opinion one of the best of investment vehicles.

Municipal bond funds are not usually actual mutual funds but rather "unit trusts" which offer a diversified portfolio of municipal bonds to purchasers. These bonds are of interest mainly because the interest they provide is not taxable.

Multi-Funds: Multi-funds offer a portfolio consisting of shares of other mutual funds. Therefore, you pay two management fees—one to the multi-fund and, indirectly, one to the managements of the funds they select. Should you buy in? Well, it can't be that much trouble to look up fund performance and select a portfolio yourself.

Closed-end Funds: The majority of mutuals are "open-ended". There is no fixed number of shares. The number of shareholders can increase as new customers want in or can decrease as net redemptions develop. Closed-end funds issue only a fixed number of shares, like other listed corporations, and these shares are purchased or sold on the open market, frequently on the New York Stock Exchange. You purchase them in the same manner as you do other securities, from a present holder and at regular exchange commission rates.

Although closed-end and open-end funds share many characteristics, there is one major difference. Open-end funds are redeemable by the investor at net asset value; the total assets of the fund divided by the number of shares equals the redemption price per share. Closed-end funds trade at negotiated prices on the marketplace and usually the shares trade at levels below the funds' actual net asset value per share. In effect, the secondary purchaser of a closed-end fund is buying shares at a discount. Be wary of new issues of closed-end funds. The shares usually do trade down from the initial offering price to some discount.

An interesting deal developed during 1973. The Eberstadt Fund, an open-end, and Surveyor, a closed-end, agreed to merge. Surveyor's shares, selling at a discount, became, according to the terms of the deal, redeemable upon consummation of the merger, at net asset value. This feature provided Surveyor's shareholders with an immediate profit to the extent of the prevailing discount on Surveyor's assets at the time the companies actually merged. The arrangement just might start a trend, inasmuch as there seems little reason for closed-end holders to endure a discount when merger with an open-end on these terms produces instant profit.

Dual Purpose Fund: Dual purpose funds originated in the United States in the mid-sixties, but, after the initial flurry, have not been very popular. These are closed-end investment companies with the usual equity portfolios. When established, their provisions called for two classes of shareholders. Capital shareholders were to receive, at a specified maturity date, all the capital gains accruing from inception of the fund to maturity. Income shareholders were to receive all income and dividends accrued over the years to the total shares, plus a fixed redemption price at maturity. The income shareholders have a prior claim on the assets to the extent of their guaranteed redemption price before the capital shareholders receive anything.

During the halcyon days of 1967-1968, capital shareholders appeared to have a good thing going. They stood to pick up the capital gain profits on double their actual holdings. The bear market, however, spelled finis to that game. By late 1973, income holders had the cards stacked in their favor. Dividend payouts have been generous and, with most shares selling at a discount from the guaranteed redemption value, current buyers of income shares stand to reap a capital gain upon redemption, which is slated for different funds at different dates in the reasonably near future. Income shareholders will pick up this profit, of course, only if the total assets of these funds remain sufficiently intact over the years to cover the redemption price. However, in most cases, current assets are approximately double the amount needed to cover redemptions, so these funds would have to lose over 50% of their present value before new purchasers could get hurt.

Table IV illustrates the return that might accrue to current purchasers of income shares in these dual-purpose funds.

TABLE IV

Fund	Market Price	Minimum Annual	Estimated Dividend 1973	Current Yield based on Estimated Dividend (a)	Redemption Price	Redemption Year	Approx. Yield to Maturity (b)
American Dual Vest	$13.00	$0.84	$0.87	6.7%	$15.00	1979	8.6%
Gemini Fund	14.00	0.56	1.19	8.5	11.00	1984	7.5
Income & Capital Shares	10.38	0.50	0.90	8.7	10.00	1982	8.4
Leverage Fund of Boston	13.12	0.75	0.97	7.4	13.72	1982	7.8
Putnam Duo Fund	17.25	1.10 (c)	1.14	6.6	19.75	1983	7.6
Scudder Duo-Vest	8.50	0.64	0.64	7.5	9.15	1982	8.1
Hemisphere Fund	7.00	0.62	0.62	8.9	11.44	1985	10.9

(a) Based on estimated dividend for 1973 divided by market price.

(b) "Yield to Maturity" is based upon estimated dividend for 1973 or minimum cumulative dividend (whichever is greater), market price, and redemption figures. No adjustments are made for possible dividend increases or decreases.

(c) Higher in future years.

(Table, Courtesy of Mr. George Peugeot, President of S.P.A. Industries, Suite 252, Willow Hill Executive Center, 540 Frontage Road, Northfield, Illinois 60093).

Hemisphere Fund in May, 1973, offered an interesting opportunity to investors to receive an 8.9% current yield plus a bonus of 4.44 points upon redemption. Purchasers of these shares stood to receive a 10.9% annual appreciation on their money at relatively little risk. (Note: January, 1974: The yield to maturity on Hemisphere had grown to approximately 14%. In other words, if you purchased Hemisphere at about 6½ and held until 1985, you would receive 14% per year on your money.)

TIMING YOUR PURCHASE

While there is something to be said for purchasing shares of mutuals and simply sitting on them over the years, profits will be maximized if investors attempt to establish positions and to liquidate in phase with important market movements. Some short term traders actually swing in and out with the no-loads on minor market moves, the lack of commission charges rendering this procedure feasible. There is another major advantage to trading no-load funds as opposed to individual securities. The diversified portfolios of mutuals are more reliable in following market moves than any individual security. An investment portfolio consisting of a diversified group of well-performing funds is almost certain to produce some profit during market upswings.

We will be discussing market indicators in Chapter 10, which should help your market timing. My book, *Winning Market Systems: 83 Ways To Beat The Market,* published by Signalert Corp. at $19.95, explores the subject in greater depth. There are also a number of advisory services which have had excellent success in calling stock market turns. Do consider at least a trial to one of these.

DOLLAR COST AVERAGING

This is probably the simplest and most effective form of systematic mutual fund investment. Dollar cost averaging involves the investment of fixed dollar amounts into funds at regular intervals. No attempt is made to forecast the market, but underlying the technique is the assumption that the stock market, ergo the fund, will at least return at some point, in the case of a decline, to the level at which you initiate the program. An ability to sustain the program must also be presumed. The method works because, with constant dollar investment, you automatically purchase more shares when prices are low, and fewer when prices are high. Dollar cost averaging has been an excellent method for setting funds aside for retirement (especially via Keogh), college expenses, etc.

TABLE V

Comparison of Dollar Cost Averaging Technique With Purchase of Fixed Amounts of Shares at Regular Intervals

	Constant Share Purchases (10 shares per purchase)		Dollar Cost Averaging ($100 per Unit)	
Price of Shares	Number of Shares	Price Per Unit	Number of Shares	Price Per Unit
$10.00	10	$100.00	10	$100.00
12.50	10	125.00	8	100.00
15.00	10	150.00	6.67	100.00
12.50	10	125.00	8	100.00
10.00	10	100.00	10	100.00
7.50	10	75.00	13.33	100.00
5.00	10	50.00	20.0	100.00
7.50	10	75.00	13.33	100.00
10.00	10	100.00	10.0	100.00
Totals	90	900.00	99.33	900.00

The purchaser of units of constant numbers of shares has accumulated 90 shares at an average price of $10 per share. With the shares returning to the level at which his program began, he shows neither a profit nor a loss.

The "dollar cost averager" has accumulated 99.33 shares at an average price of $9.06 per share and shows a profit of $93.30 or 10.4% of his total capital invested.

Both investors have placed an equal amount of money into the program over the same period of time.

DON'T BE TAKEN!

For decades, during the fifties and sixties, load funds were able to sell to the unwary, front-end loaded contractual plans, in which, during the first year, 54% of the customer's payments went for commissions and other fees, and only 46% was left working for him in actual share ownership. It normally required five years in *good markets* for the customer just to break even, and several years before the average commission rate on purchases got down to the 8½% commission, thereby completely eliminating the front-end load altogether. This still pertains. There is no reason to sign up for any front-end load contract whatsoever. If, for some reason, you cannot follow through, and even if you can but to a lesser degree, you are being screwed if you sign a front-load contract.

Just in case you do let yourself become pressured into a contractual, keep the following in mind: According to the Investment Company Act of 1970, you are entitled to a full refund of all sales charges if you terminate the plan within 45 days. If the plan carries a 50% load during the first year, 70% of the sales charge is refundable if you cancel the plan within eighteen months. However, if the plan calls for only a 20% load in each of the first three years or 16% over the first four years, you can secure no rebates. You are also supposed to receive a letter from the fund within 45 days after purchase advising you of your rights.

Notwithstanding the above, and notwithstanding the fact that there have been excellent load funds, it makes so much more sense to buy a commission free no-load that I cannot recommend any load fund purchase. Apparently, the public is beginning to agree. The net redemption of shares during 1972-1973 has occurred at the expense of the load funds. The no-loads were able to maintain a net accumulation of shares. Incidentally, you can instantly tell a load from a no-load in your newspaper by examining the quote given for the fund. Load funds will show a bid price, approximately 8½% below an asked price. When buying, you pay the asked price which includes commissions. When selling, you get the bid. No-loads will show the same price in the bid and asked column.

Funds generally advertise in the financial sections of newspapers or in other periodicals. For full information regarding past performance, addresses, amount of load, objectives and a slew of other mutual fund data, I do recommend the *Mutual Funds Almanac,* 1973 by Yale Hirsch, published at $5.95 by the Hirsch Organization, 6 Deer Trail, Old Tappen, N.J. 07675. An excellent value.

TABLE VI

TOP 50 FUNDS FOR 1967-1972 PERIOD
(Annual and Cumulative Performance)

Type	FUND	% Gain or Loss Per Share*						What $10,000
		1967	1968	1969	1970	1971	1972	Grew to:
Growth	1. Templeton Growth Fund	13.7	37.5	19.2	–6.3	21.5	67.6	$35,557
Performance	2. Rowe Price New Horizons Fd.	86.7	23.2	–6.6	–11.7	53.0	21.4	35,274
Performance	3. Mathers Fund	89.5	25.6	–5.3	2.0	19.6	15.8	31,842
Growth	4. American Ins. & Ind. Fd.	2.2	51.6	–2.8	–5.7	45.2	44.9	29,878
Performance	5. Naess & Thomas Special Fd.	96.9	8.1	–11.6	–12.3	31.9	19.0	25,900
Performance	6. Founders Special Fund	2.4	16.8	3.9	21.3	35.6	25.3	25,610
Growth	7. Putnam Investors Fund	28.9	11.4	–0.4	–2.8	32.1	28.0	23,505
Growth	8. Mairs & Power Growth Fd.	43.2	20.1	–7.7	–2.2	23.2	22.8	23,488
Growth	9. Ivy Fund	89.8	38.9	–27.8	–10.6	17.8	14.1	23,128
Growth	10. Newton Fund	40.8	25.5	–5.6	–10.7	27.7	20.2	22,865
Grw/Inc.	11. International Investors	36.2	22.6	–16.1	8.4	–5.6	57.3	22,551
Growth	12. Supervised Investors Growth	59.1	24.6	–8.5	–4.1	19.9	6.4	22,191
Performance	13. Enterprise Fund	114.6	41.7	–25.0	–26.0	23.5	6.4	22,177
Performance	14. Scudder Special Fund	69.9	22.0	–17.9	–5.4	19.9	13.3	21,870
Growth	15. Stein, Roe & Farnham-Cap. Op.	29.5	25.9	–5.9	–10.0	25.1	24.4	21,489
Growth	16. Country Capital Inv. Fd.	40.7	30.5	–7.9	–10.2	26.7	11.4	21,434
Growth	17. National Investors Corp.	31.4	8.3	4.1	–8.9	27.7	23.7	21,319
Growth	18. Johnston Mutual Fund	30.0	7.9	0.4	–5.8	28.9	24.5	21,289
Grw/Inc.	19. Istel Fund	53.4	21.2	–14.3	2.7	20.3	7.6	21,182
Growth	20. Puerto Rican Investors	34.5	56.2	–2.4	–11.3	12.3	1.8	20,793
Growth	21. American Gen'l. Growth Fd.	5.2	47.0	–5.0	–10.0	26.4	24.1	20,740
Grw/Inc.	22. Paramount Mutual Fund	13.0	31.2	–7.7	17.8	13.7	12.7	20,656
Grw/Inc.	23. David L. Babson Inv. Fd.	21.0	19.1	1.3	–0.4	15.1	23.1	20,601
Performance	24. American National Growth	52.8	20.3	–13.6	–1.4	27.6	2.6	20,502
Performance	25. Pilgrim Fund	60.6	9.2	–12.7	–4.8	26.6	11.0	20,482
Performance	26. Pilot Fund	68.1	27.9	–20.1	–6.5	21.3	4.6	20,379
Income	27. Provident Fund for Income	40.8	32.6	–19.5	3.8	27.1	1.4	20,105
Growth	28. Vance, Sanders Common Stock	9.8	25.2	0.3	1.6	17.5	21.9	20,065
Performance	29. Equity Growth Fund of Amer.	60.2	24.4	–12.1	–5.0	17.4	1.9	19,908
Performance	30. One Hundred Fund	65.1	35.3	–19.6	–2.4	11.9	1.3	19,870
Growth	31. T. Rowe Price Growth Stock Fd.	26.8	8.4	3.2	–7.9	31.3	15.4	19,795
Growth	32. Scudder Int'l Investments	22.0	21.2	4.3	–6.5	6.4	28.6	19,731
Growth	33. Canadian Fund	14.5	16.0	4.0	5.0	9.7	24.0	19,730
Growth	34. Imperial Growth Fund	58.5	13.1	–18.0	–11.7	26.6	19.8	19,686
Performance	35. Whitehall Fund	28.0	16.3	–1.8	–7.8	21.7	19.8	19,650
Growth	36. Industries Trend Fund	40.7	18.8	–15.0	–4.4	16.9	23.6	19,625
Grw/Inc.	37. Pioneer Fund	37.4	28.6	–15.3	0.7	13.2	14.9	19,602
Grw/Inc.	38. Security Investment	27.5	26.2	–16.3	15.9	16.7	7.3	19,545
Income	39. Financial Industrial Income	36.9	36.5	–16.0	–4.4	17.4	10.5	19,467
Income	40. Everest Fund	77.0	28.5	–24.9	–4.0	13.2	4.5	19,398
Income	41. Admiralty Income Fund	30.3	29.6	–20.6	8.6	27.3	4.3	19,333
Growth	42. Life Insurance Investors	1.1	28.9	–7.2	–6.4	29.1	32.3	19,314
Income	43. Decatur Income Fund	33.0	25.1	–12.9	7.8	16.4	6.1	19,293
Growth	44. Century Shares Trust	–8.5	40.4	–9.8	6.8	30.0	19.8	19,274
Growth	45. First Sierra Fund	1.2	69.5	–7.0	0.9	15.1	3.8	19,231
Performance	46. Founders Growth Fund	68.5	17.2	–28.2	–7.4	24.5	16.3	19,011
Grw/Inc.	47. Broad St. Investing	18.3	15.0	–3.7	4.3	19.7	16.2	19,006
Performance	48. Over-the-Counter Securities	37.5	30.3	–10.9	–10.3	15.8	14.1	18,919
Growth	49. Investors Research Fund	45.6	–2.6	–3.2	–7.7	24.0	20.3	18,902
Growth	50. Windsor Fund	30.7	20.6	–3.4	6.0	6.9	9.3	18,858

*Change in net asset value per share, with dividends and capital gains added. "What $10,000 Grew To" does not take into account sales charges on initial investment or any capital gains or income taxes that would have to be paid.

Source: Mutual Fund Almanac, 1973 by Yale Hirsch, The Hirsch Organization, 6 Deer Trail, Old Tappan, N.J. 07675

RECENT TOP PERFORMERS

Table VI shows the top 50 funds for the 1967-1972 period. You can observe how few funds carry superior performance over from year to year—with Templeton, Mathers, Rowe Price New Horizons exceptions in this regard.

Do not become too enamored of any fund, however, and do not expect more from it than any fund can deliver. After all, by and large, when it comes right down to it, buying mutual funds,is, essentially, buying the stock market.

Chapter 8

"Convertibles May Be The Closest Thing Yet To The Perfect Investment"

Investing In Convertible Bonds

Potential Reward, A
Potential Risk, B+
Liquidity, A
Tax Considerations, C

(Portions of this chapter have been excerpted from an article by the author appearing in *Smart Money,* July, 1973, published by the Hirsch Organization, 6 Deer Trail, Old Tappan, New Jersey 07675.)

That's right, convertible bonds offer just about everything to everybody. With convertibles, you can have the yield and safety of corporate bonds *plus* the excitement and trading action of common shares. What's more, compared to trading common stock, you enjoy lower commissions as well as increased protection. How is all this possible? Perhaps a few definitions will explain the matter.

First of all, convertible bonds share the characteristics of any bond—regular interest payments with repayment of principal in full due at a certain date. Discounted convertibles, selling below par, are available, which avoid all long term risk except corporate insolvency. Current yield and yield to maturity are computed in the usual manner.

Of course, on the basis of yield alone, convertibles would rate only a C for return, if that much. Yields at par usually run between 4½-7% in decent quality bonds. Discounted bonds, of course, do better. What makes convertibles stand out from the bond crowd are the trading possibilities. Convertibles can be traded in accordance with credit conditions and/or in accordance with the ups and downs of the shares of the issuing company. We'll get to that further below. In the meantime, consider this. The National General 4s 1993 convertible bonds traded at about $300 in mid-1970. They yielded over 13% to buyers at that time. By 1973, they had risen to $750, a gain of 150% in these years—not including the interest return!

The profit potential demonstrated by the NGC 4s 1993 illustrates the convertible bond's one unique feature, the frosting on the cake, if you will. *As an alternative to accepting repayment of the loan signified by the bond, convertible bondholders can turn their bonds in to the company and receive in lieu of interest and repayment a stipulated number of that company's common shares.* Hence, the name, "convertible bond." The following is an example of how the convertible feature works and how it can result in fine capital gains to bondholders.

Skil Corporation has a convertible bond outstanding. The Skil Corporation 5s 1992, sold in August, 1973, at $700. At that time, the bond provided a current yield of 7.1% ($50 interest divided by $700 purchase price) to purchasers, a yield to maturity of 8.1% when the $300 built-in capital gain was included for bondholders who held until 1992 for redemption at $1,000. Unless Skil goes bankrupt and/or defaults before 1992, *there is no way for patient non-margined holders of the bond to realize an annual return of less than 8.1% between 1973 and 1992.* However, they were in a position to secure much more.

Each Skil bond can be swapped for 25 shares of company stock at any time until July 1, 1992. At the time that the bonds were selling for $700, Skil common was selling for $19.50 per share. Therefore, the $700 bond could have been exchanged for 25 shares of common worth $19.50 apiece, or for a total value in common shares of $487.50. Since the bond was selling at $700 on the open market, 44% higher than its value if converted (we refer to this as a *44% premium*), it would hardly have paid to make the exchange. But suppose Skil were to rise to $44 per share, the high recorded for the stock earlier in 1973. The bond, in that case, would have to sell for at least $1,100, since each bond could be converted into $1,100 worth of Skil common (25 shares per bond times $44 per share). The bond could not sell for any less; if it did, an arbitrage situation would develop in which active and sharp traders could sell the common, purchasing bonds at prices below conversion value, converting, and delivering the shares so derived for a guaranteed profit. More likely, the bond would retain a slight premium and sell for slightly above conversion value. And, as a point of fact, the Skil Corporation 5s 1992, did sell at $1,130 in early 1973, at a time when the common sold at 44.

TO SUM UP THE UPSIDE POTENTIAL

Should the Skil common rise from 19½ to 44, the Skil 5s 1992 convertible bond must rise by at least $400 or by 57.1% of their mid-1973 price. This capital gain would accrue in addition to the 7.1% current interest yield enjoyed by mid-1973 investors. Investors do not actually have to convert the bonds to realize the gain. The price of convertible bonds on their trading markets rises to reflect increasing conversion value. The Skil bond trades on the New York Stock Exchange and is quite liquid.

O.K. So much for the upside. What if the common continues to decline? First off, let's consider the positions of holders of Skil common when the shares were selling at 44 compared to the positions during that period of four bonds convertible in total to the same 100 shares. Skil Corporation was offering a dividend of 90¢ per common share. At a price of 44, the common yielded slightly over 2%. The bonds, at $1,130, provided a yield of 4.4%, or twice that amount. Selling right at conversion value, the bonds had to rise dollar for dollar with any rise in the common. However, Skil common did not rise from the 44 level; it fell by 56%, to 19½. In the meantime, the convertible lost only 35% of its value in falling from $1,130 to $700. The yields provided by convertible bonds support their price even though a gap opens between their conversion value and selling price (see the sections on premiums). Convertible bonds selling at or near par are intrinsically safer than their underlying common shares. (Of course, should Skil rise again to 44, the common will have gained 126% while the bond gains only 57%. From that point on, both will gain at the same rate). Convertible bonds selling far below conversion value, and well below par (deep discount convertibles) offer a minimum of risk, high yield, almost guaranteed profit at maturity and the chance of a fine capital gain should the underlying common recover. At $700, the Skil bond showed a risk of perhaps a 20% further *temporary* decline, but remember, the bonds stood to be redeemed *at $1,000 in 1992; selling at $500,* they would provide a current return of 10%.

The safety of convertible bonds does decline as the bonds rise in price above par (usually $1,000). Above par, their *rate of yield* decreases, and the higher the price, the less the yield will stand as a factor to cushion any decline, at least until the price drops to a point where the yield once again assumes significance. During periods of high interest rates, and declining stock prices, convertible bonds have declined to half their face value and below, declines not ending until convertible yields become comparable to the yields of straight corporate bonds of similar quality. This floor to convertible bonds, the level where the price is determined largely by yield rather than by potential convertibility, is called the *investment value* of the bond. In no case, however, should convertibles decline at a more rapid rate than their related common. During periods of low interest rates, the floor to the price of convertible bonds rises. In this way, convertibles act similarly to any bond. However, no other bond can produce capital gains at the same rate during strong bull markets.

COMMISSIONS

Even where yield and safety are of little importance, you save on commissions by purchasing convertibles. It would now cost approximately $70.00 in commissions to purchase 100 common shares of Skil at 44. At those levels you can purchase four Skil 5s 1992 bonds, convertible into 100 shares, yielding twice as much as the common, for commission costs of $20. Pay no more than $5 per bond commissions. If your brokerage house asks more, shop around. All told, the Skil bonds provide, if nothing else, an immediate savings of approximately $50 in commission costs against straight purchase of the common.

Considering the many advantages inherent in convertible bonds, there is usually little reason to purchase common shares instead. Since that is the case, why doesn't everybody invest in convertibles rather than common? First off, convertibles exist for only a certain number of listed shares, and sometimes the common is the better buy. (Remember, if Skil rises from 19½ to 44, the common gains more than twice as much as the bond). More usually, investors are not familiar with convertible bonds and, strangely enough, are reluctant to learn, despite the many benefits.

If you have purchased this book, the odds are that you already own, have owned, or plan to own some common securities. The odds are also that you have not owned and do not plan to own convertible bonds. Be honest with yourself. Are you going to bug your broker until he checks out whether any stock he recommends provides a convertible alternative? Or are you going to remain a creature of habit and settle for second best? Don't expect your account exec to necessarily volunteer the information—not when he gets triple the commission by keeping mum. Are you going to look into the matter further to clarify any remaining questions? Or are you simply going to continue to follow the crowd—higher commission rates, lower yields and greater risks notwithstanding? Do give these questions some thought. It is, after all, *your* money.

MARGIN

Convertible bonds can be purchased, as of this writing, at 50% margin, the same as common shares. In the past, and possibly in the future, you could secure greater margin on convertibles than on common. Straight corporates can be purchased at from 25-30% margin at many houses. You can borrow up to 90-95% on high quality municipals at your bank. Maximum use of leverage is suggested for deeply discounted convertibles, purchased during periods of tight money. Risk is slight for good quality bonds, when they provide current yields of 8½-10%. Purchase bonds issued only by corporations showing definite earnings.

This applies to straight corporates as well as convertibles. A high coupon is worth only as much as the company's ability to pay.

CALLING IN BONDS

The issuing company can call in almost any bond, paying off the debt ahead of schedule by redemption of the bond, usually at a price only slightly above par. If your bond is selling below par and is called, you will have received an instant windfall. Fine. If, however, your bond is selling above par because of increased conversion value, a call-in could cost you considerable money. Your options in that case include instant sale of the bond, before the call becomes effective, or conversion of the bond into common shares. If you receive notice of a call, be certain to take the appropriate action.

CONVERTIBLE BONDS DO YIELD LESS THAN STRAIGHT BONDS OF SIMILAR PRICE

Corporations issue convertible bonds in order to save money. By supplementing yield with the conversion feature, corporations can float convertibles at lower coupon rates than they would have to pay by issuing straight corporate bonds. Most convertibles, at par, yield about 2% less than straight corporate bonds of similar quality. If high current interest income is important to you, concentrate on convertible bonds selling below par, at a discount. The upside potential is usually somewhat more limited, but risk of loss is practically nil. And you *can* secure current interest returns of 8-10%.

TAX CONSIDERATIONS

Convertibles offer no outstanding tax benefits. Interest is fully taxed as ordinary income; capital gains provisions are subject to the usual regulations. Discounted, high quality, convertibles are excellent vehicles for the Keogh Plan. Under that plan, all interest and capital gains accumulate tax free until withdrawal.

A SOPHISTICATED TECHNIQUE FOR VERY LOW RISK HEDGING WITH CONVERTIBLE BONDS THAT CAN BRING IN A 25% RETURN ANNUALLY

This is the technique which has been published in *Smart Money* and which I have employed successfully in my own account. Readers not too familiar with the convertible scene should skip ahead to the sections on *premiums* and *short selling,* before studying the special trading hedge. *The trading hedge automatically increases your return from convertible bonds,* since any substantial fluctuation in the price of the common has to result in a profit one way or the other.

DRAW A 25% RETURN AND BETTER FROM CONVERTIBLE BONDS

Let's suppose you had $2,800 to invest. And let's suppose further that you were offered for that money a license to trade a particular security as often as you wished. And let's suppose still further that the trading license virtually guaranteed you against loss on any trade, *even if your judgment was wrong.* And finally, let's suppose that the license paid 7¾% current interest with capital gain of $4,000, 162% of your initial investment at the end of nineteen years, if that long, and could return an additional capital gain annually of 25% or more. It sounds too good to be true? Presuming there are such trading licenses available, would you be interested?

Well, believe it or not, such a trading license is available. It is called a *deep discount convertible bond.* Usually thought of as conservative income investments, discounted convertibles, through the technique of the trading hedge, can produce excellent short term trading gains in addition to their interest income. Before proceeding to the description of the hedge, readers not conversant with the bond market may first wish to refer to an elementary textbook on bonds before reading further.

THE TRADING HEDGE

To institute the trading hedge, capable of producing up to and even over 25% annual return on convertible bonds virtually risk free, you take the following steps.

1. Purchase discounted bonds, convertible into sufficient shares of an active trading stock so that you can short round lots of the common against the bonds. (You can reduce this to odd lots if you are willing to pay the extra commission). Purchase sufficient bonds to offset against unusually rapid upside movement of the common (because of existing premiums over conversion) in order to protect yourself should the short go against you and the stock rise.

2. Whenever you believe the stock will decline, short it as a hedge against your long position in the bonds. If you profit on the short, cover when it appears appropriate, wait for a run-up in the common and then re-short. But, even if the stock you short rises, *the appreciation in the bonds should more than offset any loss on the short.*

3. *Treat the bond as a perpetual holding.* Remember, this bond yields a fine return and promises an ultimate capital gain. Barring corporate insolvency, you should never have to take a loss on discounted bonds. However, this technique is suitable only for investors whose temperaments and/or financial positions allow them to maintain long term positions in an investment which will fluctuate in price over the years.

4. Besides the yield from the bonds, profits will accrue each year if any of your shorts

prove profitable, *or* if the stock rises to any degree. Even if your trading judgment proves erroneous at times, *no trade will result in a loss;* your profits will simply be reduced.

Example: Short 100 shares of NGC common at 26-3/8. Buy 7 NGC 4s 1993 bonds at $620. (As a result of a tender of NGC, 1973, this hedge is no longer available.)

Cash outlay, presuming bonds are purchased at the 50% margin down payment now required for bonds, $2,187.50 (50% x $4,340 total bond price + $35 commission).

If NGC common falls to 9 (1970 bear market low) within one year.

Profit on short sale:	$1,737.50
Temporary loss on bonds (estimated price–$400, with common at $9.00):	$1,540.00
Net profit (less commission):	$ 197.50
	(plus interest from the bonds)

However, the loss on the bonds is only *temporary.* The seven bonds will be redeemable in 1993 at $1,000 each, for an ultimate total capital gain of $2,660 plus interim interest. The $1,737.50 profit on the short sale is current income for this year. Based upon the $2,187.50 cash outlay required for the hedge, the bonds on the short sale alone have provided a return of 79.4% on your investment (commissions excluded).

Suppose the short goes against you and the common rises 20 points to 46-3/8.

Loss on short sale:	$2,000.00
Profit on bonds, minimum value of $6,687.28 (20.6 shares per bond times $46.375 per share times seven bonds):	$2,347.28
Minimum profit (less commission):	$ 347.28

Rate of return–15.9%. It should actually prove higher since the bonds will probably continue to sell at some premium, should the stock rise to 46-3/8, rather than at actual conversion value. If you are correct on your short sale, you make a 79.4% annual return plus the interest return. If you are wrong, you make 15.2 plus the interest return. By altering the mix to, perhaps, six bonds long per 100 shares of common short, you will make less if the stock rises, more if it falls. *In either case, you cannot lose on the hedge.*

An Actual Illustration: On March 12, 1973, I purchased on 50% margin, for my own account, ten Sprague 4¼s 1992 convertible bonds at $550 per bond, for use in the trading hedge. Total cash outlay, $2,800. The Sprague 4¼s 1992 convertible was selected because:

1. The bond was deeply discounted. It provided, at the time of purchase, a 7.7% current return and a 9.5% return to maturity. Therefore, the margined portion cost me nothing since the yield to maturity from the bond exceeded margin carrying costs. So margined, this bond position *alone,* offered a 10%+ return on my investment if held to maturity–so long as Sprague meets its interest payments.

2. Sprague common is an actively traded, volatile issue. The best returns are secured from hedges on widely fluctuating securities.

3. Sprague appears to be a turn-around situation with improving fundamentals. The company had reported 82¢ per share earnings over the last twelve months, compared to a loss of $1.79 the previous year. The earnings irregularity is a minus in the situation, but interest payments on the bonds have been met even during hard years. (Stay with situations where the company shows definite earnings, sufficient to cover interest payments). The balance sheet is good, and current assets are 4.6 times current liabilities.

The Sprague hedge worked this way:

Each bond is convertible into 21.978 shares of Sprague common at a price of $45.50 per share. The common was selling at 14¾ at the time, so the price of the bond reflected a 70% premium. Therefore, ten bonds held long, amply covered my projected hedge since the ten bonds are convertible into 220 shares of common. To determine the proper mix of bonds to stock for a hedge play, you can do one of three things:

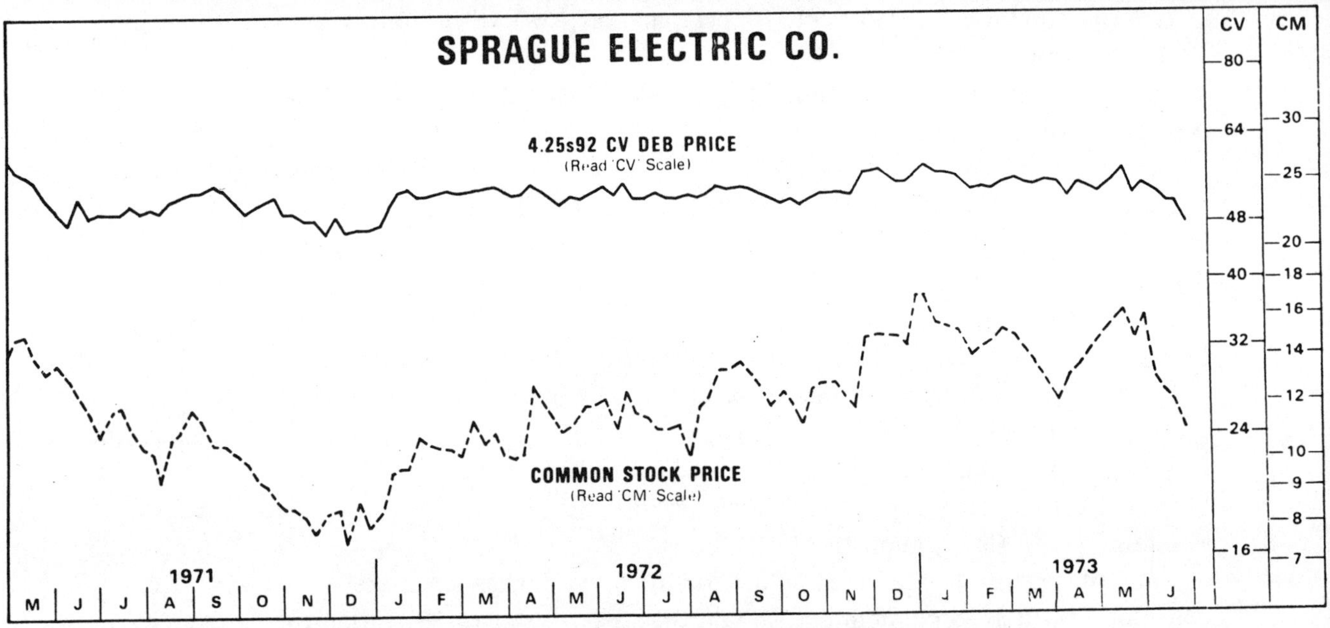

FIGURE 1: PRICE HISTORY SPRAGUE ELECTRIC CO.
Convertible Debenture and Common Stock

Source: Smart Money, July 1973, The Hirsch Organization, 6 Deer Trail, Old Tappan, N.J. 07675

A. Consult a convertible bond chart book to determine the past relationship between the price movement of the common and the bond. For example, if the last time the common moved from 15 to 18 ($300 for 100 shares), the bond rose from $550 to $585 ($350 or $35 x 10 bonds), the 10 bonds to 100 shares of common hedge is valid since the gain from the bond would have exceeded loss on any short. Adjust also for credit conditions, keeping in mind that rising interest rates exert a downward pressure on bond prices.

B. Maintain a file of back issues of *Barron's* or a similar publication to track past relationships.

C. Consult *The Value Line Convertible Survey.* (5 East 44th St., New York City, N.Y. 10017; trial $25), which maintains excellent ongoing ratios and other pertinent data.

I could have instituted a hedge by shorting the common immediately upon my bond purchase, but expected a run-up in the stock and thus an opportunity to short at higher levels. By early April, the stock had declined to 11¾, the bond to $530. I had missed a trading opportunity, but I was not concerned about the drop in the bonds, *which I treat as a long-term holding,* yielding 7.7% currently, 10% to maturity on my margined position as I wait. *That 10% return is my annual head start on the market.*

Sprague rallied from April into mid-May, partly on strength derived from a favorable report in a trade publication. On May 8, the common reached 19, up more than 3 points for the day on extremely heavy volume. This provided an excellent short-term opportunity (heavy volume following a move almost always signifies a price reversal). I, therefore, put in an order to sell 100 shares of SPE short at the opening on May 9. The short sale was executed at 18-7/8, the high for the day, only 1/8 of a point below the high for the total move.

Sprague declined to 14 on May 21. Heavy volume set in that day again, so I covered at 14¼, ¼ point above the low. My profit on the short sale was $391.64, including commissions.

The stock demonstrated only moderate strength on the subsequent rally and was reshorted at 15-3/8 on May 24. I was a little premature. The rally ultimately carried the shares as high as 16½, but by covering my original short at 14¼ and reshorting at 15-3/8, I did scalp an additional $46 profit. The stock has since sold down to 11-1/8, providing, approximately, another $375 profit on the short side.

Net Results:

Original investment:			$2,800.00
Profits on two short sales combined:		(approx.)	$ 767.00
Interest received (3 months, less margin interest)		(approx.)	$ 53.00
Total profit:		(approx.)	$ 820.00
Return on investment for 3 months:	29.3%		
Annualized rate of return:	117 %		

I still hold the Sprague bonds, the perpetual trading license described at the start of this article.

Observation: Obviously, I could have done better by selling the Sprague bonds when they reached $600.00, coincident with the stock high of May 9th, repurchasing them at $510.00, the level reached June 16th, operating on an unhedged basis. But what if I had been wrong? Suppose the Sprague common had kept rising. There is a limit to how far a stock can fall, but no limit to how far it can rise.

My hedge protected me against any loss on the short sale whatsoever. For example, if following the short sale on May 9th, Sprague common had risen to $45.50, its conversion price, the workout would take place as follows:

Loss on short (excluding commissions)	$2,662.50
Profit on ten bonds ($10,000 conversion value minus $6,000.00, total value of bond holdings at the time the short sale was executed)	$4,000.00
Net profit on the hedge if I had guessed *wrong:*	$1,337.50
	(excluding commissions & interest)

. . . or 48% of my investment.

Trading Hints:

1. Stay with actively traded bonds and volatile common stocks.
2. The price action of the convertible usually lags the price action of the common by a

day or two. You can often position yourself at an advantageous bond price to stock price ratio, if you purchase your bonds immediately following a run-up in the common.

3. If you are bearish, first short the stock and then purchase the bonds. However, it is safer to hold the bonds first.

4. Hedge positions provide less profit than unhedged positions if you are *right.* Their advantage lies in their ability to produce *some profit even when you are wrong.* Many short sellers lose money because false rallies panic them out of positions which would prove ultimately profitable. It is amazing how much more calm and objective you can remain when you are properly hedged.

5. Look for short sale opportunities at least two or three times a year, even in bull markets; this may be dangerous unhedged, but perfectly safe hedged.

6. The mix of bonds to stock is continuously variable depending upon the premium over conversion existing for the bonds at any given time. Everything else equal, the greater the premium, the greater the number of bonds required in the hedge. Stay with situations requiring no more than ten bonds per 100 shares of common short.

7. Hedge positions involving discounted convertibles require greater cash outlay for similar profit than either straight purchase or short sales of the common alone. But even where signals appear clear, I suggest the hedge. *You* may prefer to take the gamble and go unhedged.

To Sum Up: The trading hedge provides the best of both worlds. You receive high current income return and the safety derived from bond ownership, *plus* the opportunity for active short and intermediate term trading–all at minimal risk.

PREMIUM

"Premium" refers to the differential between the selling price of a convertible and its value if it were converted into common shares. The Skil bonds, mentioned above, sold at 44% premium when the bonds having a conversion value of $487.50, sold for $700. Generally, convertible bonds, at issue, are priced at a 12-20% premium over conversion value. This premium gradually evaporates as the stock, and consequently the bond, rise in price to the point where the *rate* of interest that the bond pays assumes relative insignificance compared to its conversion value. Should the common shares decline below the price of issuance, the bonds will drop too, but more slowly. Therefore, premiums expand as convertibles fall below face value (par) and contract as they rise above face value. "Deep" discounted bonds will, at first, show a rate of appreciation less than their underlying common, should the latter rise in price, since the initial rise in the common will serve, at first, to eat into the premium. As the common approaches the conversion price, and the premium disappears, the bond will appreciate virtually dollar for dollar with the common.

What are the implications of the relationship between the convertible and the common? To match the price appreciation of 100 shares selling at some distance above conversion level, you need to position yourself in only so many convertibles as would convert into 100 shares, e.g., 4 Skil bonds convert into 100 shares of common. At below conversion levels, additional bonds are required. On upside action, this represents an advantage to owners of the common. On downside action, though, the bonds still offer greater safety and yield. To repeat, at first common shares will advance more quickly than discounted bonds convertible into equivalent amounts of the common; as the rise continues, the rates of advance of the two will become more coincident.

SELLING SHORT

A short sale is the sale of a security you do not actually own. For example, suppose you believe that a stock, now 29, is going to decline in price. You can have your broker sell for you shares you *do not* own by borrowing for you shares held in the brokerage house's name for delivery on the sale. Should the price drop, say to 24, you can purchase the shares at that price, and repay the loan of the securities. The difference of 5 points between your sale price (29) and the ultimate purchase price (24), less commissions, is your profit. What if the shares rise, say to 34, and you have to reach up for the securities to repay the loan? You lose the difference. Selling short is a strategy of choice in declining markets; in bull markets, it is best avoided.

In making a short sale, you usually have to put up margin money as collateral in the same amount as if you had purchased the stock, in February, 1974, 50% of the purchase price. *However, if you own convertible bonds, outright or on margin, you can short the amount of shares into which the bonds can be converted without putting up any margin on the short sale.* Therefore, if you own 4 Skil 5s 1992, convertible into 100 shares of Skil common, you can short 100 shares of Skil without any cash outlay beyond the price of the bonds.

SUGGESTED READING

Readers interested in further pursuing hedging as a low risk investment, or convertible bonds in general, may wish to subscribe to the *Value Line Convertible Survey,* 5 East 44th Street, New York City, N.Y. 10017. This advisory service provides all essential data for convertible investment and hedge operations. The company will provide price information to inquiries.

My own advisory service, *Systems and Forecasts,* specializes in active hedge trading. Free samples can be obtained by writing to *Systems and Forecasts,* P.O. Box 1227, Old Village Station, Great Neck, N.Y. 11023. You must mention this book.

SOME CONVERTIBLES TO CONSIDER

The following convertible bonds were all selling at substantial discounts in early 1974.

All have been issued by high quality companies and, in the opinion of the author, all offer excellent safety and yield plus the opportunity for fine capital gains in the years ahead. Do request a research opinion from your brokerage house before purchasing any of these bonds. Obviously, several months pass between the preparation of a manuscript and the release of a book—even assuming that you are an early purchaser, and not reading this section sometime during 1975, 1976, or even 1980. Conditions and company fortunes do change over years, even over months.

Convertible Bond	Number of Shares Into Which It Is Convertible	Price March 1974	Yield to Maturity
Budd Co. 5-7/8s 1994	45.5	$702	9.1%
Crane Co. 5s 1993	40.0	845	6.4
Di Giorgio Corp. 5-3/4s 1993	58.8	705	9.0
Gulf and Western 5-1/4s 1987	22.9	741	8.4
Hilton Hotel Corp. 5s 1995	16.4	650	9.3
National Can Corp. 5s 1990	32.1	640	8.9
Oak Industries 4-3/8s 1987	28.8	550	11.0
Skil Corp. 5s 1992	25.0	650	8.9
Sprague Electric 4-1/4s 1992	22.0	585	8.8

You can observe within the above listing—only a fraction of what is currently available—the diversity and breadth of convertible bond situations. The minimum return from any of the above selections is 6.4% to maturity; the maximum is 11.0%. The only risk, again, to long-term holders is corporate insolvency. Many of these bonds will appreciate at more rapid rates than the yield to maturity. *Do* investigate these situations further and look further into the whole arena of convertible bonds.

I said it at the beginning of the chapter and I'll say it again, convertibles may be the closest thing yet to the perfect investment.

Chapter 9

"You'll Do At Least A Little Better Than The Dart Board"

Picking Your Own Stocks

Potential Return,	A
Risk,	D
Liquidity,	A
Tax Factors,	C

All right, so you absolutely will not stand for Gerry Tsai doing your thing. It's really more fun for you to hold your own hand in a good poker game, or to roll your own cubes. In short, you insist upon playing the stock market, and even more, you demand the right to lose your own money. Well, it is your cash; let's hope this chapter can help you hang onto a little of it.

Actually, I am preparing this section a bit reluctantly, since I frankly believe that most stock market investors would make out better in the long run selling options, setting up hedges or putting money into deep discounted convertible bonds. The majority of small investors seem to manage somehow to lose money in the stock market, which, since 1968, has been a very difficult game even for the professionals. I recently received a call from someone to inquire into the possibility of my assuming the management of his investment capital. A brief conversation revealed the all too familiar salient facts. Yes, he had been investing for several years. No, he hadn't made any money, though from time to time he'd hit it big on a trade here and there. Yes, he had changed brokers–in fact, he was on his thirteenth account exec now. Yes, he had lost a considerable amount of money during 1973. 1972 had not been so great either. Sounds familiar?

I explained to the man my concept of money management. His funds would be distributed among low risk convertible bond situations, yielding for starters, 7-10% and, in addition, each bond, barring corporate insolvency, would return a guaranteed capital gain at maturity. Periodically, I would sell call options against these bond positions or otherwise institute trading hedges. I had been handling my own money that way and had come out well ahead during 1973, for example, a difficult bear market year. However, six months, at least, had to be allowed for positions to work out. My client was enthusiastic. He was tired of losing money, and tired of playing poker. Yes, he wanted to open an account, and right away–immediately. But then, the kiss of death. Didn't I think a rally was coming and wouldn't it be a good idea to put him into a "spec" which would move "fast", and then invest his money the way I was suggesting? It was plain to see–the track was still in his blood. I referred him back to his thirteenth broker, advising him that really hedged investments might not be quite suitable for his particular temperament.

Let's make the moral clear. If you're in the market for excitement, as a lark, to prove a point or because you are masochistic, fine. Just don't expect to make money, most gamblers do not. If you're thinking of a steady, compounded return on your capital, consider safer forms of investment than the outright purchase of common shares. If you still want to be in securities, at least apply some common sense. A horse that moves "fast" is a good bet; a stock that moves "fast" may just move "fast" the wrong way.

Lest I seem unduly pessimistic, I do want to point out that systematic investors can and do make money in the stock market. The average mutual fund produced a compound return of 10.7% from 1963-1972. However, the compounded return from 1965 to mid-1973 was less than 6.8% and, at that, most funds beat the Dow. Studies have shown that over the past century, the stock market as a whole rises by 9 per cent per year. Certain stocks, of course, do better. IBM has produced a compounded rate of return of over 14% to investors since 1962; Xerox has outperformed that return. However, my experience appears to indicate that the majority of investors seem to lack the discipline and patience for long term investment, and the knowledge necessary for short term trading. Hence, I am cautious about recommending a program of investment in common shares, despite the excellent profit potential. The risks are, indeed, considerable. But, again, let's presume you do want into the stock market, and to be fair, common share equities have provided excellent rates of return from time to time.

TO INVEST OR TO SPECULATE?

Here's your choice. To put money into long term growth situations or to try to catch quickie trades on hot numbers. If you're an excellent trader, a whiz with charts and have the market killer instinct, short term trading can, indeed, prove most profitable. It does, however, require close contact with the market and if you are brave enough to seriously consider it, you will probably want to study far beyond this chapter in any case. Actually, it is possible for market neophytes to profit from in and out trading if they explicitly follow the trading suggestions of some of the better market letters. (See Chapter 20).

However, for most successful investors, the consistent profits have been made via long term investment in solid institutional quality growth stocks on the one hand, and in smaller, rapidly emerging industries and companies on the other. Growth corporations share certain common elements.

1) Their products lie in expanding innovative areas in which they have staked out early leadership, and regarding which they continue to demonstrate fine resourcefulness in marketing.

2) Their product lines are marked by fresh research, the introduction of new items, and the expansion of their products' usefulness.

3) Earnings continue to grow at both a rapid and regular pace, exceeding, at the least, 10% compound growth per year; 15-20% is even better.

IBM, Xerox and Polaroid are prime examples of long term growth stocks. Coca-Cola, Sterling Drug and Syntex are others. From time to time, industries emerge which appear to demonstrate the potentials for long term growth and staying power, but which prove in the end to be only cyclical. The mobile home industry was a strong group during the late sixties through 1971, but a shakeout occurred during 1972 and particularly 1973. Do not confuse sustained growth with temporary fads. For example, recent years have seen hot plays among the computer peripheral groups, Alaskan oil stocks, Wankel engine licenses and soft contact lens manufacturers. These were all industries with a "concept", a concept that fired the composite public imagination, but none had real staying power. Such situations are fine for speculation, but potentially dangerous for long term investment.

In the end, the single most important element for successful investment is regular and rapid growth in earnings. Companies showing these characteristics–regular earnings growth and rapid earnings growth–have consistently outperformed hign dividend paying companies and cyclical companies, companies where earnings are somewhat irregular, vacillating in gear with fluctuations in the general economy. General Motors is an example of a cyclical corporation. Drug companies, by and large, have been capable of sustained earnings improvement, and have proven to be excellent investments over the years.

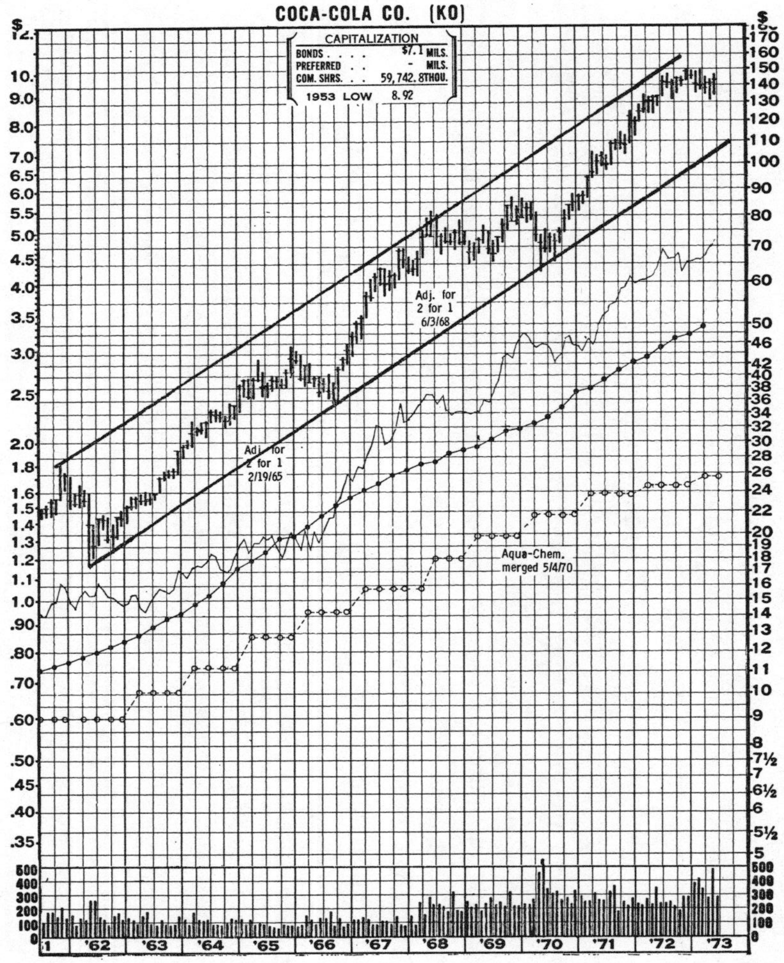

FIGURE 1

THE IDEAL GROWTH STOCK

Earnings and Price Rise In A Smooth Slope

Source: Securities Research Co., 208 Newbury St., Boston, MA 02116

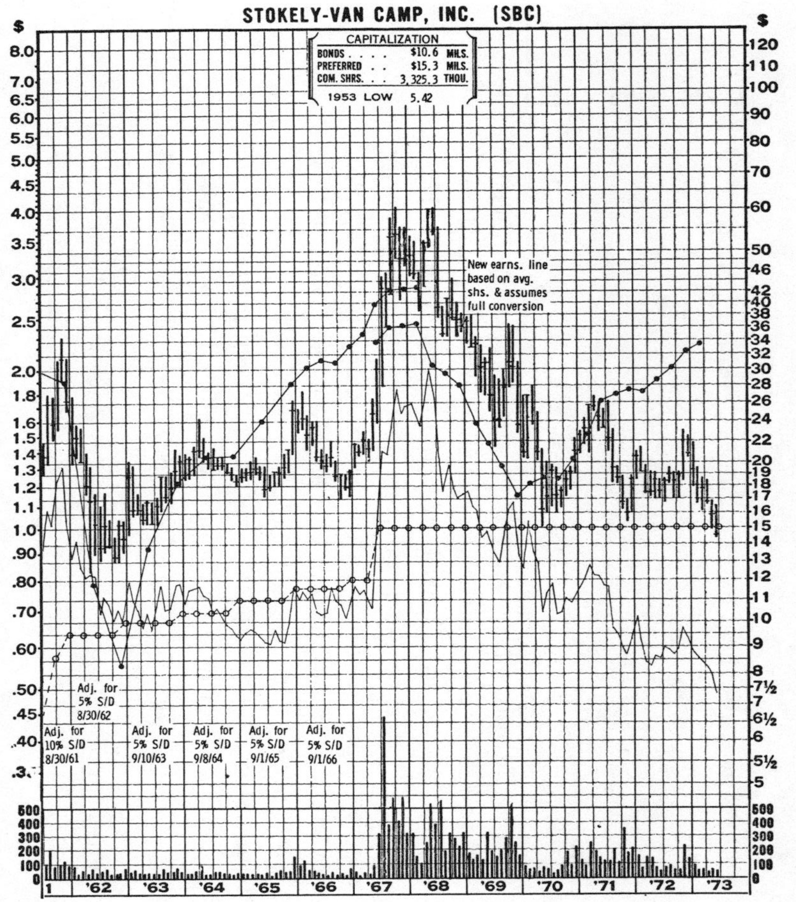

FIGURE 2

TYPICAL CYCLICAL STOCK

Irregular Earnings and an Irregular Price Pattern

Source: Securities Research Co., 208 Newbury St., Boston, MA 02116

Figure I illustrates the pattern of a typical growth company. The corporation has shown steadily rising earnings over the years (the line interspersed with heavy dots) and a concurrently rising price pattern. Stokely Van-Camp (Figure 2), on the other hand, shows a generally erratic earnings pattern. Hence, investors will not pay the premium for Stokely's shares which they pay for Coca-Cola. Notice too, that the trend in price of Coca-Cola rises at a regular rate, the slope undisturbed even by the bear markets of 1966 and 1970. Coca-Cola has been an ideal long term investment situation. Stokely has been a trading situation from time to time, but long term investors would have faired poorly.

PRICE EARNINGS MULTIPLES

The price earnings multiple of a stock is the latest price divided by the latest twelve month's earnings per share. Financial newspapers, such as the *Wall Street Journal,* carry this information for listed stocks. Each stock tends to demonstrate its own normal P/E multiple. Sometimes, the market carries the stock's price above its normal multiple; sometimes the market carries prices below its average multiple. The normal multiple for Coca-Cola in recent years has been 33. When the price has declined to a level much below 30 times earnings, the shares have been historically undervalued, and a good buy. A cautious stance has been indicated whenever the price of Coca-Cola has exceeded 40 times the previous year's earnings. Historical multiples are readily secured from your stockbroker or from advisory services such as the *Value Line Investment Survey* (5 E. 44th St., N.Y., N.Y. 10017). Review Figures 1 and 2 and observe the relationship of stock price and earnings. You can readily detect points of over and under-valuation.

TREND

Apart from the earnings history, investors should pay particular attention to the trend of any security under investigation. Growth stocks generally show well-defined patterns and slopes to their advances. Any alteration downwards in the slope of a long term advance should be treated as a signal for extreme caution. Skyline is a case in point. Here was an outstanding growth company in an outstanding industry. Notice, however, how the slope of the advance deteriorated *in advance* of the deterioration in earnings. The arrow in Figure 3 shows the danger point. Long term charts, employed herein, are relatively inexpensive and can be secured from the *Securities Research Company,* 208 Newbury St., Boston, Mass. 02116. The cost for an annual subscription has been $69.00.

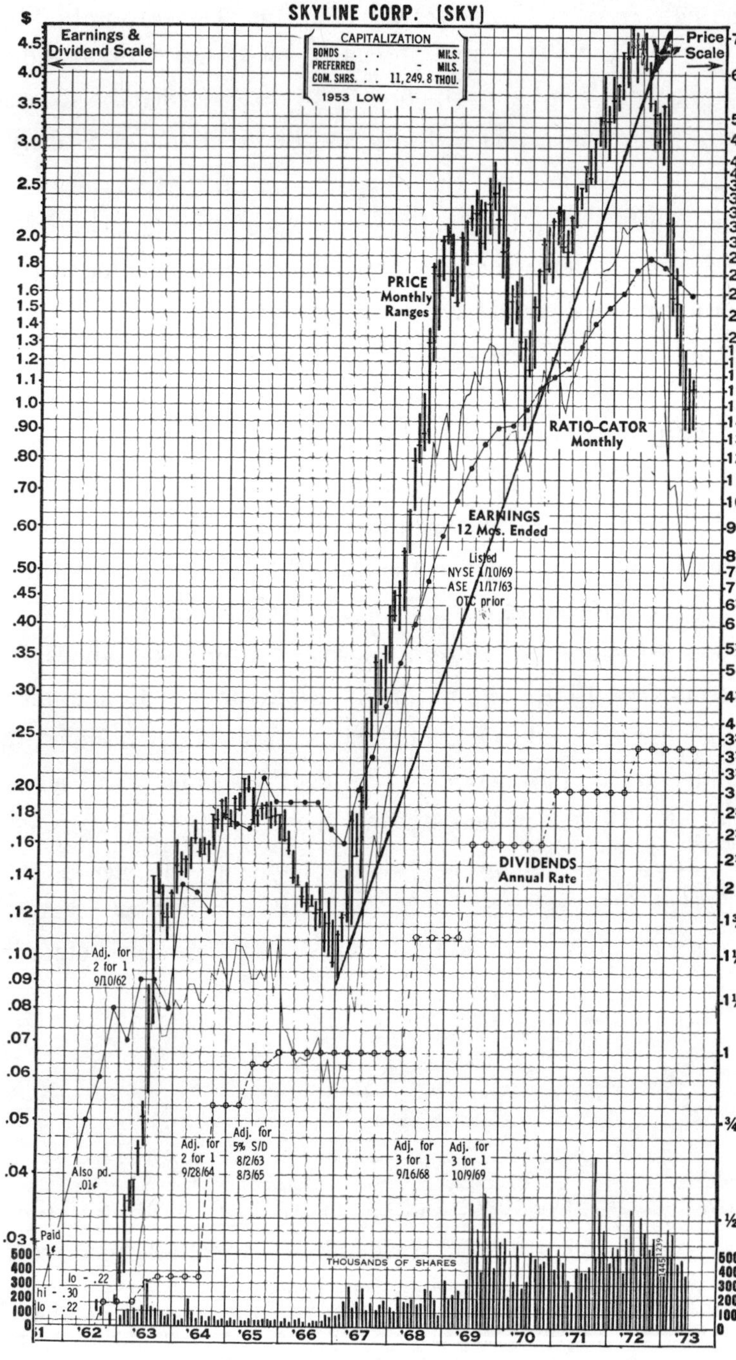

FIGURE 3

BREAKING A MAJOR TREND LINE

Skyline broke its uptrend in mid 1972, warning of the severe decline that followed.

Source: Securities Research Co., 208 Newbury St., Boston, MA 02116

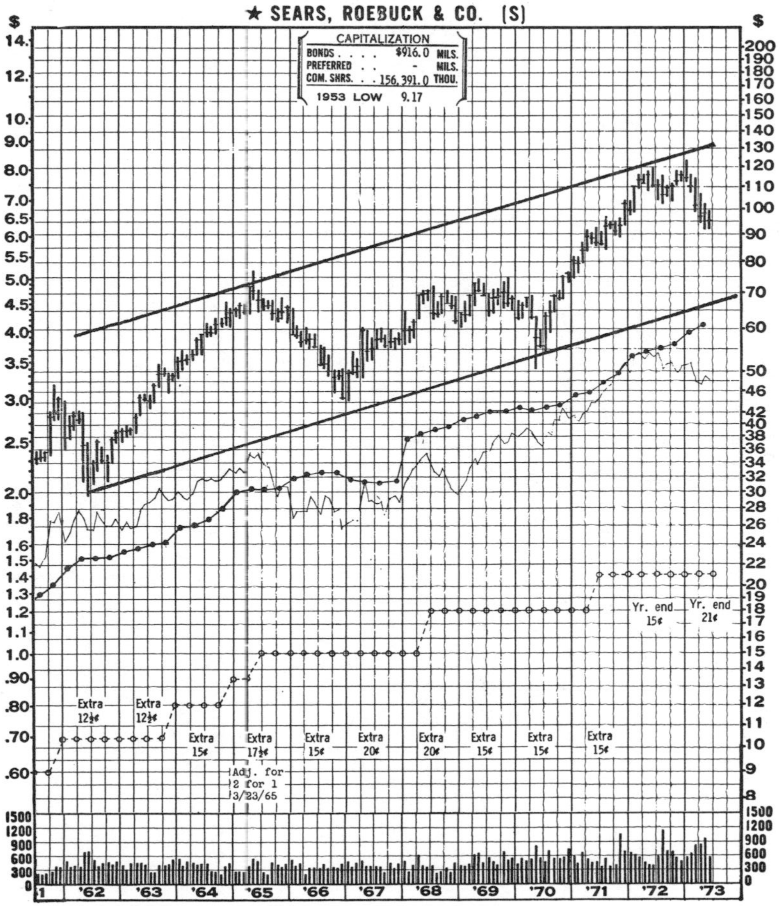

FIGURE 4

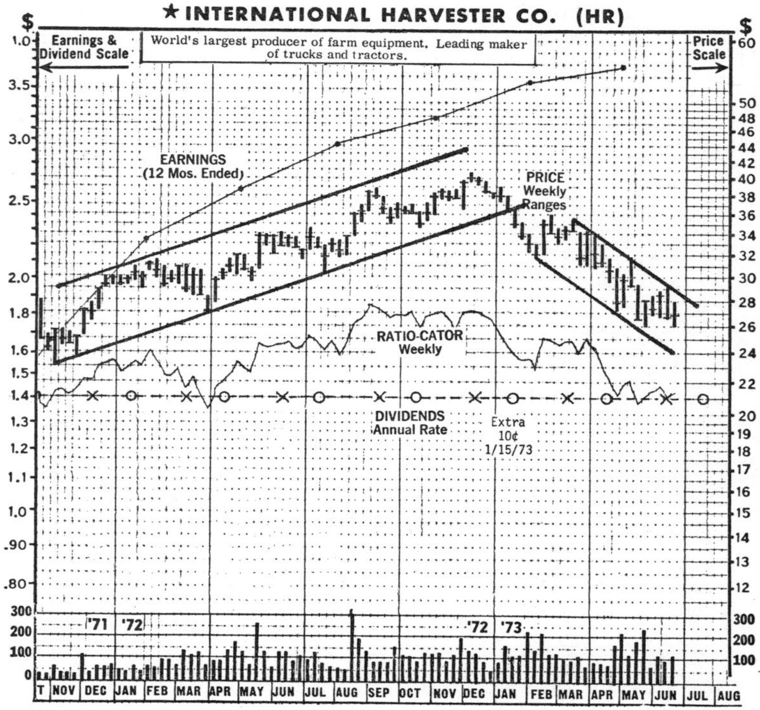

FIGURE 5

The charts of Sears, Roebuck and International Harvester reveal the long and shorter term channel for both stocks.

Source: Securities Research Co., 208 Newbury St., Boston, MA 02116

CHANNELS

The long and shorter term charts of Sears Roebuck and International Harvester reveal that the prices of these (and most) securities oscillate within well-defined boundaries, both rising and falling. The method of construction of these channels can be readily determined from study of the Figures 4 and 5. Buy near the lower boundaries of rising channels.

VOLUME

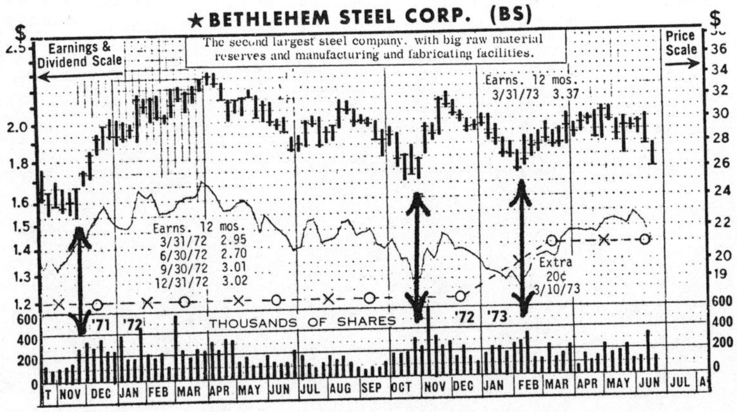

FIGURE 6

VOLUME SURGES

Each volume surge in Bethlehem Steel was followed by a price rise.

Source: Securities Research Co., 208 Newbury St., Boston, MA 02116

Volume is the number of shares traded in a security usually expressed on a daily, weekly, or monthly basis. Each security has its own particular volume configuration. For example, General Motors generally trades between 60 to 80 thousand shares per day. It usually pays to keep track of the trading volume in your securities. The following rules may help your timing:

1) A stock showing heavier than normal volume at the outset of an advance probably will continue to advance.
2) A stock that trades four times its normal volume following a period of advance probably should be sold, particularly if no further upwards motion accompanies the expansion in volume. Heavy volume, unaccompanied by price advance, usually indicates that "churning" is taking place, the distribution of stock from strong to weak hands.
3) Heavy volume at the outset of a decline indicates that the decline has further to go. Sell.
4) Heavy volume following a period of decline indicates that large money is beginning to step into a depressed situation. The decline may be nearing an end.
5) Light volume on declines is not necessarily bullish. Many declines continue on light volume for considerable periods of time.
6) Volume should increase as a stock continues to advance. A decline in volume as a stock advances indicates that the advance is losing buyer support. A decline may not be imminent, but the situation should be sold as soon as the slope of the advance becomes violated.

The *Wall Street Journal,* among other newspapers, carries daily volume figures for all listed stocks trading each day. *Barron's Financial Weekly* carries this data on a weekly basis. Figures 1-6 illustrate the volume traded for each of the stocks, shown at the bottom of the charts. Review Figure 6. You can see how volume expanded in Bethlehem Steel each time the stock reversed a decline.

DIFFERENT TRACK SYSTEMS

Everyone has his own way to bet the ponies—and the stock market as well. Systems for picking stocks multiply each year like rabbits, from the most sophisticated computer printouts of volume configurations, tick by tick, to use of the dartboard by the boys who say it's all guesswork anyhow. Probably, the single most important determinant as to whether your stock will rise on any given day, week, or month is the action of the stock market as a whole. Over the long term, earnings growth is the primary determinant. Market forecasting exotica include such gimmicks as "relative strength" (the stock should rise by a greater percentage than the market as a whole, and decline to a lesser degree than the stock market as a whole), "beta", (the relative volatility of the stock compared to the total market), and various technical chart formations. However, philosophies of trading boil essentially down to two categories.

Buy Low-Sell High

This tactic, generally speaking, involved the purchase of stocks near historical price lows or near minimum price-earnings ratios which should coincide with historically low price levels. Di Giorgio (Figure 7) qualified, in mid-1973, as a buy low, sell high candidate. The stock was selling near an eleven year low despite rising earnings and dividends, and appeared historically undervalued.

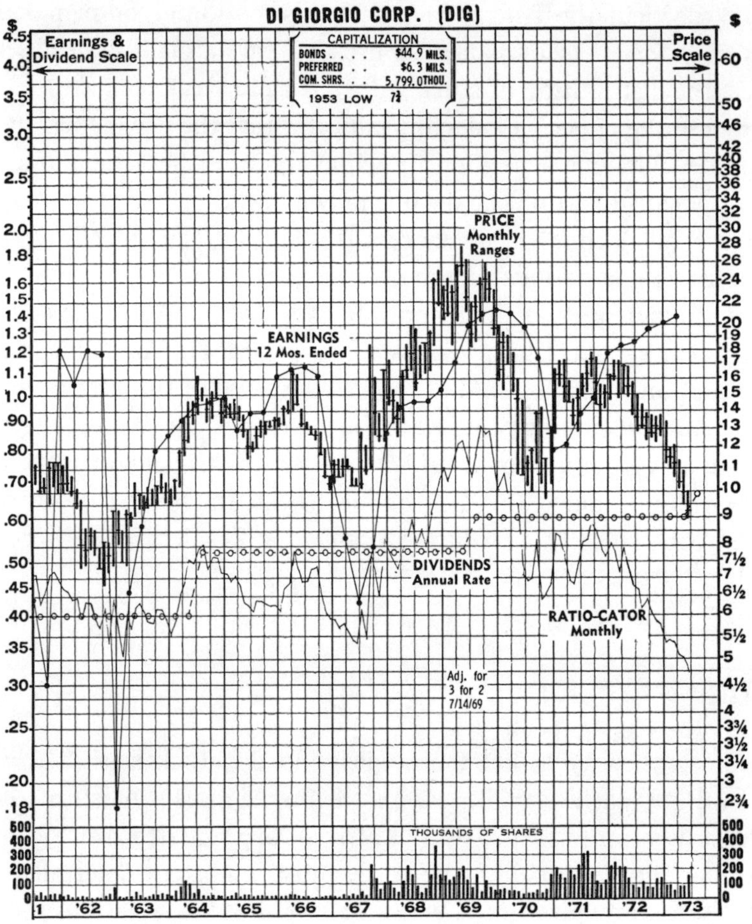

FIGURE 7

BUY LOW-SELL HIGH

Di Giorgio is in an undervalued position, in relation to its earnings and to its past price history.

Source: Securities Research Co., 208 Newbury St., Boston, MA 02116

The buy low, sell high technique is essentially conservative in nature. The general aim is to initiate positions at low price levels, where the danger of further decline is minimal, and to patiently await the price markup that usually follows. You can see how Di Giorgio, over the years, vacillated from its lower to upper price ranges. The drawbacks to the buy low, sell high strategy are the patience and time required for positions to work out. You can see, again from Figure 7, that Di Giorgio has remained at its lower levels for periods of up to one year. Some stocks can remain in a base formation for *years* at a time. However, by and large, the longer a stock remains within a trading range, the better the move once the stock does break out.

There have been several books written describing various buy low, sell high techniques. Interested readers should look up *How To Select Undervalued Stocks* by Robert and Darryl Peisner (E.P. Dutton and Co., New York, N.Y., 1973, $7.95), *How I Find Stocks That Double In a Year* by Michael R. Scott, Windsor Books, Brightwaters, N.Y., 1973, $19.95) and *The Stock Digest Price Rate Test Method to Stock Market Success* by Robert L. Robertson, Windsor Books, Brightwaters, N.Y., 1972, $12.50).

Buy High-Sell Higher

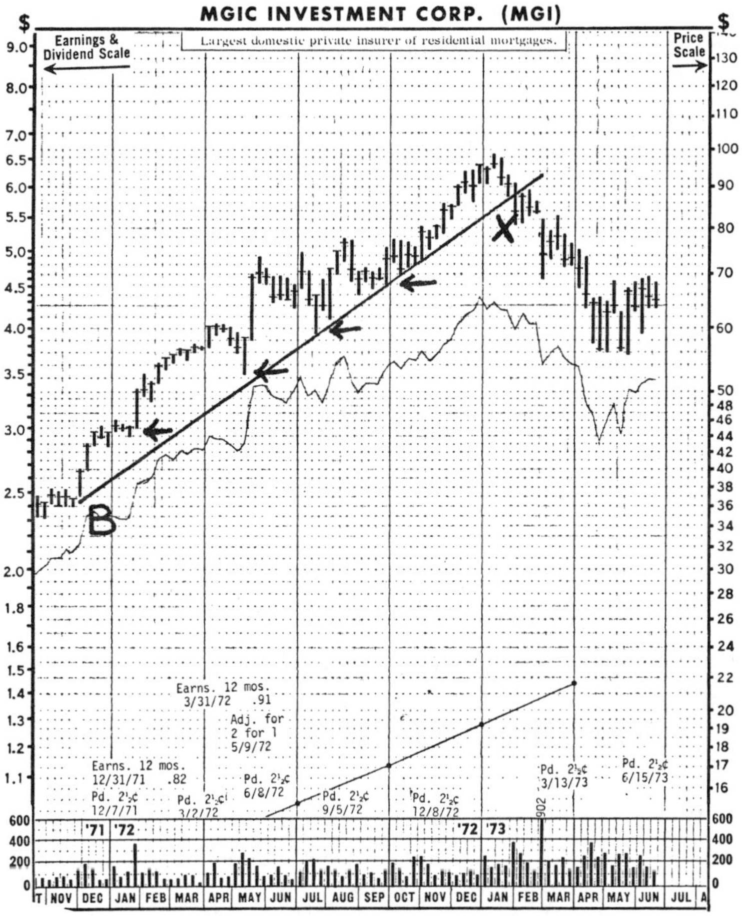

FIGURE 8: BUY LOW-SELL HIGHER

Presuming a buy at B, protective selling orders would have been placed at each arrow successively as MGIC resumed its advance. A sale would have been made at X, where the slope of the advance was broken.

Source: Securities Research Co., 208 Newbury St., Boston, MA 02116

The strategy here essentially calls for grabbing high-stepping stocks on the fly for quick action. Usually, relatively little attention is paid to fundamentals–earnings and such. Instead, the investor looks for stocks on the move for any reason, hoping to hop on and off before the public finally gets bagged.

How do you locate such animals? One technique is to check the newspapers for stocks making new highs each week. *Barron's* carries the data. Hop on board as soon as the security makes a new yearly high, especially if it is also a new historical high. Watch carefully for the first pullback in price. As soon as the stock starts upwards again, resolve to sell if it falls below the level of the first pullback. Raise your sell price as each decline phase is completed or sell upon violation of the trendline defining the upslope. Figure 8 shows the buy point (B) and sell stops (arrows) which would be employed as the stock advances. The X marks the point of sale.

Relative strength is an important aspect of this system. Buy stocks which have been outperforming the market. You can secure relative strength data from a variety of sources. One excellent source is the *Media-General Financial Weekly,* P.O. Box 26565, Richmond, Va. 23261. This is a thorough financial newspaper with slews of bond and stock data, plus a host of interesting features and articles. Readers interested in more information on the technique of picking high flyers might consult *The Haller Theory of Stock Market Trends* by Gilbert Haller (Gilbert Haller, P.O. Box 2048, Stateline, Nevada 89449, $5.00).

Summing Up: This system will at least make your broker rich. Strictly for speculators.

BUY BIG

This school for speculators suggests that you stick to large, institutional quality corporations–IBM, Atlantic-Richfield, Avon. The market is increasingly becoming monopolized by institutions which now account for 70% of all trading volume. After the 1969-1970 fiasco, these institutions became more than leery of smaller companies, since the cats and dogs simply could not be unloaded in quantity come garbage disposal time. Therefore, the institutions decided to load up on the big growth stocks, which they salt away, theoretically, for long term investment. These stocks, for the most part, held their price very well during the decline in 1973 (though not in early 1974) and performed very well from 1970-1972. Among the institutional quality growth stocks are:

J.P. Morgan
National Cash Register
First National City Corp.
Pfizer Inc.
Texas Instruments
Phillips Petroleum
Eli Lilly
American Home Products
Polaroid Corporation
General Telephone

Royal Dutch
Dow Chemical
Atlantic Richfield
Xerox Corp.
Burroughs Corp.
American Telephone
Coca Cola
Exxon Corp.
Eastman Kodak
Minnesota Mining

Bristol Meyers
Union Pacific Corp.
du Pont
Reynolds Industries
Warner Lambert
Gillette
Merck and Co.
Sperry Rand
Johnson and Johnson

A portfolio of a cross section of these securities will certainly perform as well as the stock market as a whole and most mutual funds. Institutional quality stocks enjoy broad public as well as institutional sponsorship and have not been subject to calamitous declines in recent years, although, of course, price declines do occur from time to time. Their price action is reliable since, while they will fall during bear markets, they will rise predictably during bull phases.

BUY SMALL

Another approach involves an attempt to select small, rapidly emerging growth companies early in their growth phase. Like Xerox when it was still called Haloid, or Skyline at a few dollars per share. The strategy calls for the location of companies showing compound earnings growth of 20-25% per year, purchasing and holding shares so long as this rate of growth persists. The smaller the capitalization of the company the better, since companies with fewer shares outstanding are more able to maintain large rates of earnings improvement.

Emerging growth corporations are generally not as well seasoned as larger growth companies, and, therefore, carry greater risk. *The Media-General Financial Weekly* carries compound growth data for all listed stocks and occasionally, in feature articles, segregates those stocks combining high compound earnings growth with low current price. Among the second line of growth companies in recent years have been:

- Wachovia Corporation
- U.S. Leasing Int'l
- Tropicana
- Tool Research & Engineering Corp.
- Teleprompter
- Superscope
- Sony Corp.
- Skyline Corp.
- Ryder Systems, Inc.
- Rite Aid Corp.
- Revco D.S., Inc.
- Research–Cottrell, Inc.
- Nashua Corp.
- Mc Lean Trucking Co.
- Mc Donald's Corp.
- Marriott Corp.
- Simplicity Pattern Co.

A third tier of growth situations, combining small capitalization, and growth rates in excess of 20% per year compounded, includes:

- AAR Corp.
- Action Industries
- Airborne Freight
- Altamil Corp.
- Amco Industries
- American Precision
- Benrus Corporation
- Bio Dynamics
- Coit Int'l
- Cook Industries
- El-Tronics
- Fabien Corporation
- Gray Mfg.
- GTI Corp.
- Heinicke Instruments
- Milgo Electronics
- Recrion Corp.
- Soundesign
- Sigma Instruments
- Valspar Corp.

There are, of course, many, many more which may be in the forefront of the next speculative bull market.

INSIDER TRANSACTIONS

William A. Kent (*The Smart Money,* Doubleday and Co., Inc., Garden City, N.Y., 1972, $6.95) suggests an interesting technique. The Securities and Exchange Commission publishes each month, the *Official Summary of Security Transactions and Holdings,* which can be secured for $17.40 annually by writing to the Superintendent of Documents, U.S. Government Printing Office, Washington, D.C. 20402. The publication lists the actual purchases and sales of company stock as carried out by the men in the know—corporate officials and directors, the insiders. By studying the *Summary,* you can see what insiders are actually doing with their own holdings of their company's stock. Disregard shares purchased via option benefits at prices below the market. Look for patterns of buying and selling at current market levels.

Insiders generally seek long term capital gains, and, therefore, purchase securities with the intention of maintaining long term holdings. One study of insider transactions turned up an interesting result. Between 1960 and 1966, a group of 52,000 insider transactions was analyzed. Stocks showing 1) accumulation of three or more insiders and 2) a holding period of twelve months, produced gains averaging 27.1 per cent over a twelve month holding period. By contrast, stocks marked by insider selling produced gains of only 9.6 per cent. (study by Shannon P. Pratt and Charles De Vere).

Certainly, $17.40 is not a large investment to get to the "inside".

REVERSE SPLITS

The Smart Money and *How I Find Stocks That Double In a Year* both report an interesting observation. Occasionally, stocks undergo a reverse split. That is, the number of shares outstanding is consolidated and the price per share raised. For instance, in the event you own 100 shares at 2 pre-reverse split, after the split you now will own 50 shares at a value of 4.

Reverse split situations generally decline in price during the period immediately following the reverse split. However, over a slightly longer pull, these situations do very well. Of 21 reverse splits studies by William A. Kent, the group as a whole showed a 178% increase in the eighteen months following the reverse split.

SECONDARY DISTRIBUTIONS

If your friendly stockbroker offers you a nice piece of second hand goods, commission free, tell him where to go. He's probably showing a portion of a secondary distribution, a block of stock offered at a discount price to the public by large holders, collecting their profits. Most secondaries come out at market tops and represent the distribution of shares by insiders and big money to people who ought to know better. In fact, if your account exec has a few of these around, be very cautious. The market as a whole may be topping out.

So much for the second hand goods. Ask him instead for a hot new issue and see where he tells you to go.

TAX TIP: HOW TO GET A FREE RIDE ON UNCLE SAM'S MONEY

Suppose you have a large profit on a stock, and it's time to sell. Say you're in the 40% bracket and for every thousand dollars profit you owe $400 in taxes. Consider this ploy. Don't sell your shares. Instead, sell stock short against the box, in the amount of the shares you would otherwise be selling. If you sell short against the box in this manner, your broker may possibly release up to the full amount of the proceeds of the short sale to you in cash—that's cash in your pocket. Since you have not sold the securities on which you have profit, you owe Uncle Sam nothing. Meanwhile, the profit is locked in by the short sale since, if the value of your holdings declines, you will profit by an equal amount from the short.

In the meantime, you have a free ride on the taxes owed for the price of the extra commissions. You incur no tax liability until you close out the hedged position. Check this all out with your broker, including the amount of cash his house will release on a short against the box. Odds are, he never heard of this ploy. Make him check with his back office. *Tax Tip:* If you are almost ready to take a short term profit, consider holding your shares instead and selling a call option against them. If your stock continues to rise, you'll receive an extra profit in the amount of premiums you've received for the call, plus a good chance that your short term holding will graduate into a long term capital gain. Even should your shares decline, the call premium will cushion any decline, at least to some extent, and even in the case of a severe decline, the combination of call premium plus reduced tax liabilities may still leave you ahead.

For further information regarding the selection and timing of security transactions, I refer readers to my book, *Winning Market Systems,* (Signalert Corporation, P.O. Box 1227, Old Village Station, Great Neck, N.Y. 11021, $19.95), which deals with the handling of stock market investment in considerable detail. Also, I suggest as references any and all books on the stock market cited in Chapter 20. In the meantime, try to follow the suggestions outlined here. You should at least do a little better than the dart board.

Chapter 10

"How Many Stocks Do You Know That Pay Out A 52.4 Percent Dividend?"

Investing In Stock Options

Potential Reward,	A-
Risk,	B-
Liquidity,	C-
Tax Considerations,	C

If 1973 was tough on mutuals, it saw, on the other hand, the emergence into daylight of a relatively little known form of stock market investment—the stock option. How long the fad will last is hard to say; we'll get into reasons for the sudden popularity later. *However, either way, options present excellent opportunities for the investor to draw a 15-25% long term compounded return from equity assets.* Although potential returns are excellent, until this year, the stock option vehicle of investment was employed only by relatively few stock market investors, generally the more sophisticated players. You may or may not have the temperament for the game, but before you decide, you should at least learn some of the rules. There are three major classifications of options.

CALLS

Calls represent the right of the purchaser of the call option to buy from the seller 100 shares of a stipulated stock, at a stipulated price, within a specified period of time. For example, let us presume that McDonald's Corporation is selling at 60. Some speculative soul believes that the stock will rally to 80. He purchases an option for, say, $750, which entitles him to the right to purchase from the seller 100 shares of McDonald's at 60, for a period of 6 months, 10 days from the date the option terms were settled. The $60 price is called the *striking price.* It is usually, but not always, the price of the last trade of the security. The price for the option, presume $750, is called the *premium.* In this case, the premium is 12.5% of the value of the shares ($750 premium ÷ $6,000 total share value). The *date of expiration* is the last day on which the option can be exercised, in this case 6 months, 10 days from the agreement.

What have both parties gained from the transaction? The buyer of the option, for his money, has acquired an opportunity to participate in any significant rise in the shares of the company, at limited capital investment, while incurring limited risk. Suppose McDonald's rises to 80 during the life of the option? The option holder exercises his option, buying the shares from the seller, as per the stipulation, at 60, immediately selling at 80. He has profited by $1,100 on the transaction ($2,000 gain in stock price minus $750 option cost minus approximately $150 commissions), but his position required only a $750 outlay. The return on that $750 amounted to 147%. Suppose McDonald's fell to 40, instead of rising? The purchaser of the option does not exercise and the option simply expires. The risk to the purchaser is limited to the cost of the option, and money that would otherwise be required for a position in McDonald's could be employed elsewhere. The disadvantages? McDonald's will have to rise by at least 7½ points, plus an extra 1½ points to cover commissions, for the buyer of the option to show a profit. In return for the amount of leverage and the limited risk inherent in the option maneuver, the buyer gives up a piece of the move. In this case, had McDonald's been purchased outright at 60, a buyer would realize a 20 point gain, but on a much larger investment, say, of approximately $3,040, if the shares were purchased on 50% margin, the return on capital, presuming a 20 point rise in McDonald's, would account to 60.9% (excluding interest for margin maintenance). Table I illustrates hypothetical gains and losses for the option buyer as opposed to the outright holder of McDonald's, if options are exercised or the stock is sold at the stipulated prices. Keep in mind that even if McDonald's is up by only two points at the time of expiration of the call, the option buyer will still exercise. His gains of even 2 points in this manner will offset some of the cost of the option.

TABLE I

Comparison of Results of Holding An Option On McDonald's and Outright Purchase at 50% Margin, Presuming an Initial Purchase or Striking Price of $60 a Call and a Premium of $750.

McDonald's Price at Expiration, 6 months	Gain (Loss) to Option Holder	Pct. Gain (Loss) to Option Holder	Gain (Loss) to Outright Purchaser	Pct. Gain (Loss) to Outright Purchaser
50	$- 750	-100%	$-1150	-37.8%
55	- 750	-100	- 650	-21.4
60	- 750	-100	- 150	- 4.9
65	- 400	- 53.3	+ 350	+11.5
70	+ 100	+ 13.3	+ 850	+30.0
75	+ 600	+380.0	+1350	+44.4
80	+1100	+146.7	+1850	+60.9
85	+1600	+213.3	+2350	+77.3

Commission costs of $150 are included in these calculations. McDonald's shares are presumed to be purchased at 50% margin, but interest costs are not included.

Table I demonstrates that the option purchaser will receive a superior return on capital to the outright purchaser only after the stock has made a substantial move, but that thereafter the option buyer profits greatly. On the loss side, the option buyer losses 100% of his investment unless the stock advances, but the loss is limited to $750. There is one further disadvantage to the purchase of options. Time. Once the option expires, there is no way you can recoup on the situation. Declining stocks sometimes do recover.

Historically, experience has shown that the majority of options are *not* exercised and represent complete losses to the option buyer. In evaluating the results of 36 CBOE options purchased and held between May and October, 1973, I found that only 27.8% of options purchased produced profits for holders. However, 80% of the winners produced profits in the order of 100% or better. Investing via the option purchase is clearly highly speculative, but also obviously can prove highly worthwhile. Only a limited portion of funds, however, should be committed in this manner. We will return to other aspects of option buying later.

SELLER

We have seen what the purchase of options offers and does not offer to the buyer. What about the seller? He is in a different position. Presume you have just purchased McDonald's at 60 and are contemplating the sale of an option. What is your position? You can receive, for your holding, a 12½% premium. If McDonald's rises and the stock is taken from you, you secure a profit of $600 clear ($750 minus $150 total commissions). However, let's suppose you purchase the shares on margin, capital required $3,040. You receive the $750 option money immediately upon sale of the option which can be applied to your purchase cost. Your cash out of pocket expenses are now reduced to $2,290. The rate of return to you ($600 ÷ $2,290) equals 26.2% for six months or 52.4% on an annual basis (interest charges on the margin account excluded). Unlike the buyers, who potentially can derive an unlimited rate of return from his investment, the option seller can never make more than the option premium. This is a disadvantage in selling options.

Risks? Well, suppose McDonald's declines. Since the seller has received $750 call money, his effective break-even price for the 100 shares lot is $5,400 ($600 minus $750 premium, plus $150 round trip commission costs). The seller will not lose money unless McDonald's drops below $54.00 per share. Should it drop further, he has the loss, at least partially, cushioned by the premium he has received. Should McDonald's rise by enough to offset commission costs, even if it rises by only two points, the call will be exercised and the seller receives his full $600 profit. If the stock remains at 60, the owner of McDonald's can simply await expiration and then offer another call on the stock for a second round of premiums. McDonald's pays no dividends. By selling calls, the owner of the stock has produced for himself a 52.4% annual dividend on a non-dividend paying security.

The big risk, of course, lies in the possibility of a serious decline. For instance, suppose McDonald's does decline to under 50, and the seller of the option thinks it will go lower; to some extent, he is locked in because he is obligated to deliver stock to the buyer. The seller can sell his shares and hope they do not rise again, but this is dangerous since if the stock does rise, he is obligated to deliver, or else he can sell and purchase for himself a call option, offsetting the option against him. If the stock rises and the call is exercised against him, he, in turn, exercises. (On CBOE, the call purchased by the seller simply offsets the previous call sold). Since he is purchasing his call at lower levels, it may even become possible for him to exercise his call without the other being triggered. However, the cost of this option does wipe out to a large degree the profit from the option sold by the holder of McDonald's. To repeat, *the major disadvantage to selling options lies in the fact that the seller may be locking himself into a poor situation.* Therefore, the seller of calls should be equally as bullish on the situation as the buyer. The more rapidly the options you sell are exercised, the more rapidly you can establish another position, the higher your rate of return. If the call we've discussed is exercised within ninety days instead of six months, the seller's rate of return doubles to 104.8%.

Historically, sellers of options have outperformed the gains made by the Dow Industrials and the gains achieved by the average mutual fund, despite the fact that the option premium represents a limit to profit. In the same period that only 27.8% of call buyers showed a net profit, 94.4% of call sellers achieved a profit on the same calls. However, it should be kept in mind that the stock market rose between May and October, 1973. In declining markets, both buyers and sellers would not have fared so well. Sellers must be patient, and have the temperament to neither begrudge nor regret those stocks which rise sharply and produce profits for the buyer. On average, the seller will come out better.

PUTS

Puts are the reverse of calls. The buyer receives the right to sell a stock at a stipulated price for a stipulated period of time. Let's go back to McDonald's again. Suppose a trader is bearish on the stock instead of bullish. He can purchase a put. If the stock declines from 60-40, he goes to the open market for shares at 40, and sells these shares at 60, as per agreement, to the person from whom he purchased the put. His profit is the extent of the stock's decline minus commissions and the premium. Put purchases represent a limited risk means of selling short, since no matter how high the stock rises, your loss is limited to the cost of the option. However, the premium, as in the case of the call, does reduce the extent of profit. Puts can also serve as insurance against calamitous losses in stocks which you own. A holder of McDonald's, for example, can purchase a put to guarantee his ability to sell at current market levels. He is out the put premium, but should the stock rise, he can enjoy the move.

Sellers of puts should be bullish, since they are positioning themselves for a stock purchase, albeit at a discount. If the stock declines, they will probably have to purchase the shares. A seller of a put on McDonald's at 60 will, in effect, be paying 52½ for the shares since he has a 7½ point premium in hand. If the stock rises after the option transaction, instead of falling, and the put remains unexercised, the put premium represents pure profit to the seller. The prices of put premiums are generally slightly lower than the prices of call premiums, since stocks rise most of the time.

STRADDLES

Straddles are a combination of a put and a call. They offer the purchaser the right to buy and to sell a security at a stipulated price within a stipulated time. Suppose you have purchased a straddle on McDonald's at 60. The stock declines to 40. You purchase shares on the open market at 40, sell as per the put side of the straddle at 60, pocketing the difference. The stock, still within the life of the option, then rises to 70. You then exercise the call, profiting both ways.

Generally, one side or the other of straddle options are exercised, rarely both sides. Straddles are the most popular form of option, since the buyer gets a play in both directions. Sellers are attracted to the straddle because of the higher premiums, but if you are considering selling straddles, be aware that you may be locking yourself in on the call side and obligating yourself to purchase shares on the put side.

PREMIUMS

Sellers of calls can expect to receive between 10-20% of the current stock price for six month, ten day options; ninety day options bring in 8-15% and one year options, from 15-30%. The exact amount varies depending upon the market climate, the strength and volatility of the underlying shares, and the amounts of dividends paid by the company.

Sellers of puts receive slightly less because of the upward bias of the stock market over the years.

Sellers of straddles receive somewhat less than if they sold a put and a call separately. However, straddles are the easiest to sell.

Option sellers, exercising reasonable judgment, *may expect a return on their money of approximately 15-25%,* compounded annually. Returns will naturally prove better during bull markets. I do recommend a program of option selling as a means of deriving added income from your stock portfolio. On balance, I do not recommend option purchases except in special situations. Try to purchase stock with the view of selling options following market declines, not following sustained rallies. As a seller, your timing does not have to be as precise as on the buy side.

THE MECHANICS OF THE TRANSACTION

Until 1973, options were sold exclusively through special option houses, which advertise regularly in most financial newspapers, or via the option departments of brokerage houses. The procedure is a bit complicated. If you own the securities already, you can simply call either the option house or your stockbroker and inquire as to whether any bids exist for options on your shares. If so, and the bid is acceptable to you, you simply agree on the striking price, usually the current price of the security, and the deal is made orally. Both you and the seller subsequently receive written confirmation. You also receive your premium payment immediately. Your brokerage house guarantees, in the case of a call or straddle, that you have the shares on deposit with him in case you are called upon to deliver, and that you also have on deposit any requisite cash balance required for the purchase of options which must be paid for immediately.

If the price offered is not acceptable, or if no bids exist, you may indicate your offer to sell an option and list an asked price. Possibly, you may choose to try to negotiate a compromise between the bid and the asked. This is often possible because the option dealer's profit comes from a spread of about ½ point or so between what the buyer of the option pays and what the seller receives. If you are selling, and negotiate, you can sometimes get the buyer to come up in price a bit or get the dealer to relinquish some of the spread. Another way to handle option selling is to avoid purchase of the stock until the option deal is settled. You then immediately purchase the underlying stock. It is easier to purchase common shares than to sell an option. As a buyer, you operate in reverse, looking for options available in stocks in which you have an interest.

THE CHICAGO BOARD OPTIONS EXCHANGE (CBOE)

In April 1973, a new wrinkle was added to option trading, the CBOE, which resulted in the public suddenly becoming aware of the option game. CBOE, an offshoot of the Chicago Board of Trade, which is a marketplace for various commodities, has standardized option trading. On CBOE, options are offered for four maturity dates, the last Mondays of January, April, July and October. Striking prices are fixed by the Exchange, and are based upon the price of the securities on the days that the new maturity dates become available, rounded to the nearest 5. For example, if McDonald's is trading at either 58 or 62 when a new option maturity is introduced on CBOE, the striking price of the call option will be set at 60. Should McDonald's rise to 70 at some point, a new option with a striking price of 70 may be introduced, but the 60's will continue to trade. Since the maturity dates are fixed, the purchaser in February of, say, an April option will be purchasing an option with only slightly more than two months of life left. He may have the alternative of purchasing options expiring in July and October of the same year, or January of the next year as well, but at higher premiums.

Purchases or sales of options via CBOE are simpler than through the option houses. CBOE prices appear on a ticker tape and on the quote machines of participating brokers. Since the options are standardized, fluid trading of the options themselves becomes possible. For example, suppose you purchase a call option on McDonald's for $750, striking price $60. The stock rises to 70. The option must be worth at least $10 (commission factors excluded), since a buyer could purchase a call, exercise, and sell the common at 70 (current price of common minus striking price equals minimum call price). Instead of exercising the option, you simply sell it on the Exchange for a minimum 2½ point profit, thereby saving the large commissions involved in purchasing and reselling an expensive stock. CBOE offers to the option buyer excellent leverage and the chance to make money just on option trading. In the example given above, McDonald's, in rising from 60 to 70, returned 16-2/3% to cash owners of the common, but 33-1/3% to option traders.

The procedures for selling options are simpler on CBOE, since ready buyers exist and the latest quotes are readily available. Currently, CBOE offers call options only and these are limited to 32 popular companies. Plans exist to expand the roster of companies and the variety of options for sale. *The Wall Street Journal* and *Barron's* carry CBOE quotes and the Exchange hopes that increasing activity will stimulate wider coverage. The New York and American Stock Exchanges are considering listed option transactions as well. For more information regarding CBOE procedures, margin regulations, and so forth, write to the Chicago Board Options Exchange, La Salle at Jackson, Chicago, Illinois 60604.

STRATEGIES

Successful option selling requires some sense of market timing. Obviously, calls are best sold near market bottoms, since the greatest risk to the call seller lies in the stock's declining significantly. Do not be lured by large premiums into locking yourself into positions on highly speculative securities. Be aware too, that on call options held over-the-counter, the premium you receive is reduced by the amount of dividends paid by the company during the life of the option. These dividends accrue to the buyer of the option, in the event that he exercises, in the form of a reduction in the striking price. However, on CBOE, the seller keeps the dividends. To emphasize, do not sell any option unless you like the underlying company and expect no more than a moderate drop in the market. Most professional option sellers keep selling options on their shares until someone exercises.

SELLING NAKED OPTIONS

There is one instance in which you can sell a call on a stock you don't like. Suppose you think McDonald's will decline. You can sell a call against stock you *do not own* (naked options) by putting up margin with your broker, in the amount of roughly 30% of the stock's value. Should McDonald's decline as per your expectations, the call premium is pure profit. However, should McDonald's rise, you may have to pay dearly for the shares when you are called upon to deliver. Selling naked options can be very profitable, but it is also quite risky. (Should the stock for which you have sold a naked option rise, you will have to put up additional margin to the extent of 30% of current market value, plus the amount of difference between the striking price and the new price of the stock. Puts require 25% original margin, but more money must be put up for margin as the shares decline).

Besides a few tricks here and there, option trading offers no special tax advantages. There are no ways, of any substance, to shelter profits. The only exception, perhaps, lying in custodian Keogh accounts, in which a bank acts as trustee for a variety of investments, all maintained together in the Keogh account. Some other tax ploys are discussed below.

HOW TO TURN A SHORT SALE INTO A CAPITAL GAIN

The government charges any profits made via short sales as ordinary income no matter how long the short sale has been in effect. (A short sale is the sale of stock *prior* to ownership. You sell stock borrowed from your broker. You hope the shares decline, enabling you to buy on the market, at a lower price, shares of the company that you previously sold. The difference between the sales price you received and the price you ultimately have to pay is your profit or loss). You can, however, convert a short sale into a capital gain in the following manner:

1) Instead of selling a stock short, buy a put of longer than six month's duration.

2) If the put is profitable after a six month holding period, do not exercise the put. If you sell via exercise and buy the common the same day, you pay ordinary income tax.

3) Instead, *sell the put* itself. Option dealers will purchase from you, at a slight premium, profitable options and exercise themselves. Your profit, taxwise, is based upon the purchase

and sale of the put itself. Since you have held the put longer than six months, the sale of the asset represented by the option is taxed as a capital gain. For this reason, options are timed for six month, ten day maturities.

You can turn your call purchase into a capital gain in the same manner. Instead of exercising your call, sell it after six months to an option dealer (or on CBOE) for a six month capital gain on the call itself.

HOW TO TURN A SHORT TERM CALL PROFIT INTO LONG TERM

Presume you purchase a call on McDonald's at 60 for $750 and the stock moves to 75. You show a $750 profit on the call within six months. If you exercise, the day trade is charged as ordinary income. If you sell the call, the profit on the call is still ordinary income. Solution. *Short the stock.* Should McDonald's decline, your loss of call profits will be offset by the profits on the short sale. Should McDonald's rise, your loss on the short sale will be offset by the rise in the value of the call. Either way you hold your option sufficiently long to receive favorable tax treatment.

OTHER TAX CONSIDERATIONS

If you sell a call and the call is exercised, the premium received for the call is added to the sale price of the stock in computing your profit and loss statement. If the call is not exercised, the premium from the call is treated as ordinary income.

If you sell a put which is exercised, your purchase price of the stock is the price you paid for the shares less the premium you have received. If the put is not exercised, the premium you receive is treated as ordinary income.

If you buy a call and exercise, the price to you of the stock is the price you paid plus the call premium. If you purchase any option and do not exercise, the premium you paid is treated as ordinary income loss if the option is held longer than six months or if it is held for less.

LIQUIDITY

As a form of investment, selling options does not provide a great deal of liquidity. You must either hold your securities, maintain margin, or else give up your option profit via purchases of offsetting options, should you wish to liquidate your positions. Therefore, liquidity rates only C–. CBOE option buying, however, rates an A, since you can simply trade these options in the same manner as common shares.

WHERE TO GET FURTHER INFORMATION

I have already provided the address of CBOE.

Most options are still transacted through members of the Put and Call Brokers and Dealers Association, Inc., founded in 1934. Member dealers usually offer free literature explaining in detail the option scene, and showing current quotes and availability of options. Among these dealers are:

Ragnar Option Corporation
39 Broadway
New York, New York 10006

Herzog and Company
170 Broadway
New York, New York 10038

Merkin & Company, Inc.
Godnick & Son Division
50 Broadway
New York, New York 10006

These houses frequently issue option letters describing advanced hedging strategies, favorably situated options, timing advice, new margin regulations, etc. Do write to them for further information.

SUMMING UP

There are obviously disadvantages to both option buying and selling, but option selling is, nonetheless, a sound and recommended investment strategy. Consider the income our hypothetical McDonald's owner received by selling options on his shares. After all, how many stocks do you know that pay out a 52.4% dividend?

Chapter 11

"You Probably Won't Do Any Worse Than Your Brokerage House"

Learning To Call Market Turns

Let's presume you've gotten this far. Convertible bonds entice you, you're willing to give the mutuals a chance and you've even decided to pick a few on your own. Whichever way you go, good market timing is going to help.

I'm not talking about short term scalping–grabbing a quick point or two here and there by trading the natural fluctuations of the market. That's risky at best and better left alone unless you have a hot line to the trading floor. The current high level of commission rates just puts too great a handicap on short term operations. Nor am I even talking about pin-pointing major turns to the day. I am talking, however, about putting a few minutes each week into some simple arithmetic so that you can assess, at least broadly, the current state of the market, and by so doing, up the odds in your favor when you do decide to take a

TABLE I: PRICE-EARNINGS MULTIPLES FOR THE DOW INDUSTRIALS, 1928-1972

YEAR	PRICE RANGE	EARNINGS	% CHANGE	PRICE/EARNINGS RATIOS AT HIGHS	PRICE/EARNINGS RATIOS AT LOWS	MONTH HIGHS	MONTH LOWS
1928	300–191	$15.97	+126	18.8	12.0	Dec.	Feb.
1929	381–199	19.94	+ 25	19.1	10.0	Sept.	Nov.
1930	294–158	11.02	- 45	26.7	14.3	Apr.	Dec.
1931	194– 74	4.09	- 63	47.4	18.1	Feb.	Dec.
1932	89– 41	-0.93	-100	––	––	Mar.	July
1933	109– 50	2.78	+100	39.2	18.0	July	Mar.
1934	111– 86	4.60	+ 66	24.1	18.7	Feb.	July
1935	148– 97	6.86	+ 49	21.6	14.1	Nov.	Mar.
1936	185–143	10.07	+ 68	18.4	14.2	Nov.	Jan.
1937	194–114	11.49	+ 14	16.9	9.9	Mar.	Nov.
1938	158– 99	6.01	- 48	26.3	16.5	Nov.	Mar.
1939	156–121	9.18	+ 53	17.0	13.2	Sept.	Apr.
1940	153–112	10.99	+ 20	13.9	10.2	Jan.	June
1941	134–106	11.64	+ 6	11.5	9.1	Jan.	Dec.
1942	120– 93	9.22	- 21	13.0	10.1	Dec.	Apr.
1943	146–119	9.74	+ 6	15.0	12.2	July	Jan.
1944	153–134	10.07	+ 3	15.2	13.3	Dec.	Feb.
1945	196–151	10.56	+ 5	18.6	14.3	Dec.	Jan.
1946	213–163	13.63	+ 29	15.6	12.0	May	Oct.
1947	187–163	18.80	+ 38	10.0	8.7	July	May
1948	193–165	23.07	+ 23	8.4	7.2	June	Mar.
1949	201–162	23.54	+ 2	8.5	6.9	Dec.	June
1950	235–197	30.70	+ 30	7.7	6.4	Nov.	Jan.
1951	276–239	26.59	- 13	10.4	9.0	Sept.	Jan.
1952	292–256	24.76	- 7	11.8	10.3	Dec.	May
1953	294–255	27.23	+ 10	10.8	9.4	Jan.	Sept.
1954	404–280	28.40	+ 4	14.2	9.9	Dec.	Jan.
1955	488–388	35.78	+ 26	13.6	10.8	Sept.	Jan.
1956	521–462	33.34	- 7	15.6	13.9	Apr.	Jan.
1957	521–420	36.08	+ 8	14.4	11.6	July	Oct.
1958	584–437	27.95	- 22	21.0	15.6	Dec.	Feb.
1959	679–574	34.03	+ 22	20.0	16.9	Dec.	Feb.
1960	685–566	32.50	- 5	21.1	17.4	Jan.	Oct.
1961	735–610	31.22	- 4	23.5	19.5	Dec.	Jan.
1962	726–536	36.44	+ 17	19.9	14.7	Jan.	June
1963	767–647	39.97	+ 10	19.2	16.2	Dec.	Jan.
1964	892–766	46.75	+ 17	19.1	16.4	Nov.	Jan.
1965	969–841	53.73	+ 15	18.1	15.7	Dec.	June
1966	995–744	57.68	+ 7	17.2	12.9	Feb.	Oct.
1967	943–786	53.87	- 7	17.5	14.6	Sept.	Jan.
1968	985–825	57.89	+ 7	17.0	14.2	Dec.	Mar.
1969	969–770	57.02	- 2	17.0	13.5	May	Dec.
1970	842–631	51.02	- 11	16.5	12.4	Dec.	May
1971	951–798	55.00	+ 8	17.3	14.5	Apr.	Nov.
1972	1,036–889	67.11	+ 22	15.4	13.2	Dec.	Jan.
1973E	1,200E–800E	75.00E	+ 12E	16.0E	10.7E	?	?

E-Estimated

Source: Growth Stock Outlook, P.O. Box 9911, Chevy Chase, MD 20015

mutual fund position, for instance.

Most money is lost in the stock market, not by picking wrong stocks but by picking right stocks at the wrong time. Market declines take the good with the bad; strong market advances frequently carry even the weakest issues upside. And as the public mood changes from despair to hope to reckless optimism, so does public money really get sucked in for another round of fleecing. Try to stay objective and try to keep track of at least a few of the market indicators we will be discussing. They have all shown better than average results in calling important market junctures, and none is too complicated for the average investor to track and understand.

We have already discussed the relationship between earnings and the price movement of stocks; to wit, stock prices sooner or later follow the trend in earnings. The same principle applies to the total stock market.

The price-earnings ratios for the Dow Industrial Averages are published in a variety of sources; for example, the *Barron's Financial Weekly*. This represents the price level of the Dow divided by the cumulative earnings of the 30 stocks that comprise the average. Table I shows the data for the years 1928-1972. Actually, the relationship between earnings and the Dow has not remained consistent over the years. From 1928-1955, the average P/E ratio at annual market high points was 17.5 and at market low points it was 11.8. The period between 1956 and 1964 was marked by considerable optimism, justified by economic developments. The average high P/E multiple during these years rose to 19.3 and the average low multiple rose to 15.8. Since 1961, the P/E multiple that investors have been willing to pay for stocks has eroded. 1966 saw a low multiple recorded of 12.9; 1970 saw a low of 12.4; 1974, 10. The high multiples recorded during the early 1960's have never been reached since.

At this time, it appears that a cautious stance regarding the stock market is definitely indicated any time the Dow sells above 17 times its own earnings. An optimistic position can be taken whenever the Dow sells below 10.5-13.0 times its own earnings. Keep track. Remember, optimism runs highest at market tops.

MUTUAL FUND CASH POSITION

With the increasing institutionalization of the stock market, the importance of mutual funds as a moving force has escalated. By mid-1973, funds controlled $48.6 billion in assets, and the potential buying power of these institutions, as measured by the industry cash position, augurs either well or badly for the stock market as a whole. The principle is readily comprehended. When funds have cash, they can potentially step in to buy, therefore raising prices. When the funds are low on cash, on the other hand, there is no one left to pump up prices.

Actually, mutual funds have received considerable amounts of flak lately because they are so relatively low on cash at market tops. If fund managements, the knock goes, were so clever, how come they aren't in cash at tops and fully invested at bottoms? It's really simple. Presume every fund realized that a market top was approaching. To whom could they sell?

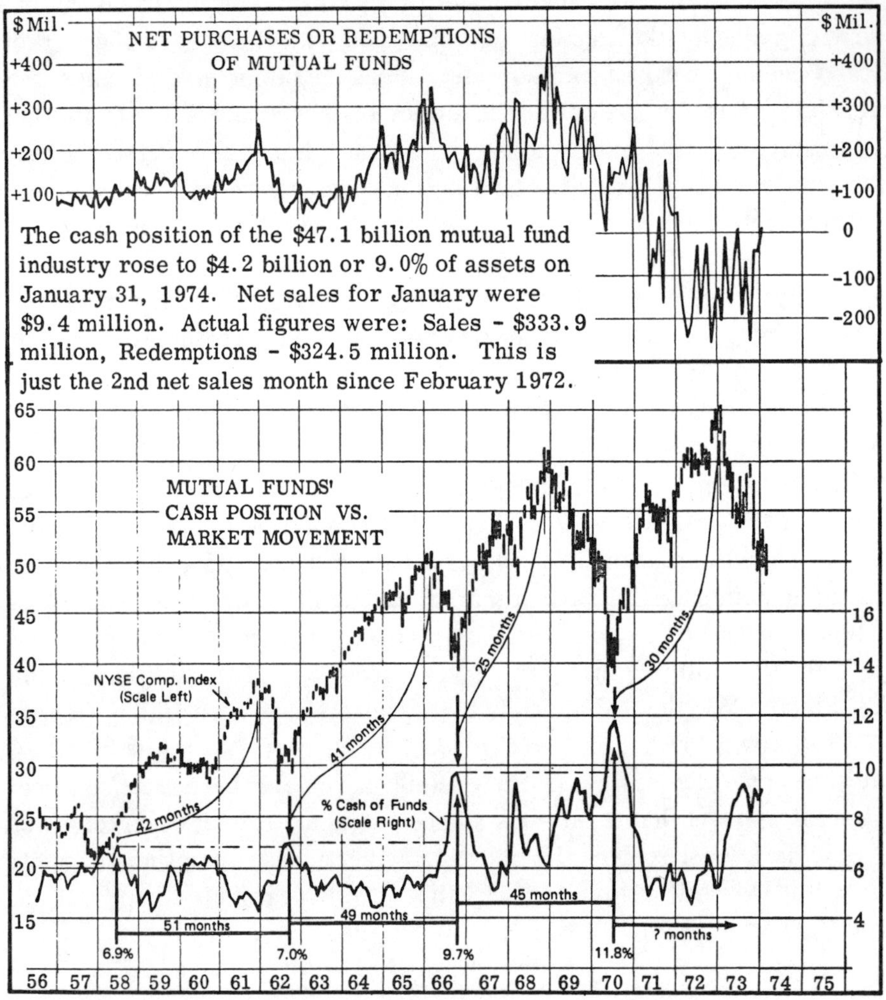

FIGURE 1
MUTUAL FUNDS CASH POSITION VS MARKET MOVEMENT
Source: Growth Fund Guide, Box 2109, San Clemente, CA 92672

If they all knew a bottom was approaching, from whom could they all buy without immediately forcing prices sky high? Obviously, while some smaller funds can move into and out of stocks rapidly, the bulk of the industry does have to remain invested for the long pull, a fact you should consider when you place money into mutuals.

In any event, a market bottom is probably approaching anytime the mutual fund cash position reaches nine per cent of their total assets. A five per cent cash position seems to mark stock market tops, but the stock market has often continued to rise for several months following the attainment of such levels. The 1973 bear market was interrupted by a major rally as the mutual fund cash position reached 9.2per cent. By early 1974, the mutual cash position had reached 9.7%.

This data is widely publicized upon its release each month.

SPECIALIST SHORT SALES

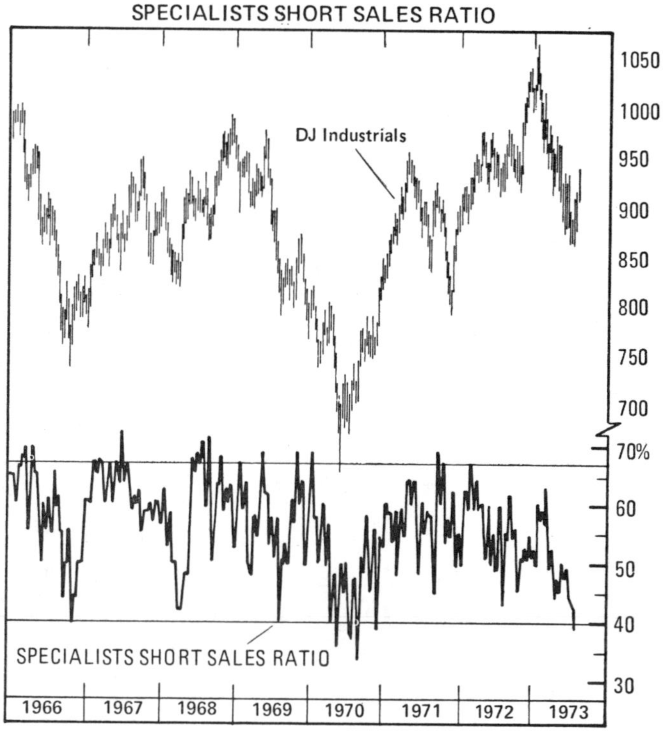

FIGURE 2
SPECIALISTS SHORT SALES
Source: Indicator Digest
Palisades Park, NJ 07650

All the trades that are made on the floors of the major exchanges have to pass through the hands of the specialists. The specialists keep books on which are recorded all open buy and sell orders for the securities they handle. Obviously, these professionals have a most informed opinion as to the future direction of the stock market.

The amount of short selling done by the specialists is published weekly, usually Mondays in *The Wall Street Journal* and in *Barron's.* When specialists, as a group, do more than sixty-seven per cent of all the short selling done on the New York Stock Exchange, important tops are close at hand. Low areas are signalled when the ratio of specialist to total short selling drops below 40 per cent. Forty per cent readings marked the low points during the bear markets of 1966, 1970, and the lows before the major advances that began in July, 1973 and February, 1974. To compute the ratio, divide the amount of specialist short sales on the

New York Stock Exchange by the amount of total short sales on that exchange each week.

Do keep in mind that the data is two weeks old when released. If specialist short sales are dropping, and the market has declined over the latest two weeks, you can usually presume a further decline in specialist shorts for the weeks not yet recorded. Vice versa for rising markets; expect the specialist shorts to increase during market advances, particularly if they have been trending upwards.

ODD-LOT SHORT SALES

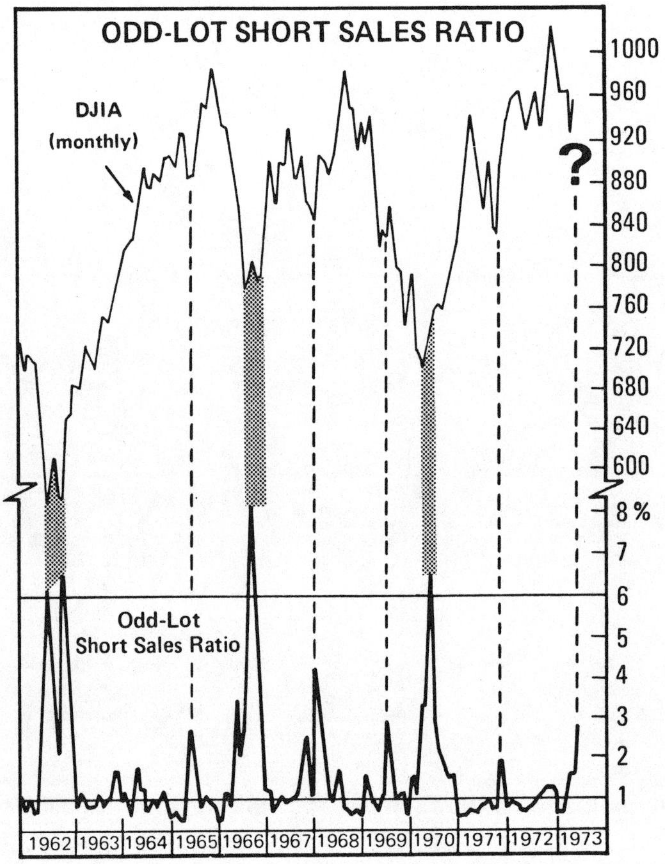

FIGURE 3
ODD-LOT SHORT SALES RATIO
Source: Indicator Digest, Palisades Park, NJ 07650

If the specialists are so smart, then who's so dumb? The odd-lotters, of course, who usually follow the crowd. The odd-lot short sales ratio is determined by dividing the amount of odd-lot short sales by the number of odd-lot sales of shares. Data appears daily in *The Wall Street*

Journal. It is quite bullish when odd-lot short sales rise to above five per cent of total odd-lot sales. Such a reading indicates mounting pessimism on the part of the most unsophisticated sector of the investment community, the person who trades in less than 100 share lots. This indicator is not as accurate in calling market tops, but it does pay to be cautious when odd-lot short sales drop below one per cent of total odd-lot sales, and particularly if they fall to the area of ½ of 1%.

Incidentally, review Figure 1 for another measure of unsophisticated opinion. You can see that the public tends to purchase mutual fund shares in greatest quantities right at market tops. Natch. That's what this chapter's all about anyhow. So you can move in the contrary direction.

CREDIT CONDITIONS

Even if coupon clipping isn't your thing, it will pay for you to keep track of the bond market. Actually, there's an interesting piece of history at play here. Stocks, historically, have traditionally provided greater yields than the ostensibly much safer bonds. As recently as 1951, the Dow Industrials provided a composite dividend yield of more than seven per cent while the *Barron's* 40 Bonds Average yielded under 3.5%. Then came the growth craze and inflation. The great post-war bull market brought with it contempt for fixed income investments, all the more since inflation has eaten into the real return from bond interest. As interest rates rose from the mid-nineteen fifties, bond prices fell so bondholders were stung both ways. As a result, the total bond market suffered a decline in popularity. At the same time, as stock prices rose, the rate of dividend payment fell. Indeed, in the halcyon days of IBM and Xerox, a company paying dividends was viewed as rather stodgy, to say the least.

By 1958, the "safer" bonds began to provide a greater yield than the "risky" stocks, a relationship which continues to exist to this day. No one minded, so long as stocks were providing capital gains of 10-15% a year. However, the stock market, since 1968, has been a new ball game, and capital gains profits have been more difficult to come by. With Triple A's now yielding 7½%, and B's up to 12%, bonds are once again offering real competition to common shares, which never recovered the luster lost five years ago. A couple of more bear markets and we may just see a return to the days when the safety of bonds was valued at a premium price. (Incidentally, market tops are close at hand whenever the Dow Industrials yield below 3-3.3 per cent in dividends).

In any event, rising interest costs, particularly if credit is tight at any price, bode badly for the stock market. The Federal Reserve Board can, and periodically does, tighten credit in a variety of ways. Margin requirements may be raised for stock purchases, which in effect, cuts into potential public purchasing power. The discount rate, the amount banks have to pay to borrow money from the Federal Reserve System, can be raised or lowered. Finally, the reserve requirements for banks can be raised or lowered. You can follow the drift of the credit scene by checking out the financial pages of your newspaper on a regular basis. As I write this,

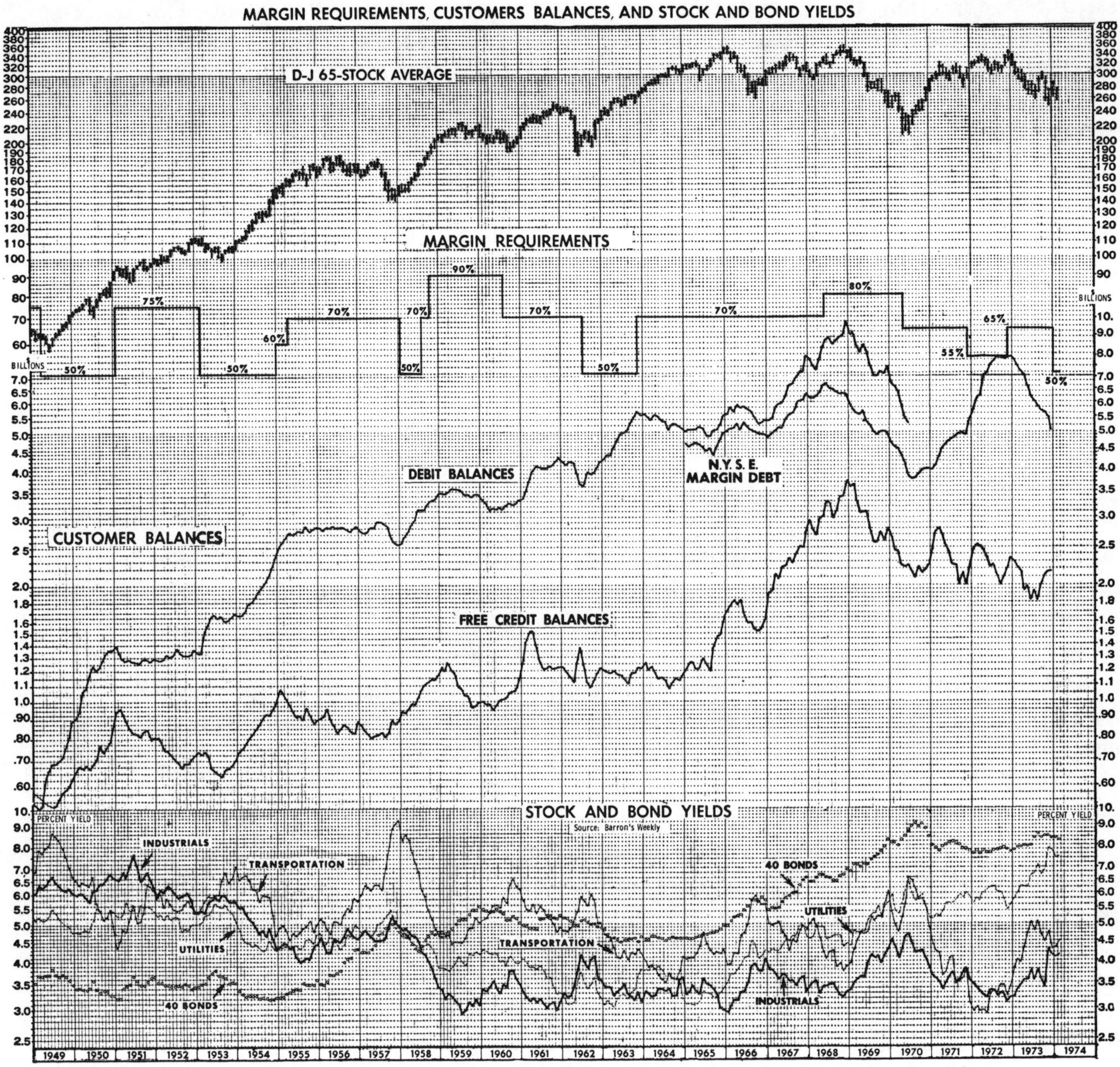

FIGURE 4

MARGIN REQUIREMENTS, CUSTOMERS BALANCES, & STOCK & BOND YIELDS

Source: Securities Research Co., 208 Newbury St., Boston, MA 02116

the prime rate has risen to 9½% and has not yet levelled off. The stock market is simultaneously falling, again demonstrating the inter-relationship between the credit and stock markets.

The discount rate is frequently an early indicator of the intentions of our national money managers. A lowering of this rate, or of stock market margin requirements, usually indicates a wish on the part of the Federal to ease credit conditions. Figure 4 shows the relationship between stock prices, margin requirements, and bond yields.

THE DOW UTILITY AVERAGE

Utility stocks are quite sensitive to credit conditions since 1) they are frequently purchased for their yields and 2) utility companies are heavy borrowers of money. Therefore, the price action of utility stocks often provides advance information as the currents of national credit, and indirectly provides a clue as to the impending direction of the stock market. The Dow Utility Average is widely published on a daily basis and will often show strength in advance of the more speculative market sectors. Weakness in the Dow Utility group presages oncoming weakness in the broader market.

THE ADVISORY SERVICES

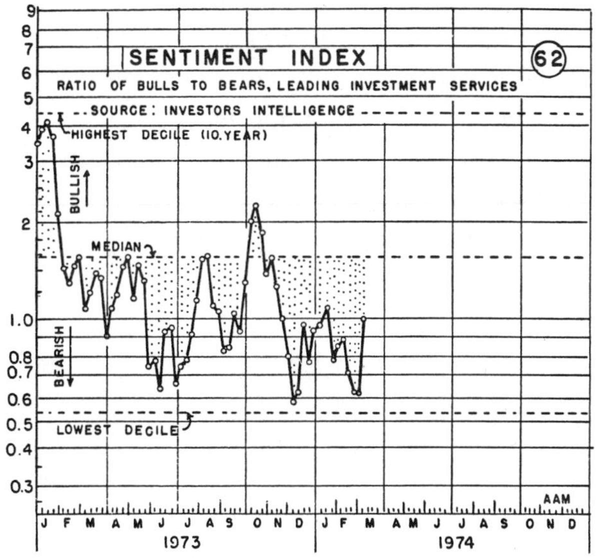

FIGURE 5

THE SENTIMENT INDEX

Source: Technical Trends, Box 228, Chappaqua, NY 10514

Advisory services have traditionally had a bullish bias—which is understandable for a number of reasons. First, the market does advance about two-thirds of the time, so a perpetual bull is less likely to be wrong than a perpetual bear. Second, subscriptions to these services rise during bull markets—so perhaps a bit of wishful thinking is involved. And, third, my advisory friends tell me that subscribers will forgive a bull who has happened to wander astray, but a bear—never. Apparently, the public would rather lose money than lose the opportunity to make money.

Investor's Intelligence, one of the more popular advisories, keeps tabs on its confreres, and the results are frequently publicized. As a group, advisories are most bullish at market tops and most bearish at bottoms. Peruse Figure 5, if you will. You will see that the "experts" were most bullish at the end of 1972, just before the 1973 decline, and most bearish in late 1973 and early 1974—prophetic of a significant bullish move.

This indicator is closely tracked by the services themselves. Each is usually quite happy to find himself in the minority. In recent years, it has paid to become bullish when about half the advisories turn bearish.

BREADTH INDICATORS

These require just a little more work. The advance-decline line is a cumulative total of issues advancing minus issues declining on the New York Stock Exchange. A healthy market should show an A-D (advance-decline) line rising in harmony with the Dow. A divergence between the two will usually resolve in favor of the A-D line. For example, since the A-D line reflects the action of the majority of stocks, it is a more accurate reflector of what the total market is doing than is the Dow Industrial Average. *Barron's* carries the data weekly.

Each week, secure the net difference between the number of stocks advancing on the N.Y.S.E. and the number declining. Add (or subtract) this total each week from the previous cumulative total. You can begin at any time at any arbitrary number. Every new high made by the Dow should be matched by a new high in the A-D line. Otherwise, it generally pays to adopt a very cautious stance. Sometimes, divergences do exist for several months at a time, before the market actually declines; but do take them seriously even when they first occur.

Related to the A-D line is the *New Highs-New Lows Index.* This is the net difference between issues making new highs each week and issues making new lows, plotted weekly. *Barron's* and many newspapers carry the data. New highs in the market averages should be accompanied by new highs in the new high-new low index. This index will usually give about a one year advance warning of the end of bull markets by failing to make new highs with the Dow. On the downside, the index will often reach its nadir some months in advance of the market averages. If the NH-NL Index fails to make new lows with the stock market, and turns up as the market averages continue to decline, expect a significant upside reversal.

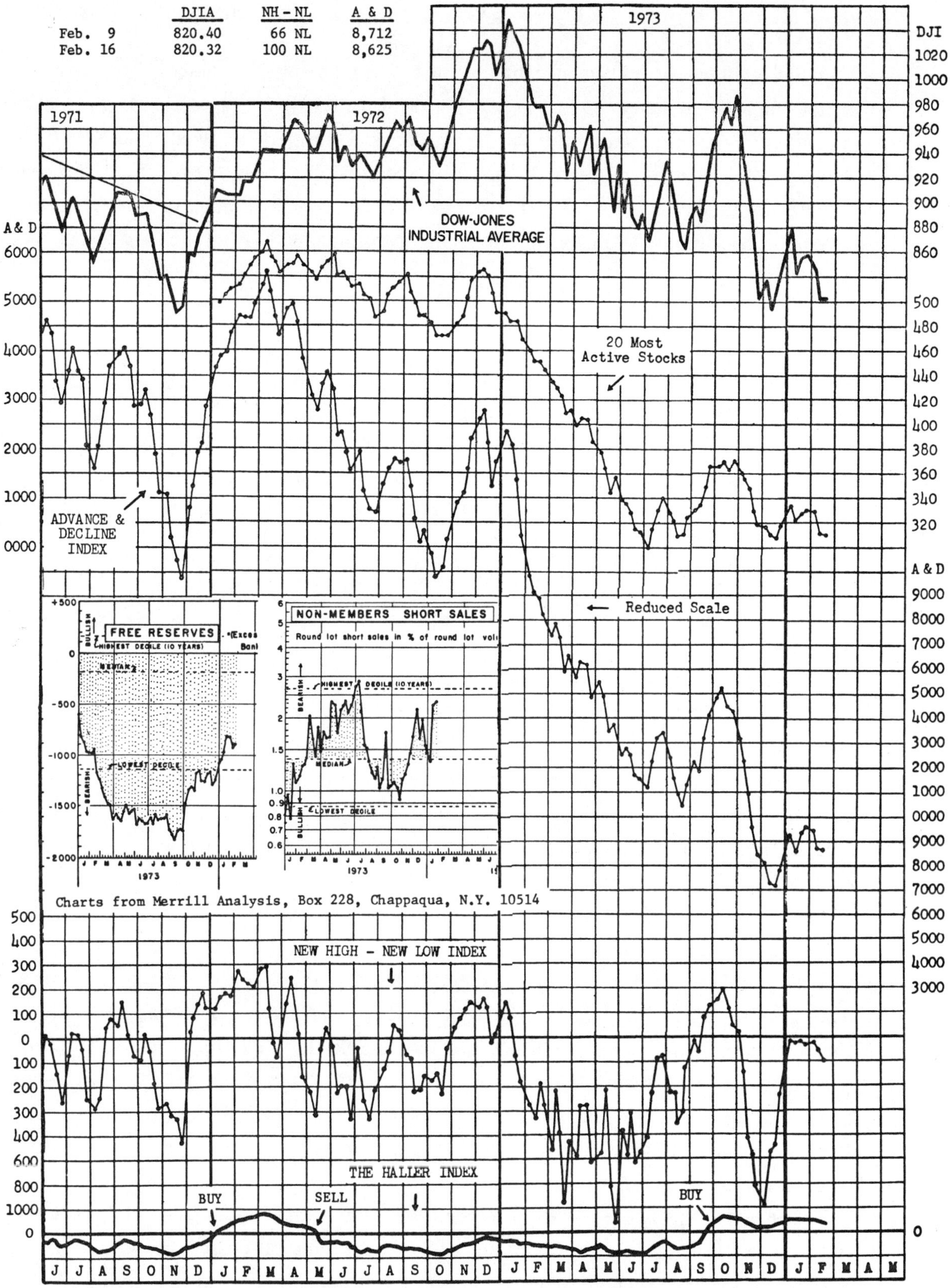

FIGURE 6: ADVANCE-DECLINE INDEX, NEW HIGH-NEW LOW INDEX, ETC.

Source: The Stongest Stocks, Box 2048, Stateline, NV 89449

Figure 6 shows the advance-decline and the new high-new low indices. The Dow advance to new highs in January, 1973 was not matched by the A-D line, which declined between December, 1972 and January, 1973. Hence, the decline that followed. The NH-NL Index likewise failed to confirm the highs made by the Dow. However, the NH-NL Index reached its low point in May, 1973, nearly six weeks before the Dow bottomed in July. These indices are simple to compute and to maintain. Highly recommended for anyone with a stake in the stock market.

TREND (See Figure 7)

We have already seen the importance of trend in individual stock selection. Figure 7 shows the application of trend and channel lines to the stock market averages. Long term investors may maintain positions so long as major trend lines remain intact, but do sell when significant uptrends are decisively broken.

A GREAT TOOL FOR CALLING MARKET TURNS

Indicator Digest (Palisades Park, N.J. 07650) has recently developed a unique indicator which has had an excellent record for calling significant market reversals. It is called the Most Active Stocks indicator, and reflects the action of the fifteen most active stocks each day on the New York Stock Exchange. The most active stocks are the stocks showing the greatest trading volume each day, the situations into and out of which large blocks of money are moving.

To compute the Most Active Stocks indicator (MAS), maintain, on a daily basis, the difference between the number of the fifteen most active stocks on the N.Y.S.E. that advance and the number that decline. If ten are up for the day, three down, and two unchanged, the daily reading is +7. Maintain a cumulative total for thirty days. The reading at the end of thirty days is the MAS. On the thirty-first day, add in that daily figure and subtract the net result thirty one days back, so you are always working with the last thirty days. A cumulative total of +9 is bullish. A reading below –9 signifies a sell signal. *Indicator Digest* suggests that these readings be divided by three and then plotted, but I consider the second step unnecessary.

The signals rendered by MAS have been highly accurate. Based upon the results of this indicator to date, no-load mutual funds can be profitably purchased and sold on its signals. Figure 8 shows the excellent sell signal given by this indicator during January of 1973.

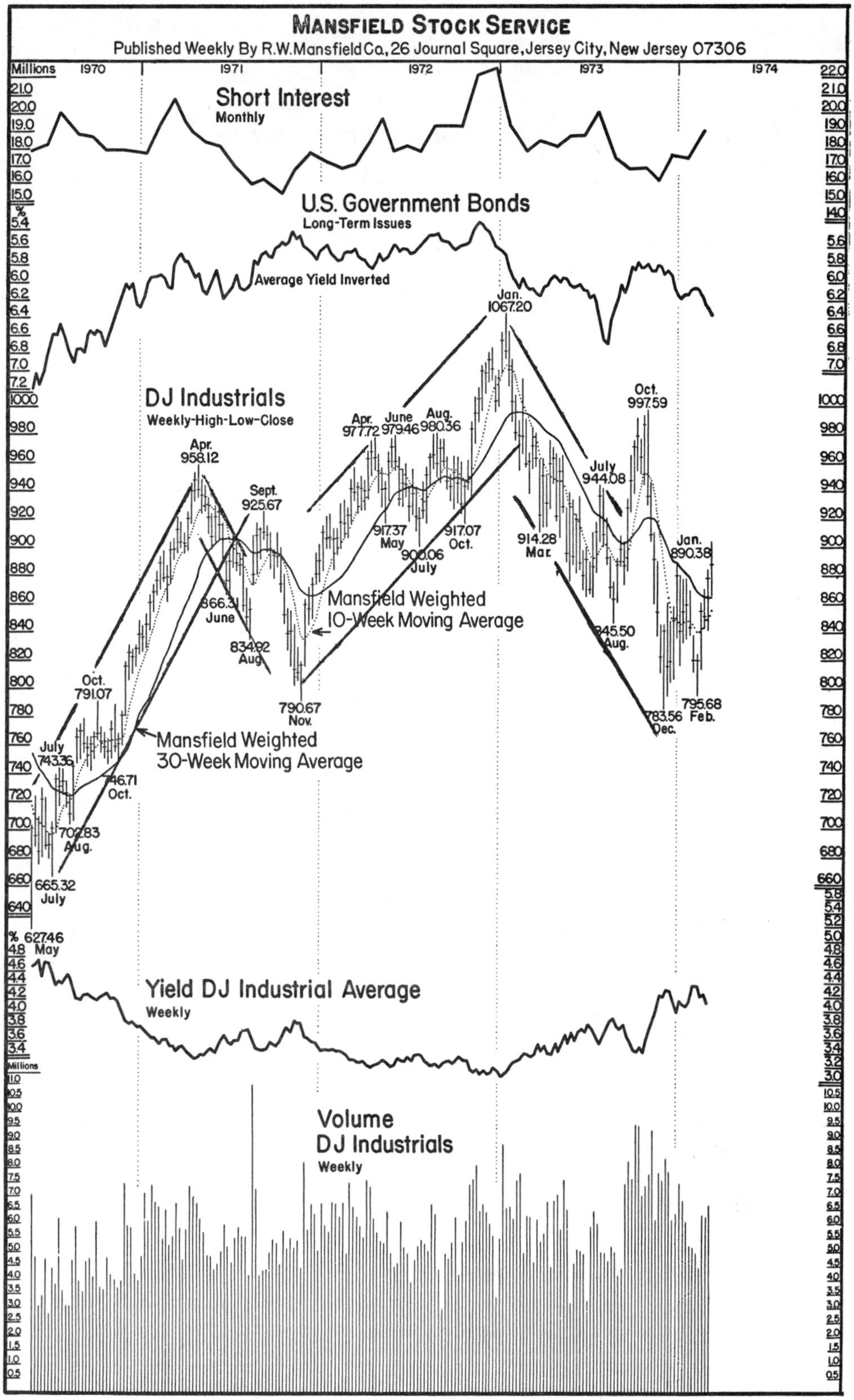

FIGURE 7: TREND CHANNELS FOR MARKET AVERAGES

Source: Mansfield Stocks Chart Service, 26 Journal Sq., Jersey City, NJ 07306

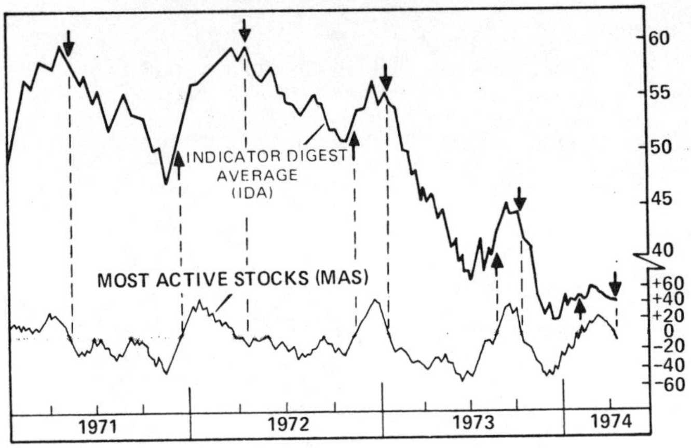

FIGURE 8
MOST ACTIVE STOCKS
Source: Indicator Digest, Palisades Park, NJ 07650

CONTRARY OPINION

This one's a bit subjective, but in the end probably the best of all. I have stressed this rule before, now I want to emphasize it once again. Move in the direction opposite to the crowd. When everyone about you loses their head—in euphoria or in despair—keep yours. Go your own lonely way. Nine times out of ten, you'll be right. Surprisingly, it's rather easy to test the direction of the crowd. Simply sample the popular investment literature. Bearish newspaper articles tend to proliferate near market bottoms; optimistic forecasts proliferate near tops. When did articles extolling the virtues of gold suddenly turn up? Right at the Zenith of gold prices, in August, 1973—naturally, and again in early 1974. Apply this rule to any investment: when the newspapers begin to provide wide coverage of a specific form of investment, it is already too late to get in.

SOME INTERESTING BITS OF SEASONAL DATA

Yale Hirsch, author of the *Stock Trader's Almanac,* has come up with some unique historical observations, which have practical as well as theoretical import. Besides, they're interesting and fun in themselves. Among Mr. Hirsch's findings:

The stock market tends to rise during presidential election years but tends to decline during post-election years. If the post-election decline does occur, odds heavily favor a strong market during the mid-term election year.

The twelve months following bear market bottoms show gains averaging 38.6%.

October and November are the best months to purchase stocks. April and May are the worst.

If January of any year shows a gain or a loss for the month, the odds are better than 4-1 that the stock market will follow suit for the total year.

Monday is the poorest performing day of the week. Friday is the best.

If Friday is a down day, the odds are 3-1 that the market will decline the following Monday.

O.K., that's it. If you're in the market, it's going to be up to you to do the work necessary to handle your own account like a pro. Try to maintain an active file on these indicators and tally up your results after a while. You probably won't do any worse than your brokerage house.

Chapter 12

"You May Not Eat Well, But You'll Certainly Sleep A Lot Better"

Investing In Corporate Bonds, C.D.'s, Commercial Paper, Etc.

Potential Reward, B+
Potential Risk, A–
Liquidity, A
Tax Considerations, B-

1973 saw the fantasies of the fifties and the speculative fever of the sixties give way, at least in part, to sanity for the seventies—the realization by investors that the stock market is not all Xerox, IBM, or some cat or dog moving only one way, up. If the 1966 bear market was nothing more than the pause that refreshes, the 1969-1970 and 1973 bear markets finally put the coup de grace on the concept that stocks must rise and that ownership of common shares is the only way to beat inflation. In fact, 1973 and, so far, early 1974 have seen just the reverse–massive inflation coupled with declining stock prices.

These have been sobering developments indeed. Most stocks peaked during 1968; only the larger institutional quality stocks, as a group, went to new highs in '72. The Amex spent most of 1973 languishing near the lows of the 1970 crash. The mutual fund industry, which produced better than a 10.5% compound growth rate from 1962-1972, has found it hard to even duplicate the return from savings bank deposits from 1966 on. In short, an 8 per cent growth rate from the stock market has once again become respectable.

Early '73, at least, saw the big play shift–from the Big Board to the commodity trading pits, as commodity prices hit the moon, to the international currency markets and into gold and silver. Less speculative souls discovered the bond market, finally becoming aware of the safety and steady, if not exciting, returns offered by bonds as investment vehicles. Sophisticated investors even began to discover some techniques for speculating in senior securities, and that's where our B+ rating for potential return comes in, not from the interest returns alone, a C+ at best. We'll get to the creative use of leverage in bond plays later on. First, some definitions and a bit of history.

WHAT ARE BONDS?

Corporate bonds are, in effect, promissory notes issued by corporations to bond buyers who, in effect, are money lenders to the corporations that issue the bonds. These notes, issued when corporations need money, stipulate, first, that repayment in full is guaranteed at a specified future date and, second, that a fixed rate of interest will be paid to the bondholder at stipulated intervals (usually semi-annual) in the interim. Bonds are generally issued in $1,000 face amounts. Their nomenclature includes the original rate of interest and the year the bond is due to be redeemed. Thus, the Alaska Interstate bond title, 6s 1996, indicates that the bond provides a $60 per year yield (6s = 6% of $1,000 face value) and that payment in full is due in 1996. Bond prices are usually quoted as a 10% proportion of actual current value. Should the Alaska bonds be quoted at 96½, it means that the current price is $965. Should they be quoted at $129, it means that they are selling at $1290. Bonds are traded on the major stock exchanges and over-the-counter. Quotations can be secured from your broker or in financial newspapers such as *Barron's, The Wall Street Journal* or the *Media-General Financial Weekly.*

SAFETY

Bonds are intrinsically safer than stocks, at least over the long pull, for many reasons. When you buy stock, you are purchasing part ownership of a company. When you purchase bonds, you are lending money to the company. In the event of liquidation, or in the event of limited profitability, the bondholders must receive their interest and principal repayment before the common or even the preferred shareholders receive anything. For this reason, bonds are often referred to as "senior securities."

The bond, of course, is ultimately no safer than the soundness of the issuing corporation. Bonds are rated for safety by such organizations as the *Standard and Poor's, Moody's* and *Fitch* bond rating services. Ratings run from Aaa (Moody's, triple A) through C. Triple A Bonds are bonds issued by prime corporations–American Telephone, General Motors, etc. B bonds (Avco, City Investing) yield considerably more but with less safety. C bonds (Tyco) are considered somewhat speculative but return the highest yield. As I write this, long-term Triple A bonds are yielding between 7½-8%, B's about 10% and C's up to 12% and even better. A rating of A or better, for practical purposes, indicates a virtually risk-free situation; almost all B's also manage to pay off on schedule.

TYPES OF COLLATERAL

The simplest method of securing the safety factor of a bond is via the bond rating, readily obtained from any bond broker. These ratings are quite reliable, and upon them depend the interest that a company will have to pay to float a bond issue. However, more compulsive or cautious investors may want to investigate further into the backing of any bond under consideration.

Mortgage Bonds are secured by realty property–buildings and land–pledged as collateral. In some cases where companies own huge tracts of valuable realty, this backing can represent a considerable safety factor. However, upon foreclosure, the bondholders may have to establish the market for and dispose of these assets, a process which can easily take several months, at a minimum.

Collateral Trust Bonds are often backed by bonds and/or common stock in the issuing and/or subsidiary corporations. These assets may possess more limited ultimate worth but are more readily liquidated, if necessary, by bondholders.

Debentures are secured by no particular assets, save the promise of the corporation to pay. Many worthwhile–and some not so worthwhile–bonds fall within this category. In the event of bankruptcy, holders of debentures have to wait on line with other creditors, until the secured notes get paid off.

Subordinated Debentures are more risky in that holders have to get on line even further back, after the previous bondholders and general creditors. A subordinated status is not reason in itself to avoid a bond. Convertible bonds are generally subordinated debentures but, as we have seen, often represent excellent investment value.

Guaranteed Bonds are bonds guaranteed by a larger, more solvent corporation and *joint bonds* are bonds issued by two or more companies.

Only the most finicky investors will want to investigate the actual backing of bonds. For most, the Moody's ratings will do very nicely. (For more information on rating companies, see *Barron's,* July 30, 1973).

THE RELATIONSHIP BETWEEN BOND PRICES AND CURRENT CREDIT CLIMATE

Bond prices do fluctuate. One cause for fluctuation lies in possible changes in the credit rating of the issuing corporation. In other words, an A bond can deteriorate to a B or even to a C. With each drop in rating, the current bondholders are assuming increasing risk by holding the note signified by the bond; therefore the rate of interest paid to these bondholders has to rise (more below). During 1973, several computer peripheral companies developed serious financial problems. Bonds of such companies as Telex, Computer Sciences and Memorex were priced to yield 20% interest per year and better. Occasionally, quality ratings of bonds are upgraded when the fortunes of the issuing corporation improve. This reduces the rate of interest required of that corporation's notes.

Far more usual are fluctuations in bond prices created by changing conditions in the credit and money markets as a whole. These fluctuations–interest rates rising as credit becomes "tight" and easing when credit loosens–affect classes of bonds clear across the board. Until 1950, stocks provided higher yields than bonds, which was natural enough since bonds were considered the safer vehicle. From 1950 on, bonds have provided the higher yields, but as we will see below, bonds fell to some degree out of favor, since the value of bonds held dropped as their yields rose. Interest rates peaked during 1970, dropped, rose sharply once again during 1973, and began to decline in early 1974. As I am writing this, banks are charging 9½% interest to prime lenders, while paying 8% and better to long-term depositors. As I said, Triple A bonds are yielding 7½%, and B and C bonds are yielding over 10 and 12 percent respectively. Should interest rates peak soon, bonds purchased now will return both fine yields and excellent capital gains. Don't expect, however, a return to the 3½% yields of the early 1950's. As you can see from Figure 1, one way we have accommodated to permanent inflation is by living with chronically high interest rates.

HOW BOND PRICES FLUCTUATE WITH INTEREST RATES

A bond, once issued, continues to pay a fixed *amount* of interest. The number of dollars paid in interest to bondholders remains fixed over the years. But the price of the bond, as we have seen, does vary. Why? Well, let's suppose that American Telephone had issued a bond during 1959 paying $50 interest or 5 percent, perhaps the prevailing rate at the time. Let's suppose further that a few years later, American Telephone issues another bond, during a period of tighter credit. In order to float the bond, they have to offer $70 or 7 percent interest. (As a point of fact, American Telephone has listed on the current market, bonds ranging in coupon rate from 2-5/8 percent to 8.7 percent). What will happen to the value of the first bond? Holders will be inclined to sell it, of course, in order to purchase the new, higher yielding note. The rush of sellers will drive the price of the low coupon bond down on the open market. To where? To approximately $714 at which point the bond will be yielding 7 percent interest ($50 amount of yield divided by $714 bond price). Actually, the going price would end up somewhere higher than $714, since the

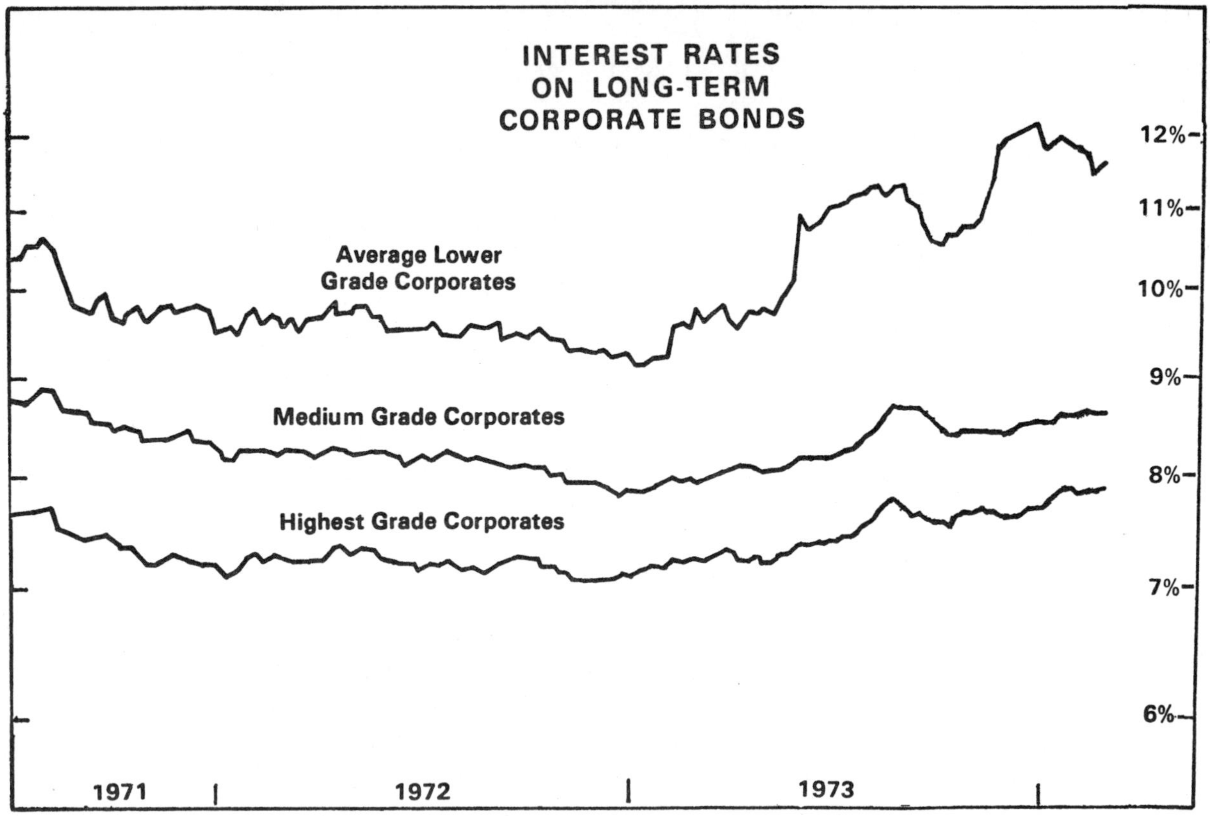

FIGURE 1
INTEREST RATES ON LONG-TERM CORPORATE BONDS
Source: Value Line Convertible Survey, 5 E. 44th St., NY, NY 10017

purchaser at $714 also stands to receive a capital gain of $286 when the bond falls due and the $1,000 note is repaid in full. The total return from a bond includes both the current yield and any capital gain (or loss, if the bond currently sells above face value), the two together, computed according to the time left before repayment, comprising the total *yield to maturity.* Your broker can provide the yield to maturity for any bond you are considering from special yield tables.

In the decades from 1950-1970, most bondholders saw the value of their holdings erode as rising interest rates forced the current value of these bonds down—although, of course, these bonds would still be redeemable at $1,000 when it came time to cash in. However, bonds purchased when interest rates are high rise in value when later issues provide lesser yield. 1970 provided an excellent opportunity for bond speculators, and 1974, in retrospect, may do likewise.

Table I shows what will happen to the price of a bond, all else being equal, as prevailing interest rates in the credit market vary.

TABLE I

Presuming a $1,000 Bond Yielding $60 or 6% Interest At Issue

1. If prevailing interest rates for similar quality bonds drop to 5%, the price of the bond will rise to $1,200.
2. If prevailing interest rates for similar quality bonds remain at 6%, the price of the bond will remain at $1,000.
3. If prevailing interest rates for similar quality bonds rise to 7%, the price of the bond will fall to approximately $857.
4. If prevailing interest rates for similar quality bonds rise to 8%, the price of the bond will fall to approximately $750.

We can see then, that even a 1% increase in prevailing interest rates can cost bondholders dearly, easily the value of two year's interest payments should the bonds have to be liquidated prior to maturity. That's why the bond market resembled a graveyard all through the fifties and sixties. Just too many people were hurt, as interest rates continued to rise. But suppose you purchase bonds when interest rates are at 8% and sell them when interest rates fall to 7%. Now, we have another story, a $107 or 14.3% capital gain on top of the interest received. The secret? Timing. Try to accumulate bond positions during periods of tight money or just after interest rates peak.

You do not have to hold a directorship in Chase Manhattan to stay on top of the situation. Daily newspapers carry extensive coverage of the money markets. It will probably be safe to take positions when you read: (1) that the Federal Reserve Board announces it plans to ease up on credit. These boys usually do not lie, although wishful thinkers like to hope they do. (2) The Federal Reserve Board announces actual steps to ease credit. The discount rate is lowered at least once or preferably twice in succession; reserve requirements are reduced, and the margin required for stock purchases is lowered. All point to an easing of credit conditions and to lower prevailing interest rates. (3) Banks across the country begin to announce reductions in the interest rates charged to prime creditors (the prime rate). Two reductions in a row in the prime rate will probably indicate a trend.

Do learn to trade the bond market. Despite fluctuations in price, good quality bonds are intrinsically much safer than stocks. The interest they pay does provide a floor to their price, and even if you guess wrong on credit conditions, you do have interest payments coming in to ease your boredom and pain while you await maturity and the ultimate repayment of the face amount of the note.

USING LEVERAGE FOR REALLY FANTASTIC PROFITS

Bonds are sufficiently safe to allow for profitable use of leverage in bond trading. You can readily borrow from 75-90% from a bank on listed Triple A and/or municipal bonds, and very close to that on BBB bonds, which together comprise about 90% of the bond market. Brokerage houses will let you buy listed bonds at 25% margin. At present, however, convertible bonds require 50% margin.

Suppose you purchase twelve Avco 7½s 1993 bonds, recently yielding in the area of 10.7%. You purchase the bond at 75% margin. (Price, $700). This means that you have to put up only 25% of the price. In many brokerage houses, you are required to deposit at least $2,000 to open a margin account; some require more. As I said, the prime rate has recently stood at 9½%. Margin costs at most houses are about 1¾% above prime rate (depending upon the size of your account). Banks will just about match that on loans secured by bond collateral. Therefore, the interest you receive from the bonds you purchase on margin (slightly over 10.7%) will just about offset the interest you pay to carry them. You will, of course, receive 10.7% interest from the portion of your purchase that represents your own equity in the account. In addition, each Avco bond will return $1,000 in 1993, representing an additional capital gain of $300 or 42.9% of your investment at the end of twenty years. That capital gain is a free ride also on the margined portion of your holdings. The Avco 7½s 1993 sold for $880 early in 1973. Let's presume that, within a year from that period, credit conditions had eased and the bonds returned in price to early 1973 levels.

RETURN FROM UNMARGINED POSITION

Purchase three bonds at $700. Total cost including purchase commissions, $2,115.

Interest Received during a one year holding period, $225 ($75 per bond times three bonds).

Capital Gain if bond returns to $880, $540 ($180 per bond times three bonds).

Total Return $765.

Less commissions to buy and sell, $30.

Net Return, $735 or 35%. Not too bad at all. The risk is relatively small. Should interest rates continue to rise, so that Avco yields 12.7% instead of 10.7%, the price of the bond will decline to $590, a 15.7% loss. This loss will be almost offset by one year's interest yield, and will not pertain at all if the bond is held to maturity.

Now, let's see what happens if the position is margined. Purchase twelve Avco 7½s 1993 bonds at $700, at 25% margin through a bank. The total purchase cost equals $8460, including commissions. Your cash out of pocket outlay is 25% of that, or $2115.

Interest Received during a one-year holding period, $900.

Interest Paid to bank at 11¼%, on $6345 margin debit ($8460 minus $2115), $715.81.

Capital Gain if bond returns to $880, $2160 ($180 per bond times twelve bonds).

Less Commissions to buy and sell, $120.

Total Net Return, $2226.19 or over 105% net profit! The risks, of course, are multiplied by leveraging bonds in this manner, *but only if you have to liquidate prior to maturity.*

Should the price of the bonds drop to $590, your capital loss, if you sell at the end of one year, amounts to about $1220 or approximately 58% of your investment. However, if you hold until maturity, you will be receiving approximately 10% interest on the cash you put up *plus* a $3600 capital gain at the end of 20 years, or about 123% of your original investment. If you are willing to wait, your only risk is corporate insolvency.

Do consider the use of leverage in the purchase of sound bonds. Just be certain that the total return from the bonds—interest plus capital gain—exceeds or is very close to your margin-carrying costs.

You can deduct brokerage or bank interest paid out on your income tax statement, but you must declare interest received. The capital gains, when taken, are taxed at favorable capital gain rates, if you have held the position for at least six months.

OTHER FORMS OF INCOME INVESTMENTS

Periods of tight money provide ample opportunity for short term, high yield investment. The following are suggested as temporary havens for your money only. The returns are not, in my opinion, large enough to justify long term investment, particularly since the income received usually varies from between 6-8 percent, barely more than the savings account. Still, another percent or two doesn't hurt, and periodically, tight credit conditions produce fine, safe payoffs.

CERTIFICATES OF DEPOSIT

This is for the well-heeled only. In mid-1973, banks were offering as much as 10¾% interest on $100,000 issues of 90-day negotiable certificates of deposit. If you need your cash in a hurry, there is a secondary market in C.D.'s. For $25,000, you could buy ***banker's acceptances,*** rates from 1 to 180 days quoted at 9% interest, sold by major banks for $20 commission.

Still in the multi-thousand dollar category, you could have secured better than 9% last year by purchasing *commercial paper,* unsecured short term notes issued by large blue chip corporations needing short term funds. These promissory notes are backed only by the issuing corporation's good name, not by assets. However, only top companies (e.g. GMAC) are able to float their paper, so the deal's pretty safe. The investor often has a say in determining the maturity of the note, generally between one and nine months from issue, but there is no certain secondary market if the money is needed prior to maturity. Commercial paper has risen in popularity in recent years. In 1960 there was less than $5 billion worth of commercial paper outstanding; this amount rose to nearly $40 billion by 1970.

The rates of income achievable from these media vary with credit conditions. However, at all times these will provide better returns than money deposited in short term savings accounts. Check with your local banker for procedures and current rates—but first be certain that you have at least $25,000 for ante. Even if you aren't in the big lending league, track current rates. They are available weekly in *Barron's.* In 1970, the credit crunch ended when certificates of deposit yielded 8.1%, and commercial paper, 9.1%. These rates were already exceeded by August, 1973. A reversal or two in the trend of rising rates may indicate a topping of interest rates in general and an excellent opportunity to purchase bonds. Table II shows the prevailing rates of income provided by a variety of vehicles during late October, 1973, a time of tight money. By early 1974, rates had already begun to decline.

TABLE II

MONEY RATES

	October 25, 1973	One Year Previous
Banker's Acceptances: 1-180 days	9 – 8-3/4%	5-5/8 – 5-3/8%
Call Money: (renewals)	9-3/4 – 10-1/4	5-3/8 – 5-3/4
Commercial Paper: 30-270 days	9-1/8 – 9-1/2	4-7/8 – 5-3/8
Certificates of Deposit: ($100,000)		
One Month	8-5/8	
Two Months	8-1/2	
Three Months	8-1/4	
Six Months	7-1/2	
One Year	7	
Federal Reserve Discount Rate:	7-1/2	4-1/2

Source: *Barron's*, October 29, 1973.

U.S. TREASURY BILLS

Another excellent refuge for short term money are 90 or 180-day U.S. Treasury bills, the safest forms of debt since they are backed by the full taxing power of the U.S. Government. In addition, the interest Treasury bills pay is not taxable by states having a state income tax or by local taxing authority, except for estate, inheritance, gift or other excise taxes. Like the securities above, T-bills frequently provide a higher return than short term savings accounts. They are also fully negotiable, actively traded, and can be used for leverage plays in case you want to speculate on a decline in interest rates. In fact, there is a good chance that you can borrow up to 90-95% of the face value of Treasury bills, which means that you can operate on 5-10% margin. Be careful though. At such margined positions, a 10% decline in price wipes you out completely.

Treasury bills, in mid-1973, were yielding over 8%, climbing to 8½% by May, 1974. In 1970, they peaked at 8.1%. These bills, to be precise, pay no interest. They are sold at a

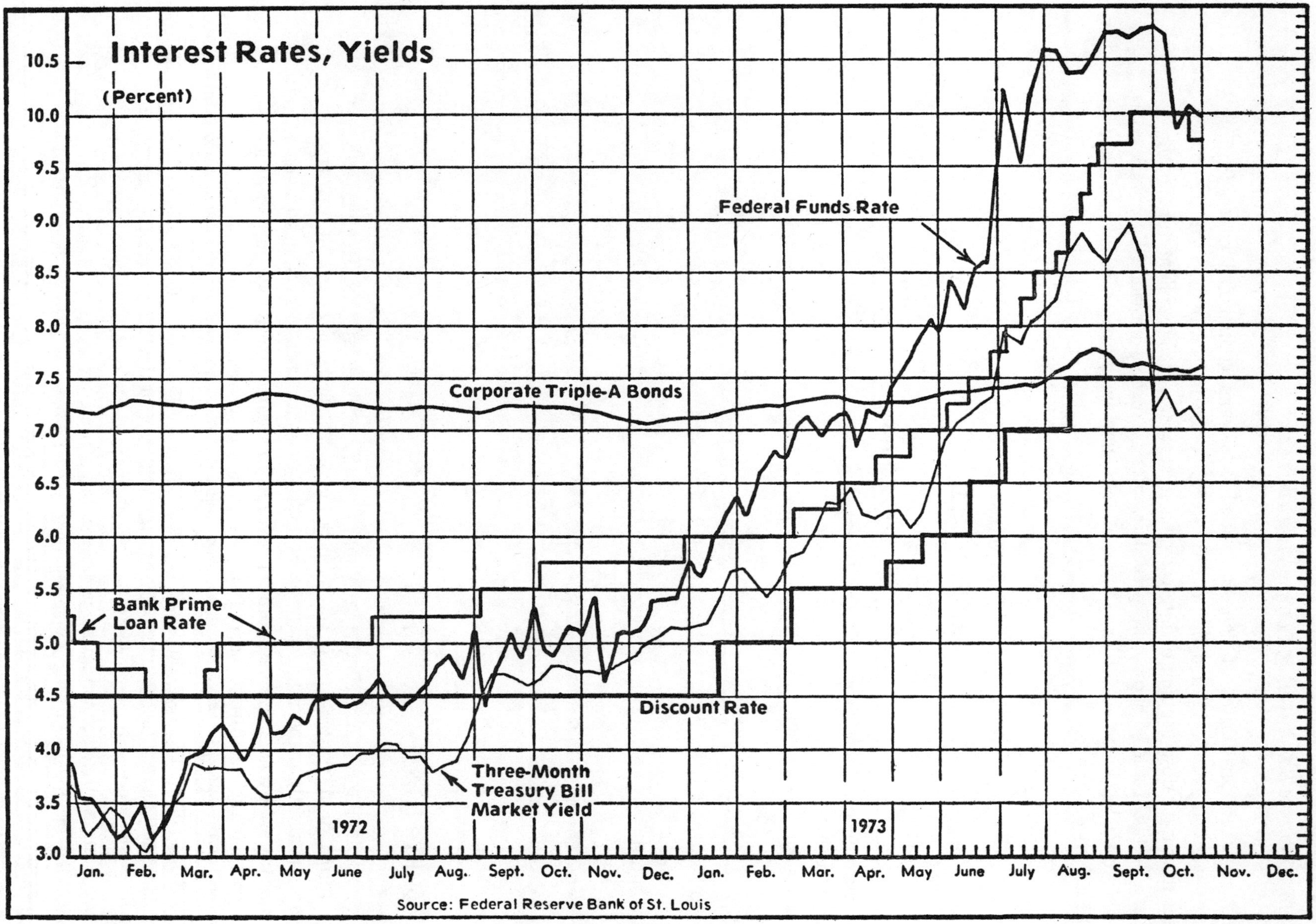

FIGURE 2: INTEREST RATES, YIELDS

Source: Media–General Financial Weekly, 119 N. Third St., Richmond, VA 23261

discount from par and redeemed at par. The rate of "interest" you secure is computed by taking the differential between the discount and face value (your profits) and dividing by the price you pay, adjusting for the length of the holding period—e.g. 2% profit for a three month holding period equals an "interest rate" of 8 percent. The profit from Treasury bills is always treated as ordinary, not capital gain, income—no matter how long the holding period.

Treasury bills can be purchased two ways. Your bank or a stockbroker can secure them for you, but will charge commissions—usually between $15-25 which does cut into your yield. Sometimes, you can negotiate a lower rate for yourself, depending upon the size of your transaction. Your broker can also buy T-bills for you in the secondary market, but again you pay commissions.

However, there is a better way yet to pick up Treasury bills. Locate in the telephone book your local Federal Reserve Bank branch (large metropolitan areas only). Auctions of T-bills held by the Fed are announced on Thursdays and held Mondays at noon. On Monday morning, go down to the office and fill out a "tender," depositing $20 for each bill you wish to buy (maximum, $200,000). You are, in effect, submitting a "non-competitive" bid. The price you pay will be determined based upon the average competitive bid arrived at during the auction. On Thursday, you are expected to produce either cash or a *Federal Funds check* sufficient to cover your purchase. No personal checks. Minimum transaction, 10 bonds or $10,000. It should even be possible to handle the transaction through the mail. You receive a different form for each bill offered of varying time and length. Check the procedures with your local Federal Reserve branch. By buying direct from the Fed, *you save all commissions.* Treasury bills are in "bearer form." Whoever holds them is presumed to be the owner. So either leave them with your broker or keep them in a vault, serial numbers recorded.

If you think all this is a lot of trouble to save a percent or two, just figure out how much an extra two percent on $10,000 adds up to over a period of years.

A WAY TO PURCHASE SMALLER AMOUNTS

The Fed will accept bids only for a minimum order of $10,000. However, the *American Board of Trade* (286 Fifth Avenue, New York, N.Y. 10001, # 212-736-9740) will handle smaller orders for a slight service charge, and will liquidate positions for you at the market for a total commission cost of $10 for up to $50,000 in T-bills.

FLOWER BONDS

Certain "flower bonds" or U.S. Estate Tax Bonds are redeemable at par plus accrued interest when owned by a decedent and left as part of his estate, if they are applied against Federal estate tax liabilities. For example, suppose you purchase such a bond for $700, below par as most of them are. Upon your death, your estate can turn these bonds in as partial or full payment of estate taxes, receiving at least $1,000 credit for each bond–original cost to you, $700. In the interim, you collect interest. Flower bonds are decreasing in numbers as their maturities come due, but a number are still available. Check with your bond broker for current listings and prices.

No need to bother unless you expect to leave an estate of $120,000 or better. However, if you apply some of the tactics described in this book–well, who knows?

BOND FUNDS

There are a number of mutual funds now specializing in bonds. The concept achieved some popularity early in 1973, but frankly I don't see too much point in paying an 8½% sales commission to purchase an investment vehicle yielding 7½% or so. With just a little research, you can secure for yourself a balanced portfolio of high grade bonds. Convertible and municipal bond funds may hold more interest for investors, however.

Periodically, brokerage houses have offered shares in "trusts," which may have some appeal to investors seeking highest quality, fully U.S. government backed bonds. Participation in such trusts allows smaller investors to accumulate positions in these bonds, which are normally available only to large scale lenders. For example, Merrill-Lynch, in June, 1973, offered units in the ML Government Guaranteed Securities Trust. Price per unit, $5,000. Estimated current return, 7.21%. Merrill-Lynch plans to maintain a secondary market for these units.

I, personally, cannot become too enthused about the deal. In my opinion, the degree of safety involved may be more than necessary, and the ongoing liquidity of these units may be questionable. Merrill-Lynch charges no management fees for operating the trust but there is a 2½% sales charge. *Summing Up:* May be O.K. for the ultra cautious, but higher yields are available from good corporates, and effectively from municipal bonds.

A UNIQUE CASH HAVEN

A new no-load fund achieved considerable popularity in mid-1973–the Reserve Fund, which was designed specifically as an investment vehicle for short term money, and which can be employed by small as well as large investors.

The Reserve Fund seeks current income and preservation of capital by investing solely in short term obligations issued or guaranteed by the U.S. Government and its agencies and in certificates of deposits and other bank obligations. The minimum investment in the fund is only $1,000, and for that the little guy can get a piece of the action that is usually confined to the "fat cat." Even better, interest payments are declared daily and invested automatically. What's more, you can go into and out of the fund at any time, receiving interest on a daily basis for as long as you hold your positions.

There are no commission costs involved, buying or selling. The management receives a fee of ½ of 1% of total assets, plus another ½ of 1% for expenses.

In mid-July, 1973, the fund was paying to shareholders a return of 9¼% interest on their money! Of course, when credit eased, this rate of return dropped proportionately. The fund grew from $400,000 in assets, end of 1972, to over $13,000,000 in assets, July, 1973.

A prospectus can be secured by writing to the Reserve Fund, 1301 Avenue of the Americas, New York, N.Y. 10019. Similar funds are now in the process of, or have already completed formation. Check *Barron's* for ads.

We will be discussing municipals and convertibles in succeeding chapters. In the meantime, do consider putting at least a portion of your investment portfolio in good quality bonds. In the worst cases, you may not eat well, but you'll certainly sleep a lot better.

Chapter 13

"If Nothing Else, They're One Way To Beat The Government"

Investing In Municipal Bonds

Potential Reward,	B
Potential Risk,	A
Liquidity,	A
Tax Considerations,	A

Okay, you've struck it rich on raw land, and your apartment houses have waiting lists of prospective tenants. In between, some $2 stock ran to 50 and you managed to pick up some corporates just as interest rates topped out. Now that you've made it, you're looking for places to stash the profits—only it's too soon for "flower bonds". Well, why not consider municipals? On August 15, 1973, New York City issued $50 million worth of Budget Notes, priced to yield 7%, due for repayment on July 31, 1974. The interest on these bonds was exempt from all federal, state and city income taxes. To the individual in the 48% tax bracket, this 7% *tax exempt yield* was equivalent to a 13.46% return from income taxed at ordinary rates.

Therein lies the special attraction of municipal bonds—the opportunity to receive regular interest payments from an investment second only to U.S. Government securities in quality—completely tax free. All that's required at your end is a little investigation to establish quality, clipping the coupons, and cashing the checks. Usually, investors don't get rich via the municipal route (though you can up the return considerably if you time your purchases properly and buy on margin). Municipals usually represent a means of holding on to the rewards from what you have achieved before. However, even a small, if conservative, investor should consider sticking a municipal or two into his safe deposit box. The returns, considering the tax relief, almost always beat out the savings account.

I'm rating the bonds B for reward. For most investors, the returns will approximate about 9-10% taxable income (a B– or C). However, the possibilities of successful bond trading lead me to increase the rating to a B. Risk is A only if you are prepared to hold to maturity.

WHAT ARE MUNICIPALS?

They are bonds, and share all the characteristics of bonds previously noted—interest payments, repayment of principal at the due date—in short a promissory note. Except that in the case of municipals, the borrower is not a corporation. The borrower is rather a state, county, city, school district or special authority who needs money to finance streets, hospitals, highways or any other capital or other governmental expense. The lenders may be corporations, banks, or individuals who purchase the bonds when issued and/or who subsequently make purchases in the secondary markets. Unlike corporates, municipal bonds are very frequently issued in $5,000 denominations. The 7% bond described above was issued in $25,000, $50,000 and $100,000 denominations. As I write this, over $132 billion worth of municipals are outstanding in the United States. Commercial banks are the largest single group of bondholders, followed by individuals and insurance companies in that order.

THE TAX EXEMPT FEATURE

The Internal Revenue Code has allowed tax exemptions for the interest paid by municipals since 1913, and this exemption has so far survived all efforts made by tax reformers to make municipal investors kick in a portion of their returns to the community kitty. Why the exemption? One good reason is that municipals yield less than corporate bonds of similar quality. Were the interest fully taxable, communities would have to pay interest rates competitive with private industry to borrow money. In the end, the taxpaying body as a whole would have to pay back, in the form of higher borrowing expenses, the money gained by hitting municipal bondholders with income taxes on their interest. Elimination of the Federal exemption would, in effect, create Federal taxation of municipal projects. There is no express Constitutional prohibition against the Federal government taxing state and municipal operations; nor is there any express provision forbidding local and state governments from taxing Federal operations. However, from the mid-nineteenth century on, a Constitutional doctrine of reciprocal immunity has been recognized as necessary to preserve the dual sovereignty of local and Federal government. Should the Federal government tax New York State Municipal bonds, New York State might just decide to try to tax the local post office.

Keep in mind, however, that only interest payments are tax free. Should you sell the bond at a profit, either in the secondary market or by redemption at maturity, the profit from the resale is taxable—at ordinary or long term capital gain rates, depending upon how long you have held the bond.

THE MATHEMATICS OF TAX EXEMPTION

Lebenthal and Co., 1 State Street Plaza, New York, N.Y. 10004, has been offering various forms of information to prospective purchasers of municipals. One gadget they've been sending for the asking is a disc showing the price you really pay in pre-tax dollars for various goods and services. Among the items mentioned:

If you are in the 66% bracket, a $4,000 freshman year at Harvard will cost you $11,764 in pre-tax dollars. A $5.00 shampoo will set you back $14.71. And you'll have to earn $20.59 to pay for a fifth of J & B, retailing for seven bills.

Are you a 57% taxpayer? How about 38¢ of real earnings for a New York Times? Or $1.28 for a 55¢ hamburger? Or $19.53 for $8.40 worth of gasoline?

Don't think you're much better off if you're in the lowly 31% bracket. A 50¢ shoe shine will still set you back 72¢ in pre-tax dollars. A $100 dental bill costs you $144.93 in hard labor, and $6 worth of babysitting means $8.70 you had to pick up at the office.

In short, anything you save on taxes is one for your side. Table I tells the story more completely.

If you are in the 36% tax bracket, you would need a 10.94% return taxed at ordinary rates to provide the equivalent of a 7% return from tax free municipal bonds. If you are in the 45% bracket, you will require a 7.27% return to equal a 4% tax free return.

TABLE I

The Per Cent Of Taxable Return Needed To Provide a Real Return Equivalent To Municipal Bond Tax Free Income

Investor Tax Bracket	28%	32%	36%	40%	45%	50%	60%	70%
Municipal Bond Yield				**Equivalent Taxable Income**				
3.00%	4.17	4.41	4.69	5.00	5.45	6.00	7.50	10.00
3.50	4.86	5.15	5.47	5.83	6.36	7.00	8.75	11.67
4.00	5.56	5.88	6.25	6.67	7.27	8.00	10.00	13.33
4.50	6.25	6.62	7.03	7.50	8.18	9.00	11.25	15.00
5.00	6.94	7.35	7.81	8.33	9.09	10.00	12.50	16.67
5.50	7.64	8.09	8.59	9.17	10.00	11.00	13.75	18.33
6.00	8.33	8.82	9.37	10.00	10.91	12.00	15.00	20.00
6.50	9.03	9.56	10.16	10.83	11.82	13.00	16.25	21.67
7.00	9.72	10.29	10.94	11.67	12.73	14.00	17.50	23.33
7.50	10.42	11.03	11.72	12.50	13.64	15.00	18.75	25.00
8.00	11.11	11.76	12.50	13.33	14.55	16.00	20.00	26.67
8.50	11.81	12.50	13.28	14.17	15.45	17.00	21.25	28.33

CONSIDER DISCOUNTED MUNICIPALS

At any given time, investors have the option of purchasing municipals of varying dates of maturity and of varying coupon rates. We have seen how, when interest rates rise, the prices of existing bonds fall. We have also seen how bond prices rise when interest rates fall. This results in the market offering a selection of bonds originally issued during periods of very high interest rates, possibly selling above par, and bonds issued when interest rates were low, dropping in price and selling *at a discount,* below par as interest rates rise.

Bonds selling at or above par generally *provide a higher rate* of *current income* or interest than discounted bonds, but the capital gain inherent in discounted bonds usually results in discounted bonds providing a higher total return, *if they are held to maturity.* The discrepancy occurs because current money generally is more valued by investors than future money. The increased total yield to maturity of discounted bonds usually pertains even when the capital gains taxes, due upon sale, are considered. Incidentally, in considering discounted bonds, do not be put off by a nominally low coupon rate. The *rate* of interest paid may be substantial if the discount is sufficiently great. For instance, the Maine Turnpike 4s 1989 sold in August 1973 at $830. At that price, their actual yield was 4.82%, ($40 ÷ 830) plus the $170 capital gain due in 1989. By contrast, the New Jersey Turnpike 7s 2009 sold at $1,105, and provided a current yield, not of 7%, but of 6.33%. In addition, there was a built in *capital loss* of $105, since at maturity, the bond holder would receive back, not $1,105, but only $1,000. The high current yield had propelled the bond's price above par. Many municipal bond dealers will provide lists of bonds, including current yields, yields to maturity, and safety ratings. *Lebenthal,* mentioned above, will send regular listings if you ask to be put on their mailing list.

Discounted bonds are recommended if (1) you plan to hold long term for the life of the bond and (2) you do not need current income. Try to buy bonds having maturity dates coincident with your need for the money. You might try mixing maturities, short maturity for maximum liquidity and longer maturity for maximum total yield. Incidentally, in mid-1973, the average municipal bond was yielding close to 6%–tax free. *Barron's Municipal Bond Yield Index* reached 7% in 1970.

SAFETY RATINGS

Municipals, like corporates, are only as good as the issuer. Actually, municipals have an excellent record. Even during the depression, 98 per cent of municipals paid on schedule. Only Arkansas, among the states, defaulted. Still, bonds are usually purchased for safety and possibly for retirement income, so don't be so dazzled by high yields that you overlook the possibility of defaults.

Most tax exempt bonds fall within the following classifications:

General Obligation Bonds: These bonds are secured by the full faith, credit and taxing power of the issuing state, city or county. Often, for instance in the case of school district bonds, an additional pledge of property is made, in addition to the tax revenue–so the bonds are doubly collateralized.

Limited and Special Tax Bonds: These are similar to the above, but not backed by as broad a taxing power. These bonds may be backed by the proceeds of a special tax, for instance, a gasoline tax. Since the proceeds from the pledged taxation usually far surpass the indebtedness incurred by the bonds, these bonds are generally quite secure, if not quite as safe as general obligation bonds.

Revenue Bonds: Revenue bonds are issued by special authorities created by a state or municipality, and are backed by the revenue of the project, not by taxing power, e.g., turnpike bonds. Riskier and, therefore, higher yielding than the above.

New Housing Authority Bonds: Highest quality. Issued by local housing authorities but backed by the U.S. Government for the purpose of financing low-cost housing.

Double-Barrelled Bonds: Bonds secured by a pledge backed by two or more guarantees of payment. For example, many special tax bonds are also backed by the full faith and taxing power of the issuer. Very safe.

Of course, municipals are also rated by the bond services, Moody's and Standard and Poor's, subject to certain size restrictions. Many non-rated bonds are quite sound, but do steer away from low rated bonds if safety is important.

Comparative ratings are:

Moody's	Standard and Poor's
Aaa	AAA
Aa	AA
A	A
Baa	BBB
Ba	BB
B	B
C	CCC
	D (default)

Dun and Bradstreet rates from 01 (best) to 22. The majority of acceptable bonds are rated BBB or better.

Coupon Bonds: "Coupon bonds" or bearer bonds are the most marketable. The holder or bearer of the bond, presumed to be the owner, clips and redeems interest coupons on interest dates (usually every six months). The principal and interest due on municipal bonds is payable at the paying agent's office, generally a designated bank or some treasurer's office. Often, your own bank will handle the transmittal for you. Transfer of ownership is effected merely by delivery of the bonds. These bonds are very readily used as collateral; banks will lend up to 95% of the value of good quality municipals. *Tax Caution:* The interest you pay on loans secured by tax-exempt securities such as municipals is *not* tax deductible. Otherwise, investors could really clean up by margining municipals–receiving tax free income while securing a tax deduction on the margin interest.

Registered Bonds: "Registered bonds" are registered in the owner's name, which appears on the bond. The registrar sends interest, when due, by check. In some cases, only the original or principal owner can be so registered. These bonds are neither as marketable nor as readily used for collateral as bearer bonds.

Bearer bonds should be accorded maximum protection against theft. They are the most marketable of securities. There is an active and fluid market for municipals which are a highly liquid form of investment. Municipal bonds can be purchased and sold through many banks and brokerage houses.

Tax Exempt Bond Funds: Tax exempt bond funds are registered unit investment trusts, the assets of which are invested in a diversified portfolio of interest bearing municipal bonds. They provide the advantage of diversification for the investor. Many brokerage houses sponsor such funds, including Merrill Lynch. Check with your broker, if you are interested.

TRADING MUNICIPAL BONDS

Like any bond, municipals vary in price depending upon the prevailing credit conditions.

1974 will probably be recorded as a good year to have accumulated municipals, since interest rates were at historically high levels. Traded in the manner described in the previous chapter, municipals offer excellent possibilities for capital gain. And, of course, good quality municipals purchased at a discount are very unlikely to show any loss ever, if held until maturity. Maximum leverage can be employed with fair safety, so long as your interest costs (non-deductible) do not exceed the real, effective yield from the bonds.

MUNICIPALS AND THE STOCK MARKET

The stock market and municipal bond yields usually move in inverse directions. The market tends to drop as municipal yields rise and vice versa. The action of municipals often leads the stock market by several weeks. Look for a strong stock market if municipal yields begin to decline. *Barron's* carries the data each week.

SOME TAX PLOYS

If your state has an income tax, try to purchase bonds which originate within that state. Your interest will receive state as well as federal tax exemption. Should your city have an income tax, try to concentrate on bonds issued by that municipality to secure city as well as state and federal exemption.

SWAPPING BONDS

Periodically, you may want to swap your bond holdings—to upgrade your portfolio, to revise your mix of current income versus deferred income via discounted bonds, and/or to alter maturity dates in accordance to changes in your needs.

One very good reason to swap is to establish a "capital loss". Here and there, despite your best efforts at timing, you may purchase bonds only to see them drop in price. You can readily exchange the bonds for bonds of similar quality and yield, at small commission charges. By so doing, you have established a capital loss, the difference between what you paid for the bonds, and what you have received. If you have held the bonds less than six months, excess losses over gains can be applied against ordinary income in amounts up to $1,000 per year. Losses in excess of $1,000 can be carried forward indefinitely and applied against future gains, or taken $1,000 per year at a time.

Bonds held longer than six months are subject to regulations concerning long term capital losses. These can be used to offset long term capital gains, or one-half of such losses can be applied against ordinary income. In this case, $2,000 worth of losses can be deducted, which will offset $1,000 ordinary income.

High commission costs usually make tax loss selling of common stock unprofitable.

Municipals may be another matter. Commissions are low and capital gains can be deferred until retirement, when your tax bracket is lowest, while losses can be taken when the tax savings can really help.

KEOGH PLAN

Many brokerage houses sponsor Keogh Plans by which you purchase municipals. This affords no additional tax saving, however, above regular corporates channelled into a Keogh Plan, since the interest under Keogh is not taxed in either case. In fact, corporate bonds will probably be the better buy under Keogh since they pay higher rates of interest. However, if safety is the prime consideration, you may prefer to put away the highest grade municipals.

MAJOR TAX CAVEAT

I have already mentioned that if you borrow money to finance the purchase of tax exempt bonds, the interest charges on that loan will not be considered tax deductible. Recent interpretations by the Internal Revenue Service have resulted in a nasty tax trap for unwary investors.

Suppose you own some municipals and decide to enter the real estate game. You buy an apartment house, and blithely attempt to enter a deduction for mortgage interest. Although the borrowing was not directly for the purpose of buying the tax exempts, the IRS may disallow part or all of your interest deduction on the grounds that you could have sold your municipal bonds instead of borrowing to meet your mortgage. The same reasoning may be held against you if you own municipals and attempt, say, to deduct interest on a stock margin account.

This warning does not pertain if your municipal holdings represent less than 2 per cent of your total investment and business assets. Nor does it apply to your home mortgage, unless the mortgage was taken out during the same period of time that tax exempts were purchased, so that a connection between the two could be established. Basically, the ruling applies not to personal but to investment interest deductions.

In general, the IRS will disallow interest deductions to the extent that municipals comprise a proportion of your total assets. For example, let's presume that your total assets amount to $300,000. Your tax exempts amount to $100,000 or 1/3 of total assets. You try to claim a $4,500 deduction for interest on an investment property. The IRS may disallow 1/3 of the deduction or $1,500.

Do check your own situation out with your accountant. But, do also stand on notice; taxpayer beware!

To sum up, municipals offer high liquidity, maximum safety and excellent, after tax, yields plus the opportunity for astute bond traders to secure an occasional capital gain. The Ohio Turnpike 3¼s 1992 may not have the glamour of Polaroid, but if nothing else, they're one way to beat the government.

Chapter 14

"All That Glitters Is Not Gold, But Gold Certainly Does Glitter"

Investing In Gold Coins

Potential Reward,	B+	
Potential Risk,	B	
Liquidity,	C+ (coins),	A (gold mining shares)
Tax Considerations,	C	

If 1967 and 1968 were years for common shares, 1973 was the year for precious metals and commodities. Gold soared up to about $130 per ounce on the free market by mid-1973, more than double the prices that pertained near the beginning of the year, before correcting to around $90 per ounce at mid-year. By early 1974, prices had soared to $175 per ounce.

What late 1974 onwards will bring is obviously a matter for some conjecture. Gold prices have, in the past, moved in irregular spurts. Early 1968 saw a flurry of gold speculation, 1971 another. However, the gold bugs really hit the jackpot in '73 as the price of gold set new records week after week, only to be bettered again six months later.

Will the price of gold whither in the years ahead? Compared to most commodities–and gold is a commodity–gold remains undervalued in terms of the inflation that has taken place since the early 1930's. Many experts predict prices upwards of $200-$250 per ounce by 1975, hardly a pie in the sky estimate in view of recent monetary developments. No less a monetary expert than Dr. Franz Pick now predicts the price of gold to reach $400 an ounce within the next two years (he also predicts an inflation rate of 15-20%, an unemployment figure of 12-14 million, rioting in the streets, general turmoil and a dictatorship–all by 1975).

As I write this, a number of rumors abound which may become reality by the time this book goes to press. The official price of gold has risen twice since December 18, 1971–from $35 an ounce to $38 per ounce to $44.22 an ounce. Another multi-national devaluation is a distinct possibility–with nations in concert raising the official price of gold–this time to near $100 an ounce! Will this halt gold speculation? Perhaps, for a time. The irregularity in the price of gold shares taking place as I write this suggests that at least some large international money speculators expect a period of quiescence. However, this has happened before (1968, 1971) and gold has always regained its luster.

Whatever the immediate future, gold and gold related items have, indeed, proven to be among the finest of investments in recent decades. Gold mining shares–particularly the South African–rose to new highs during 1974. Gold coins, treasured both for their intrinsic and numismatic value, have risen by an average of more than 16% per year over the last decade. Many individual coins have, of course, done much better. For example, the $5 Indian 1909 gained 220% between 1963-1973, and the $5 Liberty 1892-0 gained 629% within that ten year period! *Barron's* has reported that rare numismatic coins ranked first in appreciation among all investments for the year 1972.

Temporary international settlements to the contrary, gold coins have achieved strong price increases over the years, and more important, have had a history of maintaining the gains made. Not that gold coins can be purchased indiscriminately. Poor timing can tie up capital non-productively for years at a stretch. Gold, however, has always come back, and until this country corrects its long-term inflationary trends and balance of payments deficits, odds are that it will continue to do so.

A BRIEF HISTORY OF GOLD

Why the continuing strength over centuries in the yellow metal? Gold has been employed as the basis for monetary units dating back to the Babylonian and ancient Chinese cultures. The very properties of the metal–its softness, beauty, permanence, and virtual indestructibility–have made it highly suitable as a medium for coinage since antiquity. Coupled with its qualities as material for artisans, the scarcity of gold has added to its suitability as a monetary base.

As a result, from ancient times on, gold has always been accepted as a measure of value—to be treasured and hoarded whenever possible, by nations and individuals. And over the centuries, paper money has always been accepted as having value basically in proportion to its convertibility into gold. Departure from gold backing has, in the end, always resulted in the debasement of unbacked currency. For an example, we need only consider the fate of the dollar in recent years.

The dollar has, indeed, had its ups and downs as the U.S. Government has flirted from time to time over the centuries since our founding with unbacked money (all that's needed is a printing press). In 1900, matters stabilized for a time; the United States passed the Gold Standard Act. This set an official value in the United States of $20.67 per ounce of gold, a ratio that dated back to 1837. The gold coins minted by our government between 1838-1933 contained amounts of gold in ounces roughly equal to the face value of the coin as a proportion of $20.67. Thus, a $5 coin would contain roughly ¼ ounce of gold, and a $20 coin would contain roughly .97 ounces of gold. This practice ultimately resulted in the intrinsic value of these coins today. With gold selling on the free market at $100 per ounce, a coin holding .97 ounces of gold has to be worth a *minimum* of $97. As we shall see, these coins are worth considerably more.

In 1934, the American dollar was devalued—from $20.67 per ounce to $35 per ounce of gold. Instead of receiving one ounce of gold for $20.67 in paper money, $35 in paper money became required. The Gold Reserve Act of 1934 also prohibited United States citizens from owning gold bullion; the convertibility of gold, even at $35 an ounce, was limited to foreign holders of paper dollars.

This was one step in the erosion of the dollar; by the Act of 1934 our government no longer guaranteed, to its own citizens, the conversion of dollars to gold. Silver certificates eventually went the same route in 1965. Foreign convertibility has eroded as well, as a result of worldwide gold speculation and the gradual depletion of our national gold reserves. Until March 18, 1968, we continued to honor foreign held dollars by guaranteeing to foreign holders convertibility of their dollars into gold at $35 per ounce. However, on that date, we announced that we would honor only official government transactions with gold backing; on the private market, gold was to be set free to find its own level. The U.S. Government no longer gives gold for dollars to private foreign individuals.

The quietus wrought by this move proved only temporary. Various developments, notably balance of payment deficits, fostered further weakness in the dollar, and on August 15, 1971, President Nixon announced that the dollar was no longer officially convertible into gold. Later that year, we settled on a 7.89% devaluation, the price of gold pegged at $38 per ounce (though still not guaranteed in exchange for paper dollars). On February 13, 1973, another devaluation saw the official price of gold raised to $42.22 an ounce. As I said before, there is strong speculation that the official price of gold will soon again rise—to $100 an ounce, which, of course, would immediately increase by approximately 138% the official value in paper dollars of our remaining gold reserves.

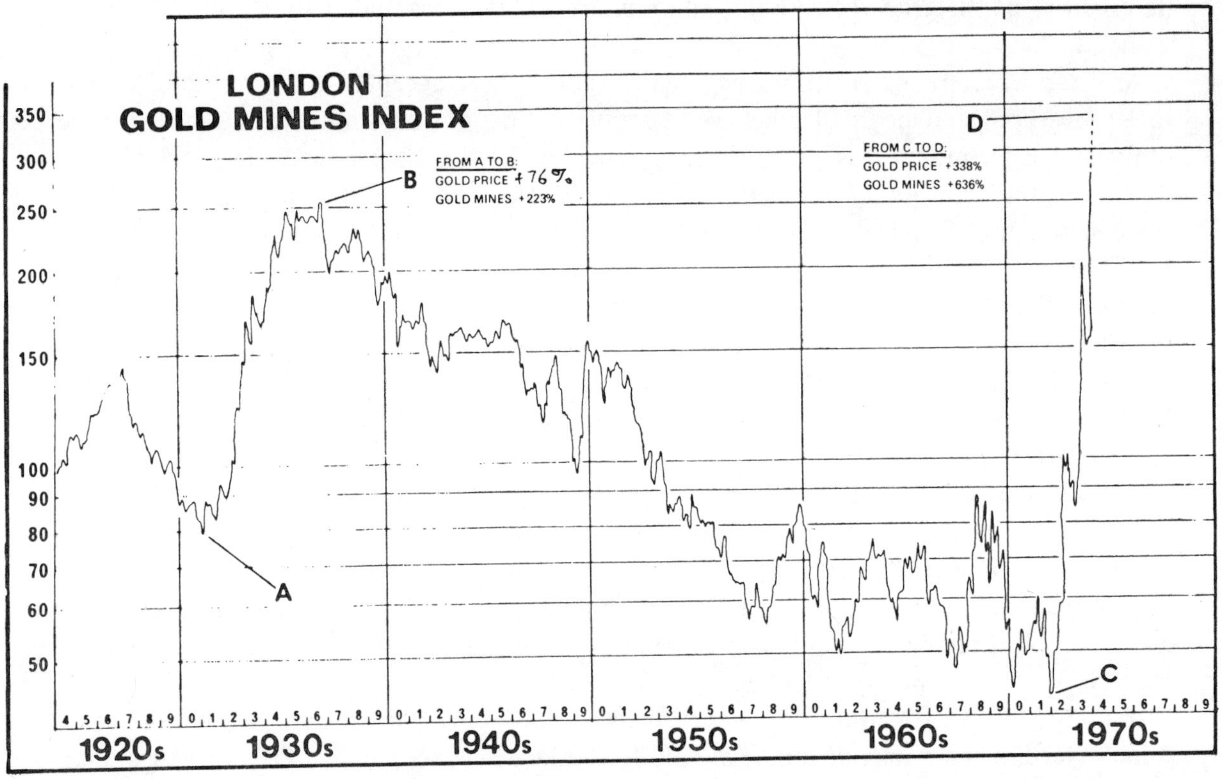

FIGURE 1

LONDON GOLD MINES INDEX

Source: Stock Market Alert, 189 DeLaWarr Rd., Boxhill-on-Sea, Sussex, TN402JY, England

In the meantime, the value of U.S. gold reserves has declined by over 50% since 1940. We own, currently (1974), approximately $10 billion in gold reserves. Official estimates place European dollar holdings at about $70 billion. In other words, were dollars still convertible into gold, we would owe out seven times our current reserves. In plain English, we are now bankrupt, and have solved the problem by defaulting on our debts. Nor have attempts to separate money from gold succeeded; the result has been inflation within the United States and a reluctance on the part of other nations to invest here. The dollar has shown weakness for months on end in recent years in comparison to the Swiss franc and the German mark (improvement took place from late '73 to early '74). Small wonder that gold has continued to maintain respect as a true store of value, and that currencies well backed by gold have continued firm while the value of ours has become, at least, uncertain.

Needless to say, while the official price of gold appears to rise significantly with each monetary crisis, *it does not drop* significantly when crises subside (just glance at Figure 2). Therefore, the floor to gold prices—and, consequently, the rock-bottom value of gold investments—continues to move in only one direction, up. Not too many investments can

FIGURE 2
LONDON GOLD
Source:
Commodity Research Bureau,
1 Liberty Plaza,
NY, NY 10006

boast of such a sustained uptrend. And, of course, should Dr. Pick's more dire predictions come to pass, and this nation be beset by hyperinflation to a degree heretofore never experienced in this country (the Europeans are familiar with such calamities and the hoarding of gold is common practice there), then gold may become your only lifeline to survival. Should the cost of living continue to rise here—not by 5, 10 or even 20 per cent, but by 100, 200, or 1,000 per cent—what will a paper dollar really be worth? In Germany, at the height of the inflation during the 1920's, workers were paid daily because by Friday, Monday's paycheck had been rendered nearly worthless. Many monetary experts believe that were such events to transpire, the only money items of real worth would be actual gold and silver—the monetary units that have withstood the tests of bad times throughout history. Not only for investment then—but as a form of fiduciary insurance, possibly as a matter of survival—we suggest that readers secure and salt away at least some gold and silver coins.

GOLD AS A COMMODITY

Even apart from its role in monetary matters, gold as a pure commodity has wide industrial use. Basic demand for gold for industry, jewelry and the like has been exceeding current new production by many millions of dollars per year. Nonetheless, the convertibility of dollars into gold prevented any rise in the price of the metal until this convertibility was finally threatened and suspended.

HOW TO CASH IN

Let's presume two things: 1) that you are by now convinced that gold has been and will continue to be an excellent vehicle for investment and 2) that you want to stake out a claim of your own. What avenues should you explore?

Truly rare gold coins–coins from ancient civilizations, and examples of scarce latter-day coinage–have appreciated very strongly in recent years. But, and it's a big but, this is no area for the novice. Counterfeiting of such coinage has been rampant, and the liquidity of such investments leaves much to be desired. You either have to sell to a dealer at wholesale prices, or put your portfolio up for auction. Furthermore, the value of select numismatic, collector pieces is to a large extent dependent upon collector fad and the availability of surplus capital in quantities sufficient to support price rises in such discretionary items. Collectibles often seem to peak in price after a time; sharp price rises do not continue forever. Furthermore, a depression is bound to affect numismatic coin values adversely.

Gold artifacts–statuary, music boxes and jewelry–pose similar liquidity problems, besides which the investor pays a heavy premium over the value of the actual gold content within for the workmanship and scarcity involved. Again, this is no arena for the novice.

Gold mining shares have been fine long-term investments, although stock certificates will not offer much solace should doomsday really arrive. We'll look at some of the better grade mines in a subsequent section.

I do recommend the purchase of garden variety gold coinage–coins which are relatively plentiful by collector standards, and in which a large proportion of value is represented by the actual gold content within. These are the coins which will rise with any appreciation in the price of gold itself, and which fall surprisingly little as the price of gold declines. Such coins are readily purchased and sold through reputable coin dealers and brokers and can be selected by inexperienced coin traders with relative safety.

BUT IS IT LEGAL?

Yes, indeed. The Gold Reserve Act of 1934 forbade U.S. citizens from holding gold bullion. However, the Act specifically exempted gold coins of "recognized special value to collectors." Over the years, this has come to be interpreted to mean that all gold coins, U.S. and foreign, minted prior to 1933, are bona fide collector items. The Treasury has ruled in this manner on a number of occasions. Some post-1933 foreign coins have been exempted as well, providing that the Treasury Department has granted them an import license.

Donald J. Hoppe, a leading expert in this area, estimates that current supplies exist in values of $8 billion for pre-1934 American coins and $25.50 billion for pre-1934 foreign coins (*The Investing Professional,* April, 1973). A list of legal post-1934 foreign coins plus the latest regulations, can be obtained free of charge from the U.S. Treasury, Office of Domestic Gold and Silver Operations, Washington, D.C., 20220.

DO THEY ALSO HAVE COLLECTOR VALUE?

They certainly do. When I suggest that most investors stick to "garden variety" coins, it should be understood both that the bulk of these coins are over forty years old, and that the supply of them is fixed for all time. Even the most common gold coins have considerable collector value, if they are in good condition. It's a matter of relative degree. Coins prized more for scarcity and numismatic interest may have, say, 80-90 percent of their value as a result of these factors, with only 10-20% of their worth based upon the intrinsic value of their gold content. Ancient coins show an even greater proportion of value as a result of scarcity alone.

On the other hand, "common" coins will have from 40-80 percent of their value attributable to their actual gold content, only 10-60 percent attributable to numismatic considerations. However, do not overlook the possibilities of price increases based upon rising numismatic value alone. Remember, the supply of coins is fixed, and as more and more hoarding takes place, these coins will increase in scarcity, fluctuations in the price of gold apart. Coins purchased primarily for their intrinsic gold value have always shown a premium over the value of their gold content alone. For example, in early 1973, with gold at $70 per ounce, 20 dollar U.S. coins sold at approximately 22 percent premium above their intrinsic gold value, and 10 dollar coins sold at more than a 50 percent premium. Lower price U.S. coins command an even greater premium. Among U.S. coins, the $5 Indian and the $2½ Liberty have high numismatic value. If you want gold for the sake of pure gold, stick to Mexican 50 peso pieces, British Sovereigns (pre-1934) and Columbian 5 pesos. If you prefer to add a little collector class to your gold lode, consider conversation pieces such as $20 Liberty 1855-0, the $10 Indian 1933 or the Indian 1914.

However, expect to plunk down a thousand, minimum, per coin, if you're playing in that sort of league (on February 21, 1973, a 1927-D Double Eagle, one of seven in the world, was auctioned off at $60,000).

Frankly, again, except for persons with genuine interest in coin collecting, I do not particularly recommend playing the rare coin game. Common coins are probably more readily disposed of; valuable collections are less liquid than coins having high intrinsic gold value, and, most important, coins like art are a field of specialized knowledge. Until and unless you develop some expertise in the area, you will be completely at the mercy of your coin dealer. However, should ownership of classy coinage pique your interest, any demurrer from my end will be slight. Such coins have done quite well over the years, indeed.

SECURE THE BEST CONDITION COINS YOU CAN

Gold coin experts appear virtually unanimous on this one. Make every effort to secure the highest grade of coin possible. Circulated, rubbed down coins can be secured at lower prices in relation to their gold content (although small amounts of gold are lost by wear and usage). However, you are paying anywhere from a 20-60 percent premium for numismatic value, and collectors greatly prefer coinage in excellent condition. *Brilliant Uncirculated* is the highest category. *Almost Uncirculated* and *Extremely Fine* are next. Try for the BU's. If you don't know the one from the other, enlist the services of a reliable coin broker or dealer, and do take steps to corroborate that you are receiving coins of the quality you order. As usual, when the public becomes involved in a heretofore private game, shady operators begin to move in, and one shady practice in recent years has involved the pawning off of coins of low quality for high on unsophisticated investors.

INTRINSIC VALUES OF POPULAR GOLD COINS

Table I shows the approximate intrinsic values of popular gold coins based upon their gold content alone. For example, the U.S. $20 gold coins (Liberty and St. Gaudens) contain .9675 actual ounces of pure gold. If gold were selling on the free market at $50 per ounce, each coin would contain a minimum of $48.37 in actual gold (rounded off here to $50). *The Guide Book of United States Coins,* published annually and available from coin dealers, can provide recent price levels for coins, although exact up-to-date quotes have to be secured via the latest teletype bids.

Premiums over intrinsic gold content vary considerably coin by coin. The more common British Sovereigns have been selling at about 12 percent over their intrinsic value, while the U.S. $20 coins have been selling at premiums of 20 percent and up. By contrast, 15 Ruble Russian pieces have been commanding premiums of 150 percent and better, depending upon the particular coinage and condition. Remember, in the end, you and only you can determine how much to put into gold per se and how much you are willing to add for numismatic value. The difference between the intrinsic gold value and the price you actually pay for the coin represents the numismatic value. I would suggest, at this point, a mix of higher intrinsic to numismatic value, in a ratio of at least 60-40.

SAMPLE PORTFOLIOS

On September 13, 1972, *The Forecaster* (edited by John Kamin, 19623 Ventura Boulevard, Tarzana, California, 91356) published the following suggested portfolio of gold coins. These were selected by Donald Hoppe. Prices have risen since these portfolios were compiled; check with your coin dealer for recent quotes.

Model $600-$800 Coin Portfolio

1 U.S. $20 St. Gaudens
1 U.S. $20 Liberty
1 U.S. $10 Liberty

TABLE I

Type of Coin	Intrinsic Value of Coin With Gold Price At:						
	$50 oz.	$60 oz.	$70 oz.	$100 oz.	$150 oz.	$200 oz.	$250 oz.
10 Corona (Austria)	$ 4.83	$ 5.79	$ 6.76	$ 9.66	$ 14.49	$ 19.32	$ 24.15
20 Franc (Belgium)	9.34	11.20	13.07	18.67	28.00	37.34	46.68
5 Pesos (Columbia)	11.77	14.12	16.48	23.54	35.31	47.08	58.85
1 Ducat (Czechoslovakia)	5.55	6.65	7.76	11.09	16.64	22.18	27.73
20 Kroner (Denmark)	12.97	15.56	18.15	25.93	38.90	51.86	64.83
20 Francs (France)	9.34	11.20	13.07	18.67	28.00	37.34	46.48
20 Marks (Germany)	11.53	13.83	16.14	23.05	34.58	46.10	57.63
20 Corona (Hungary)	9.80	11.76	13.72	19.60	29.41	39.20	49.00
10 Lire (Italy)	4.67	5.60	6.53	9.33	14.00	18.66	23.33
20 Lire (Italy)	9.34	11.20	13.07	18.67	28.00	37.34	46.68
10 Guilders-King (Netherlands)	9.74	11.68	13.63	19.47	29.21	38.94	48.68
10 Guilders-Queen (Netherlands)	9.74	11.68	13.63	19.47	29.21	38.94	48.68
1 Ducat (Nether-East Indies)	5.55	6.65	7.76	11.09	16.64	22.18	27.73
1 Libra (Peru)	11.77	14.12	16.48	23.54	35.31	47.08	58.85
5 Rubles (Russia)	6.22	7.47	8.71	12.45	18.67	24.90	31.13
7½ Rubles (Russia)	9.33	11.20	13.07	18.67	28.00	37.34	46.68
10 Rubles (Russia)	12.45	14.93	17.42	24.89	37.34	49.78	62.23
15 Rubles (Russia)	18.67	22.40	26.14	37.34	56.01	74.68	93.35
20 Francs (Switzerland)	9.34	11.20	13.07	18.67	28.00	37.34	46.68
20 Francs (Tunisia)	9.34	11.20	13.07	18.67	28.00	37.34	46.68
50 Pesos (Mexico)	60.00	72.00	84.00	120.00	180.00	240.00	300.00
20 Pesos (Mexico)	24.12	28.95	33.76	48.23	72.35	96.46	120.58
10 Pesos (Mexico)	12.06	14.47	16.88	24.11	36.17	48.22	60.28
5 Pesos (Mexico)	6.03	7.24	8.44	12.06	18.09	24.12	30.15
2½ Pesos (Mexico)	3.01	3.61	4.22	6.03	9.04	12.06	15.08
2 Pesos (Mexico)	2.41	2.89	3.37	4.82	7.23	9.64	12.05
Sovereigns (British)	11.75	14.10	16.45	23.50	35.30	47.00	58.75
20 Dollar (U.S.A.)	50.00	60.00	70.00	100.00	150.00	200.00	250.00
10 Dollar (U.S.A.)	25.00	30.00	35.00	50.00	75.00	100.00	125.00
5 Dollar (U.S.A.)	12.50	15.00	17.50	25.00	37.50	50.00	62.60
2½ Dollar (U.S.A.)	6.25	7.50	8.75	12.50	18.75	25.00	31.25
1 Dollar (U.S.A.)	2.50	3.00	3.50	5.00	7.50	10.00	12.50

1 U.S. $5 Liberty
1 U.S. $2½ Liberty
1 each, Mexican 50, 20, 10, 5, 2½ and 2 pesos
1 British Sovereign
1 Russian 5 Rubles

Model $1,000-$1,500 Coin Portfolio

2 U.S. $20 St. Gaudens
2 U.S. $20 Liberty
Mexican Gold type set: 6 coins–50 pesos, 20 pesos, 10 pesos, 5 pesos, 2½ pesos, 2 pesos
U.S. Liberty Gold type set: 4 coins–$20, $10, $5, $2½
British Sovereigns: ten different types and mintmarks
Mixed European coins (inexpensive varieties)

A selection of the above provides a good balance between numismatic and intrinsic value

GOLD COIN FUNDS

Recently, a number of organizations have sprung up offering plans whereby investors put up varying sums of money to purchase pre-selected portfolios of gold coins. Some even guarantee to return your money if, after a year or so, you are not satisfied. This type of offer sounds better than it is. You've lost a year's interest on your outlay, plus another 6-8%, at the least, through inflation. I cannot evaluate the merits of any particular coin fund. However, as a concept, coin funds strike me as having limited appeal. In essence, the funds are acting as dealers, buying wholesale and selling retail, and so far as I know, the purchaser receives no guarantees as to the conditions of the coins he is receiving or whether lower prices can be secured elsewhere. Should any reader have some interest in such plans, I strongly suggest that you first secure the specifics of what you are being sold and then comparison shop before you make any commitments.

Coins can be purchased from dealers who profit from markups, or from coin brokers who can often pick up coins for their customers at near wholesale prices, plus a 5% buy and/or sell commission. I would, in most cases, suggest brokers over dealers, since dealers have a built-in interest in promoting what they hold in inventory. However, this is not a hard and fast judgment; a reliable dealer can prove to be an excellent asset. Do compare prices before making any purchase, and, if possible, secure a written representation as to your coin's condition.

TIMING

Last summer, I was able to call the turn on gold, just prior to the August sell-off. Writing for the *Entrepreneur's Early Warning System,* published by the *Capitalist Reporter,* I repeatedly warned subscribers throughout late July and August to steer clear of gold for the time being. In August, the price of gold suddenly plummeted 30 percent from around $130 per ounce to $90. Did I have a secret pipeline to Zurich? Not at all. I was simply applying the basic rule of contrary opinion, set forth in Chapter 2. Everyone–just about everyone–and their uncle was talking gold. Coin funds were springing up like crazy and my mailbox reeled from mail order ads for gold coins. Popular magazines were pushing the stuff and every born loser I knew was inquiring about gold and currency speculation. *When the public and the public media get in* and in with a vengeance, it's about always time to get out.

Long term, gold has proven out as a fine investment. However, for safety's sake, take positions only when gold is out of the headlines. Prices on American and South African gold stocks are published daily in *The Wall Street Journal.* Keep track of them. The prices of gold coins will move in tandem with the prices of gold shares. Begin to accumulate gold coins as the trading volume of the American gold stocks dries up and prices begin to stabilize. Then, wait patiently, averaging down, if necessary, should your initial purchases cost a little too much. Remember, gold is basically a long-term investment, even though nimble traders can often catch a swing or two.

If you do accumulate gold coins, be sure to keep them in a safe place, and do not advertise their presence if you do decide to keep them at home.

DISADVANTAGES

Although gold comes close–at least long term–no investment is a one way street. There are disadvantages even to gold coin collecting, to wit:

1) Gold coins pay no interest or dividends. You receive no income from your investment while you await the development of capital gains. In the meantime, your capital remains tied up.

2) Most coins now sell at a considerable premium over their intrinsic gold value. Gold coins have been a hot collector's item in recent years, but should public interest decline for any reason, these premiums may evaporate, leaving investors with at least temporary losses.

3) Any collection of appreciable value may have to be sold at wholesale prices to dealers or at auction. In either case, investors will not receive the full market value of their holdings.

4) It is just possible that some international currency agreement will be reached which will successfully undermine the importance of gold for considerable periods of time. Should this result in a stabilization in the price of gold, your holdings may lie stagnant insofar as any profit is concerned.

5) In the near future, at least, high bond yields will offer tough competition to alternative forms of investment, 1973 and 1974 may have been the years to *both buy and sell gold.* The profit taking in August, 1973, was attributed, in part, to European speculators shifting their capital from gold and currency speculation into high yield bonds available in the United States. Money flowed back into gold later in the year, but gold shares weakened again in early '74, which may yet turn out to have been the period to accumulate bonds.

Do diversify your entire investment portfolio.

GOLD MINING SHARES

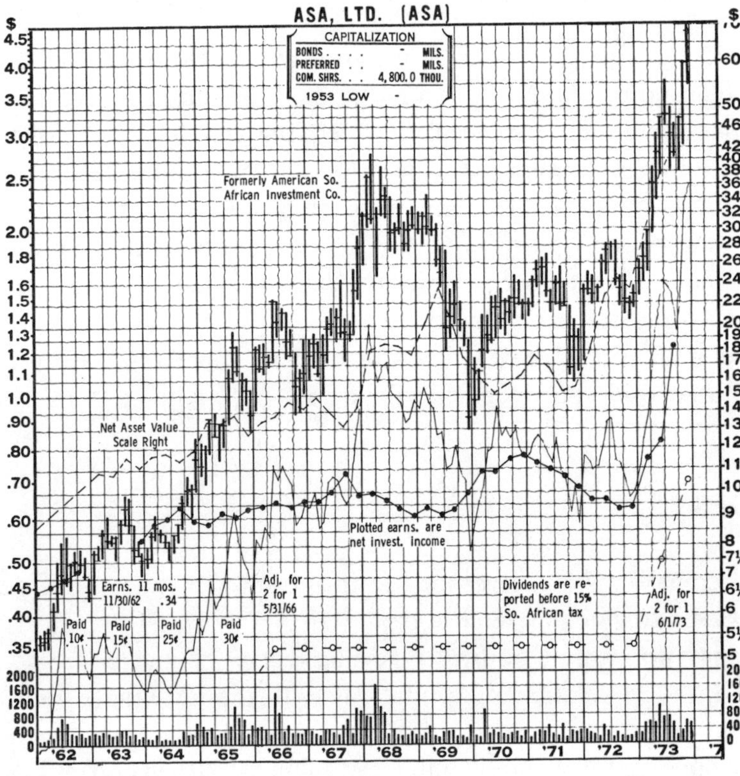

FIGURE 3
PRICE HISTORY ASA, LTD.
Source: Securities Research Co., 208 Newbury St., Boston, MA 02116

Some of the disadvantages inherent in gold coin collecting can be alleviated by playing the gold field via shares in gold mining corporations. In America, the best known is A.S.A. Industries, a closed end investment company, 50% of whose assets are in South African gold mining shares. A.S.A. is traded on the New York Stock Exchange. The company has been a good buy in the past when it has traded below its net asset value per share; it has been a poor buy when it has traded at about 50-75 percent above its net asset value. And as A.S.A. goes, so goes the whole gold arena—coins included.

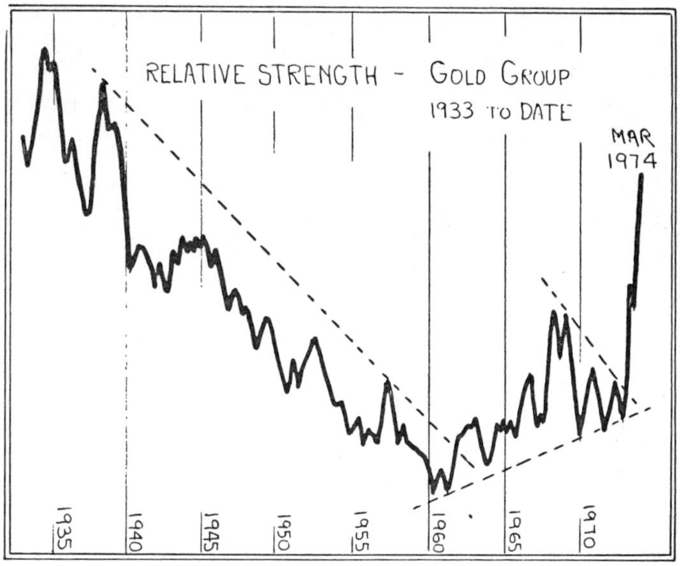

FIGURE 4
RELATIVE STRENGTH—GOLD GROUP
Source: Dow Theory Letters, Box 1759, LaJolla, CA 92037

Excellent yields and long-term growth can be expected from the following South African gold mining companies. All of these are long life mines, with many years of profitable mining ahead. Accumulate these shares on price weakness only. Be certain to specify American Depository Receipts (ADR's) when placing your order.

One drawback: if the worst social calamities do come to pass, there will be no way for you to spend stock certificates, and the payment you receive, should you sell, will turn out to be only *paper dollars* in the end.

LONG LIFE SOUTH AFRICAN SHARES

These companies have a long remaining lode life, and pay high dividends. Purchase them during periods of quiescence and specify ADR's when ordering. Your broker can provide the latest prices and dividend payouts.

- Kinross Mines
- Kloof Gold Mining Co.
- Vaal Reefs Exploration and Mining Co.
- Western Deep Levels
- Hartebeesfontein Gold Mining Co.
- St. Helena Gold Mines
- West Driefontein Gold Mining Co.
- Southvaal Holdings
- Doornfontein Gold Mining Co.
- President Brand Gold Mining Co.

CANADIAN GOLD MINES

Canadian gold shares, by and large, are of lower quality than the South African, and investment therein is more speculative. However, stock in these companies should appreciate in tune with rises in the price of gold.

Campbell Red Lake	McIntyre Porcupine Mines Ltd.
Dome Mines Ltd.	Lake Shore Mines
Agnico-Eagle Mines Ltd.	Little Long Lac
Goldex	Camflo Mines Ltd.

One way or another, gold coins or gold stocks, do take some position. All that glitters is not gold, but based upon past performance, gold certainly does glitter.

Chapter 15

"As I Said, All That Glitters Is Not Gold"

Investing In Silver And Silver Coins

Potential Reward,	A
Potential Risk,	B-
Liquidity,	A
Tax Considerations,	C+

For the sake of argument, let's presume that you are interested in a solid hedge against inflation, but that you can do without all that numismatic exotica. In fact, you couldn't care less whether your investments are "brilliant uncirculated" or grimy with dirt and palm sweat—just so long as they make you money. As an added kicker, perhaps you dig a little leverage play—not too feasible with gold coins (unless you actually take out a side loan), but very possible with gold's kissing cousin, silver.

Just in case you haven't guessed by now, I'm referring to an investment in a unique commodity future—silver coins. Why do I say unique? Because it's the one commodity future you might want deposited on your doorstep. A bag or two of silver half-dollars or quarters won't do nearly the damage to your lawn that you'll suffer from a few tons of soybeans, and just in case doomsday does arrive, you'll be able to spend your hoard. More about *that* later. In addition, silver coins, unlike most commodities, provide a fixed floor to your risk while sharing with other commodities the possibilities of super-leverage. And, finally, you can start as large or as small as you like—contracts are available in all sizes.

WHAT MAKES SILVER RUN?

The profit potential of silver is based upon two factors: (1) silver has served in a secondary manner to gold, historically, as a backing for and as a vehicle with which to hedge against the debasement of paper money and (2) it is actively employed in various industrial usages—world consumption rising steadily, at a faster pace than world supply.

Silver coins, like gold coins, derive their potential appreciation from the actual amounts of precious metallic content within and the feasibility of melting the coins down in order to recover their silver. Unlike gold coins, however, silver coins purchased with this end in mind have little or no numismatic value whatsoever. The coins in question are pre-1964 U.S. coins —dimes, quarters and half-dollars—not delivered carefully polished in presentation cases to the investor, but stuffed unceremoniously into canvas bags, $1000 worth of coins per bag—just large enough to bulge out a mattress or two. Collectible silver coins are another matter altogether, and have to be considered in an entirely different light.

HISTORY

Silver, like gold, has been a medium for coinage and precious artifacts since antiquity. In fact, in ancient times silver probably enjoyed a greater role as a monetary medium than today; certainly, its value relative to gold has been greater than at present. For decades the price relationship between gold and silver in the United States stood at 16-1. This ratio then rose to and remained at 27-1 for many years, finally rising to as high as close to 50-1 at some points during 1973. At current levels, *silver remains historically undervalued in relation to gold,* and in relation to many other commodities as well.

There are, furthermore, strong possibilities that heavy industrial shortages of the metal may develop, exacerbated by speculative hoarding. Should this come to pass, the price of silver could easily soar to record heights—$7 or $8 per ounce, perhaps even higher. Some experts are predicting price levels over $8 per ounce within the coming years. Silver contracts have already sold at a record $6 per ounce, approximately triple price levels that pertained during 1972, and approximately seven times the 90¢ per ounce price level that existed as recently as 1962.

Silver has not always been quite so shiny. Until the 1960's, in fact, the U.S. Treasury had to purchase silver to keep the mines operating, since production far exceeded demand, even allowing for the silver coinage then taking place. A gap existed between the monetary value of silver ($1.29 per ounce) and the free market price (90¢ per ounce). Paper dollars were backed by silver at $1.29 per ounce and those old dollars were called, for that reason, silver certificates. By 1959, the demand for silver had increased to the point where the Treasury was becoming a net seller of silver, but sales were temporarily suspended in 1961. Silver certificates were eventually replaced by unbacked Federal Reserve Notes, because the Treasury was running low on the metal. However, silver coins did remain a bastion of metal-backed currency until their demise. Hopes for an end to the silver price explosion faded, however, and by 1963 the Treasury resumed selling silver at $1.29 an ounce, in order to forestall the melting of coinage for the silver content within. Despite these measures, continuing demand forced the Treasury's hand. In 1965, Congress authorized the silverless halves, quarters and dimes that are in use today. In May 1967, the Treasury stopped selling silver at $1.29 an ounce, although it continued to dispose of silver holdings at auctions. All told, the Treasury's reserves of silver have dwindled from approximately 2 billion ounces (1959) to under 150 million ounces. President Nixon has proposed the further sale of 117.8 million ounces of the current reserve, which, if it takes place, will finally remove the U.S. Treasury as a major source of silver supply for the free market. With demand rising and supply diminishing, the implications are plain for the price movement of silver. Need I say more?

IS THE TREND LIKELY TO REVERSE?

Anything's possible, but I wouldn't count on it. Thus far, increases in price have not led to increases in silver production. The bulk of silver produced in the United States is not mined directly, but is extracted as a by-product from the production of other metals, mainly copper. Copper has recently risen appreciably in price itself, and if increased copper production should develop as a result, silver production could increase as a secondary effect. Peter C. White, writing in *Commodities* (June 1973), estimates that production costs will keep low paying silver mines inoperative until and unless the price of silver stabilizes at, at least, $4 per ounce. This has not yet developed. In fact, the reverse has developed; U.S. silver production actually *declined* between 1970 (45 million ounces) and 1972 (38 million ounces). Consumption, on the other hand, increased in the United States from 132 million ounces (1971) to 149 million ounces (1972).

Nor are we likely to receive much solace from other nations. The gap between worldwide production and consumption has continued, (See Figure 1). India and Pakistan hold between them possibly more than 4 billion ounces, but a heavy proportion of this is in processed form —national treasures unlikely to be released. Supplies from these nations are potentially high, however, but are also expensive to American buyers because of the dollar devaluations.

FIGURE 2
SILVER COINS WEEKLY FUTURES

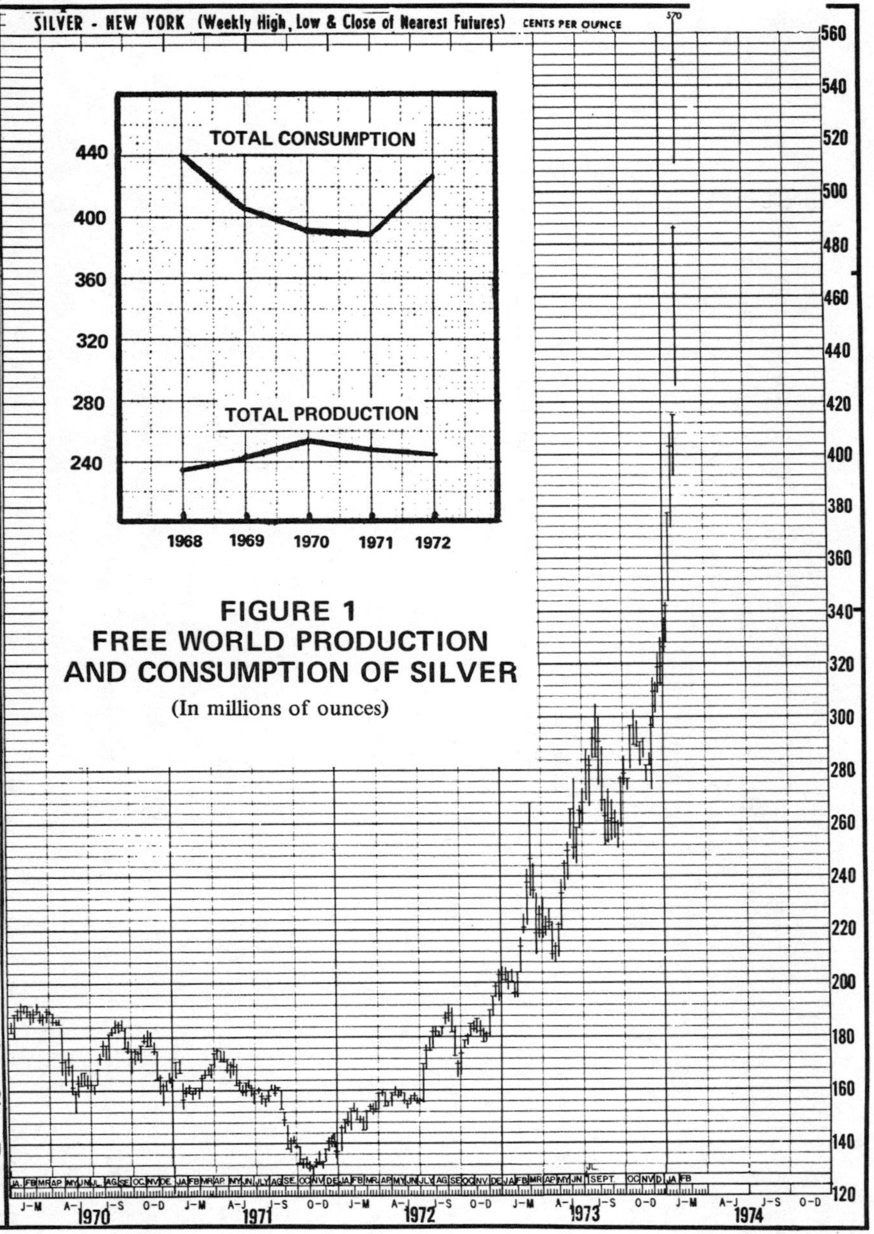

FIGURE 1
FREE WORLD PRODUCTION AND CONSUMPTION OF SILVER
(In millions of ounces)

FIGURE 3
SILVER WEEKLY FUTURES

Source for Figures 2 & 3: Commodity Research Bureau, 1 Liberty Plaza, NY, NY 10006

Canada is now the free world's largest producer of silver, followed by Peru, the United States and Mexico. The total free world production of silver amounted to only 243 million ounces during 1972, compared to consumption of 427 million ounces.

SALVAGE POSSIBILITIES

It is possible to salvage silver from scrap sources such as photographic film, electronic parts and, of course, silver coins. In fact, salvage silver has risen to over 50 million ounces (1972) from only 12 million ounces (1969), the result of shortages and rising production costs. It is also possible that photographic suppliers may develop either film using less or no silver or new processes for the recovery of silver from old film. In the United States, photography consumes the most silver, followed by electrical products and sterling. However, the amount of salvageable silver is fixed and long term trends will probably not be altered by salvage from current processed material. Short term, silver has enjoyed strong moves already. (See Figures 2-4). Try to take positions during price reactions.

CURRENT RESERVES

Estimates place the total amount of free world silver reserves at slightly more than 800 million ounces, or approximately two years supply. The N.Y. Commodity Exchange holds approximately 68 million ounces (lowest since 1968); the Chicago Board of Trade, 24 million and the London Exchange, 7 million. *Silver coins represent the largest source of potential reserve, 350 million ounces.* Reserves are not increasing; they are dwindling.

ONE FINAL THOUGHT

Compared to gold, the world of silver is a poor relative. Even at $4 per ounce, the entire free world production of silver in 1972 had a total valuation of only $972 million dollars. Should the large international speculators really decide to play the silver game, a speculative corner on the market could readily develop, crowding the industrial users, and sending prices clear out of sight. These fellows have wrought havoc on the currencies of whole nations, not to mention what they've done to the price of gold. Imagine, if you will, the impact if Zurich should suddenly discover silver.

A LITTLE DOOMSDAY THINKING

Just in case everything does go to pot, and your wife ends up needing a larger shopping bag for her paper dollars than for the goods they can buy, silver coins may become a major lifeline to essential goods and supplies, even better in many ways than gold coins, since silver coins are far more common and readily understood by the man in the street. It may sound far fetched but such currency debasements have occurred in the past in other nations. Remember, they said we would never devalue the dollar and for a time during 1971, Americans travelling abroad found themselves in the unusual and embarrassing position of not having a currency acceptable to Europeans.

HOW TO PLAY YOUR CHIPS

Convinced by now? I hope so. Silver may indeed prove to be an excellent play in the years to come.

Investors can, of course, shoot their silver bullets via the bullion route, purchasing neat little bars for storage (they are being offered now as small as Hershey bars, but avoid them—hard to sell). Another alternative for the stout of heart involves the purchase of silver contracts on the various futures markets. On the New York Commodity Exchange, you could purchase in October 1973, a 10,000 ounce (.999 fine) contract for as little as $3,000 down for margin. At $3 per ounce, such a contract is worth $30,000. You can play for lower stakes on the Chicago Exchange: $1,500 down secured a 5,000 ounce contract. But keep this in mind. When I said these alternatives were for the stout of heart, I meant it. Silver looks good as a long term holding. Short term fluctuations, however, can thoroughly wipe out a fully margined account in a few days. At $3,000 margin for a $30,000 contract, a 10% drop does the job. It can and does happen frequently. Don't take my word for it; ask any commodity trader. If you must operate fully leveraged, treat your investment as a gamble, using only speculative funds, or be prepared with plenty of back-up money should you be hit with margin calls.

More conservative souls might want to consider outright purchase of spot silver bullion for immediate delivery. Silver bullion can be purchased in quantities of as little as one 1,000 ounce bar (roughly $4,000 at the time of this writing) through various sources. The American Board of Trade, Inc., 286 Fifth Ave., N.Y.C. 10001 has been issuing such offerings, and will arrange for storage should you wish ($24 per year per bar). Commission and other charges range on the ABT from $21 for one bar to $130, or under 0.5%, for ten bars. Silver bullion is readily used as collateral for loans from various sources; you could probably borrow up to 70% current value in a pinch.

The ABT has also been offering penny ante silver futures contracts in smaller sizes than either the New York or Chicago exchanges. Contracts have been offered for as little as $300 down for the 1,000 ounce size; commissions, $10 round trip. Although this commission is low by stock exchange standards, it is higher pro rata than the Chicago contract (round trip, $30) and the New York (round trip, $45).

Incidentally, just in case this year's commodity killings haven't already piqued your interest, a futures contract represents a commitment to either buy or sell a specified amount of a commodity at a specified time, usually some months into the future. Quantities run from a mere 100 ounces (paladium) to 100 tons (that's right tons) of sorghum/milo. In case you're considering taking delivery, sugar contracts run to 112,000 pounds and soybean oil to 60,000. Silver, at 10,000 ounces and down, is a very modest contract—at least in terms of pure bulk. When you purchase an April 1975 silver futures contract you are agreeing to purchase the stipulated quantity of silver when the contract expires (April 1975) at the price you agreed upon when you assumed the position. Rarely does the commodity speculator actually take delivery; that is left for the actual meat, soybean and sugar processors. One way or another, your intent will probably be the disposal of the contract prior to the delivery date. In the meantime, you hope that prices rise, so that the silver which you, for instance, purchased at $4 per ounce, becomes valued at, say, $5 within the period before your contract falls due. If all goes well, you sell the contract at $5 an ounce, clearing a profit of $1 per ounce on the quantity you purchased. Should the going price drop, the difference between what you paid and what you realize from the sale represents your loss.

The futures market can be played in reverse, too. Suppose you expect silver to drop in price. You sell a contract at today's prices. Should the price drop, you cover your short position by purchasing a contract, nullifying your obligation to deliver. If you can purchase silver in the future more cheaply than you have sold at the present, you profit by the difference. If silver keeps rising in price and you have to pay above today's prices to make good on your commitment—well, you've learned one fact of life about commodites.

There are, incidentally, no interest charges involved in purchasing commodities on margin. The purchase of a contract is not a purchase of an actual item; it is simply the assumption of a commitment to make a purchase in the future. When you purchase stocks or bonds on margin, in contrast you are actually taking ownership of a security.

One very astute fellow I know had a partnership in the coffee business, and had the sort of fundamental knowledge of the coffee and cocoa markets that comes only from long experience in purchasing, selling and actually processing these commodities. One year, he sold his share of the business, receiving about $100,000, which he promptly put into a long position in cocoa. Cocoa immediately dropped, and he was forced to scramble to borrow another $100,000 for additional margin. Clever fellow. Cocoa eventually took off and he made $3 million within a few months. This happy tale is meant to bolster the courage of readers who want to take a flyer of this sort. Rate commodity trading A+ for return and D- for risk. *The majority of commodity traders lose money,* and lose it quickly. You cannot hold a "growth commodity" long term, and wait for a good market—in the meantime collecting dividends. A number of commodity brokers have confided in me to the effect that almost all their customers get hurt in the end, although some brokers somewhere, I am sure, do consistently make money for their people.

In short, again, I am not recommending any commodity trading on a short term basis, except for speculative souls who are really itching to play a long shot and are willing and able to assume the risks involved. In no case should you risk more than 10 per cent of your capital on any single position.

BACK TO BASICS

So much for get rich quick schemes. Silver coins, in contrast to silver bullion futures, have offered, in the past, an excellent limited risk vehicle for speculating in silver. Unfortunately, at recent price levels, investors have to be willing to risk at least 60% of their investment on an unleveraged basis; even more leveraged. However, should silver prices drop by any appreciable degree, the amount of risk involved in silver coins would likewise drop considerably. The key to the fixed amount of risk in silver coins lies with the fact that the coins themselves can be used as money in their own right. It figures that bags containing $1,000 face value silver coins can never be worth less than $1,000, no matter what happens to the price of silver. Therefore, there is a fixed limit to your loss, but no limit to potential profit.

Each bag of $1,000 face value silver coins contains approximately 720 fine troy ounces of silver, and these coins can be legally melted down to regain this silver content. Table I shows the value in pure silver of $1,000 bags of coins at various price levels for silver.

TABLE I

Price of Silver Per Ounce	Value of $1,000 Face Amount of Silver Coins, Containing 720 Ounces of Silver
$6.00	$4320.00
5.00	3600.00
4.75	3420.00
4.50	3240.00
4.25	3060.00
4.00	2880.00
3.75	2700.00
3.50	2520.00
3.25	2340.00
3.00	2160.00
2.75	1980.00
2.50	1800.00
2.25	1620.00
2.00	1440.00
1.75	1260.00
1.50	1080.00
1.25	900.00

Were pure silver to sell at $3.25 per ounce, the actual silver content in a bag would be worth $2,340.00, (720 x 3.25). Bags have been selling at levels commensurate with Table I, in fact at premiums over their intrinsic silver value, because of the floor to the risk inherent in silver coin investment. Premiums have persisted even when the intrinsic value of the silver in bags fell below $1,000, and despite the fact that there are expenses involved in melting down silver. Because of melting expenses, holders of bags of silver coins would not, in actual practice, realize the full value of their holdings, should melting actually become necessary.

Silver coins have sold at their greatest premiums at times when silver prices have been depressed. When silver sold at $1.29 an ounce, bags of coins containing approximately $930 worth of actual silver sold at about $1,050–1,070, or at a 14% premium over their actual silver content. This represents the virtual floor to silver coin prices; a drop, as I said, of approximately 65% from recent levels. In the unlikely event that silver does retrace to the $1.30 area, do mortgage your house, hock the jewels, moonlight, do anything, but somehow get your hands on the money to take a position. Your risk can never amount to more than 7 per cent, against a very possible double or triple on the upside.

HOW TO BUY SILVER COINS

Silver coins are traded as futures on the New York Mercantile Exchange and can be purchased through any commodity brokerage firm. Contracts consist of ten bags (each containing $1,000 face value in coins). Margin requirements: roughly about 8 per cent of current value. Obviously, this sort of margin play does carry short term risks similar to margin speculation in silver bullion, though the track does run a little slower. Your ultimate risk, again, in silver coins can never exceed the difference between the cost of the futures contract and $10,000, the face value of the 10 bags. It may be, depending on the price, safe enough to speculate on margin, leaving the differential in a bank to gather interest. Just be ready with the cash in case of a sell-off. Commissions are cheap enough; $35 covers a ten bag contract, buying and selling combined.

Sources do exist for smaller purchases, but at higher purchase costs. The American Board of Trade offers contracts as small as one bag, but commission costs amount to $10, and margin requirements are higher, pro rata, than on the New York Mercantile. You can purchase one bag of coins for $300 margin on the ABT.

The escalation in precious metals has spawned the inevitable profusion of organizations promoting and selling silver and gold coins, offering various plans and charging various costs. *The Pacific Coast Coin Exchange* is one of the best known. *Barron's* usually carries a multitude of ads and addresses. Coins purchased through these outfits are usually for delivery, not for futures trading, although for an additional fee, many firms will arrange storage for you. The cheapest way to speculate in coins is via the futures market. You incur no shipping costs until and unless you take delivery and you pay no interest charges on margined purchases. When the delivery date does come due, you may simply sell your contract and purchase a new one for a more distant month. Commission costs usually run higher when you purchase from a coin company or through a broker. For example, the Pacific Coast Coin Exchange has charged 2 per cent commission for buying and for selling. At current prices, commission costs amount to over $80 per bag there, against $35 for ten bags for actual delivery and you are liable for interest charges. Some question has arisen regarding the pricing practices of such "exchanges", and whether investors have a ready and equitable resale market outside of the regular futures exchanges.

Against lower costs you have to weigh the security of actually holding spendable silver in your possession, the peace of mind that comes with outright purchase and the elimination of any danger that the company that sells you coins won't deliver if and when you demand delivery. Certainly, a bag or two on hand will offer some protection in the event of monetary chaos.

COMMODITY OPTIONS

Certain firms have been offering commodity options, roughly similar to stock options, on various commodities, including silver. Despite scandals associated with at least one house specializing in commodity options, options purchased from reliable houses do provide a limited risk means of speculating in silver; however, option maneuvers are quite speculative. Consult *Barron's* or *The Wall Street Journal* for advertisements and write to option houses for further information.

TAXES

Profits and losses occurring from ventures in silver will be taxed according to the usual rules pertaining to capital profits and losses. Silver coins should be treated as long term investments and profits will be taxed as long term capital gains, if long positions are held for at least six months.

SILVER MINING STOCKS

In the event that you prefer to approach silver via the stock market route, the following companies are among those with large stakes in the metal, and their earnings should rise appreciably should the price of silver continue to climb.

	Exchange	**Price February 1974**
Callahan Mining	NYSE	18 1/8
Rosario Resources	NYSE	50 1/8
Sunshine Mining	NYSE	21 3/4
Day Mines	ASE	11 3/4
Fresnillo Company	ASE	40 7/8
Hecla Mining	NYSE	29 5/8
United Park City	NYSE	3 5/8

These are all actively traded listed issues. Your stockbroker can supply up-to-date prices and the latest Standard and Poor's reports of recent fundamental developments.

DISADVANTAGES

Silver does look good, long term. However, there are certain risks and caveats associated with silver investments regarding which potential investors should be aware.

1) Silver, like gold, provides no income while you await developments. In fact, you have to plan on storage costs for silver bullion (about $24 per year per bar), packing and delivery costs, and re-assay expenses when you sell. Such charges pertain for coins as well.

2) The price history of silver has been erratic, and overly bullish investors have been disappointed at times in the past. For example, prices shot up from $1.29 to $2.56 an ounce (1968) after the U.S. Treasury stopped selling silver at $1.29 to all comers in 1967. However, during 1971 prices retraced to the $1.29 level. What might trigger such a price reaction from current levels? Changing technology for one. Perhaps the development of silverless photography. Or suppose speculators decide to take profits and dump their holdings. Or India and Pakistan decide to throw vast amounts of silver onto the open market. All unlikely, but nonetheless possible. Remedy: Take positions when the precious metals are out of public view and lying quiescent.

3) The risks in highly leveraged bullion and coin positions that have already been mentioned.

4) There are long term commitments which tie up your capital. Should you borrow, using silver bullion or coins as collateral, you have to consider your interest charges as an investment expense.

5) Every fad spawns offshoots. The precious metal boom has spawned medallion sets, special dishes, mini-bars of silver, coin funds–you name it. Medallions and silver plates contain relatively limited amounts of silver. While it is possible that these "collector editions" will appreciate someday, such appreciation will not be based upon their intrinsic silver content. Mini-bars will be difficult to sell when the time comes. Always be leery of clever side promotions.

A SUPER-SAFE WAY TO PLAY THE GAME

Occasionally, price spreads between spot and future prices develop sufficiently enough to provide excellent arbitrage opportunities and profit with almost no risk. It works this way. On the silver futures markets, contracts for distant months generally sell for more than contracts for near months or for purchases for immediate delivery. For example, on August 10, 1973, silver futures for delivery that month sold for $2.67 an ounce, while silver slated for delivery in October, 1974 sold for $2.92. This spread represents partly the storage costs for a 14-month period and partly the fact that a purchaser of a futures contract does not have to tie up capital in actual inventory, whereas the outright purchaser does. To profit from this situation, you purchase, say, 1,000 ounces of August 1973 silver at $2.67, taking delivery, and simultaneously sell an October 1974 contract at $2.92. Comes next October, you simply deliver the silver you purchased this year. Profit, 25¢ per ounce or about 9% over 14 months, less expenses. Not exciting, but quite safe, and if you keep your eyes open, higher profit arbitrage situations sometimes do develop.

Do look into silver investing in one form or another, particularly if bags of silver coins drop again into the \$1,500 price range or below. Odd dimes and quarters may not have the glamour of a Russian gold Ruble, but one maxim is worth keeping in mind—all that glitters is not gold.

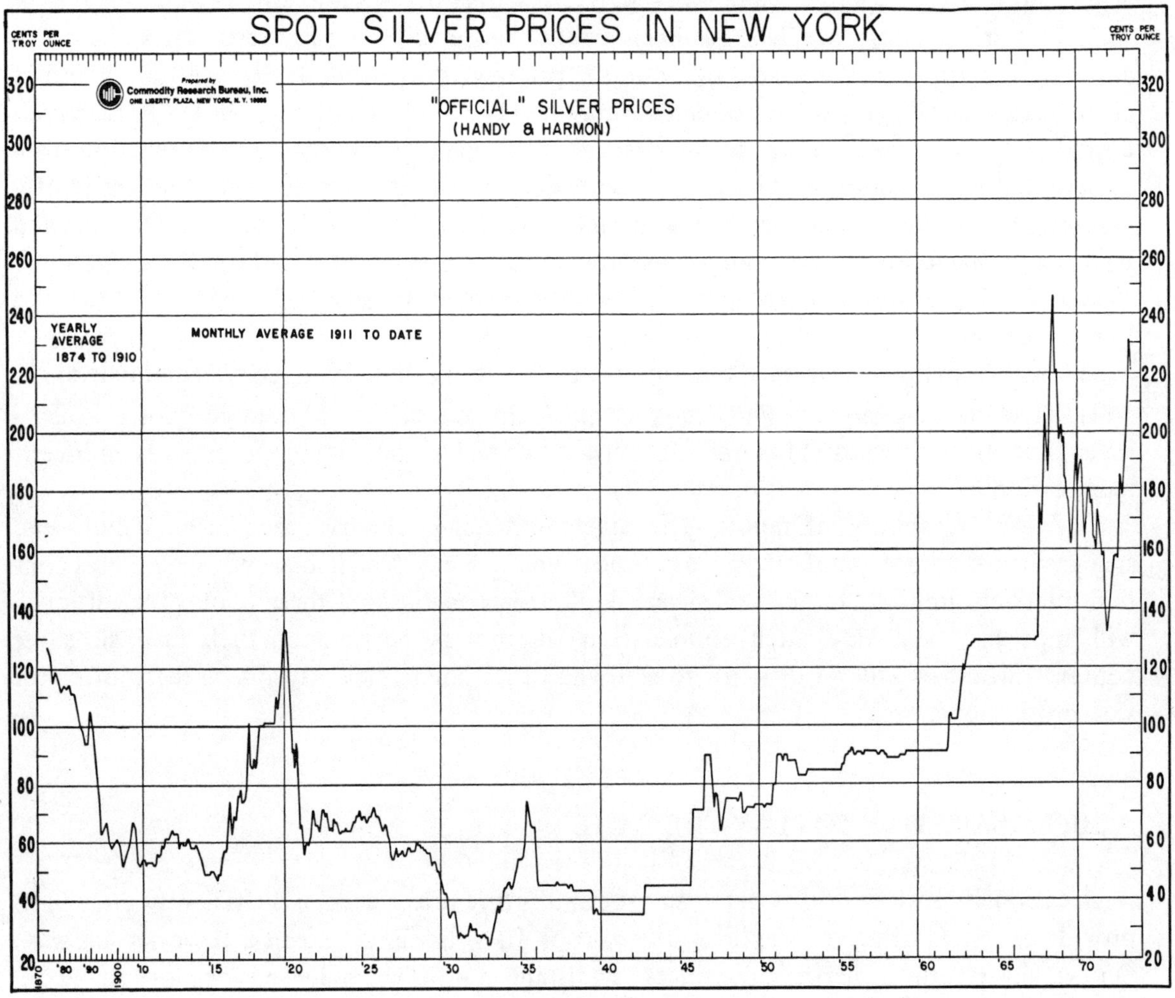

FIGURE 4

LONG TERM PRICE HISTORY OF SILVER

Source: Commodity Research Bureau Inc., 1 Liberty Plaza, NY, NY 10006

Chapter 16

"To Tell The Truth Though, I Would Rather Drink The Stuff Myself"

Investing In Scotch Whiskey

Potential Reward,	A
Potential Risk,	Grain C–, Malt B
Liquidity,	C
Tax Considerations,	B+

No guarantees, but this just may be the time to take a flyer in one of the drinkables—Scotch whiskey. Please don't hold me to it too strongly and definitely don't put in your life savings. Scotch, in my opinion, has been a greatly over-rated investment. In recent years in particular, it has not brought in anywhere near the returns promised by glowing mail order promotions, backed by sweetheart articles in such media as *Medical Economics* and *Moneysworth.* Why the present cautious optimism then? Contrary opinion. After years of favorable reporting, the tide of public opinion seems to have turned. Following a lukewarm article in *The Capitalist Reporter* this year, *Money Magazine* and *Changing Times* suggested caution, at best, regarding Scotch whiskey investments. To boot, the S.E.C., with much fanfare, has been getting after some of the shadier promoters and appears on the verge of establishing whiskey investment as a regulated arena. When things look so bad, when the publicity begins turning consistently unfavorable, it's usually time to begin taking a fresh look. In the case of Scotch at this time, there may be more than just a good drink. In any event, whiskey investment does make a great conversation piece and, at the least, is certainly a more snobbish way to lose money than in the stock market.

HOW IT WORKS

The basic maneuver consists simply of the following: (1) You purchase a quantity of preblended Scotch malt or grain whiskey through a broker or dealer. (2) This whiskey is kept *at your expense* in barrels in Scotland, to age. (3) The hope is that the whiskey will appreciate as it ages, so that you can ultimately sell to a blender or to another investor at a price sufficient to bring in a profit after all expenses.

We will consider further details later on, along with specifics of results over the last decade. At this point, let's just note that there have been periods of time when whiskey has produced strong snorts of profit, and other times when grain in particular, and malt to a lesser extent, have turned out to be evil spirits indeed.

THE FUNDAMENTAL PICTURE

The case for Scotch whiskey essentially rests upon the consistent rise in world consumption of Scotch that has taken place over the last decade. Promoters of whiskey capers point with pride to the worldwide escalation of intoxication that has taken place over the last twenty years, and the figures bear them out. Whiskey consumption, worldwide, has risen from 25 million gallons (1952-1953) to over 100 million gallons per year—and that's a lot of Glenlivet down the spout no matter how you look at it.

The United States is the largest single consumer of Scotch, the 35.6 million gallons downed here during 1971 representing more than triple the consumption of our closest competitor (?), the United Kingdom. However, we're far from earning top honors as the nation of drunkards. Per capita consumption is greater in the United Kingdom. The biggest drinkers of all? South Africa. Their rate of consumption is nearly double ours. And though their rates of consumption of Scotch remain relatively small, Japan, Australia, and Brazil, of all places, show the greatest increases in national Scotch imbibition.

Table 1. Scotch Whisky Consumption

	1966 000's Evaporated Gallons	1971 000's Evaporated Gallons	1971 Per Capita Consumption (Bottles)	5 year Compound Growth Rate %
U.K.	9,048	11,087	1.66	4.1
U.S.	22,654	35,565	1.39	9.4
France	1,711	3,179	0.52	13.2
W. Germany	1,453	3,169	0.45	16.9
Italy	711	2,131	0.33	24.8
Australia	963	1,807	1.27	13.4
Canada	1,079	1,444	0.58	6.0
Belgium	1,082	2,380	1.17	5.0
Japan	468	2,139	0.17	35.5
Spain	472	1,131	0.28	19.1
South Africa	630	1,230	2.46	14.3
Venezuela	671	677	0.60	0.2
Sweden	852	733	0.76	—
Argentina	516	944	0.33	12.9
Brazil	212	1,079	0.05	38.7
Netherlands	328	638	0.41	14.2
Switzerland	306	604	0.81	14.6
Denmark	341	506	0.85	8.2
Others	7,147	11,962		10.8

Source: The Investing Professional, 420 Lexington Ave., NY, NY 10017, July 1973. "Scotch Whiskey, A Turnaround Investment Situation" by Maurice L. Schoenwald.

Whiskey investment enjoyed its heyday during the early fifties, and those mail pieces promising 20% annual appreciation draw that profit potential by averaging in the sharp gains made during 1959-1963 period. Whiskey did, in fact, produce some fancy capital gains during that decade. Grains selling for $1.33 per gallon new during 1954, fetched $5.72 only four years later. Malts ran from $1.95 to $5.20 per gallon during the same period. These gains were largely the result of underproduction during World War II when facilities were used for military purposes, coupled with a 56 per cent increase in consumption between 1952 and 1958. Scotch whiskey is usually blended and bottled at 4, 8, and 12 year ages so a considerable time lag exists between original production and consumption.

The joyride ended in 1964. Bottlers and speculators pushed up the market, fostering overproduction between 1964-1966, which resulted finally in the great whiskey glut of the late 60's. Grain that sold new for $1.89 in 1964 fetched only $1.17 four years later and by 1972, was still worth only $1.35. In between, holders were responsible for storage and insurance costs, not inconsiderable amounts over eight years. Malts fared somewhat better, but as we shall see, represented no great bargain either.

From 1968-1971, production of grain decreased and the coming years may see what might become the final absorption of surplus grain reserves spilling over from the overproduction of the mid-sixties. A number of blenders are believed to have been using eight and nine year old grain in four year old blends, and some experts are beginning to foresee a shortage of four year old and older grain developing in the mid-seventies. However, such predictions are standard in the industry. Were such a shortage to develop, or were surplus stocks to be finally absorbed, we could well see a return to past price structures when 4 year old grains and malts sold for at least $3-4 per gallon.

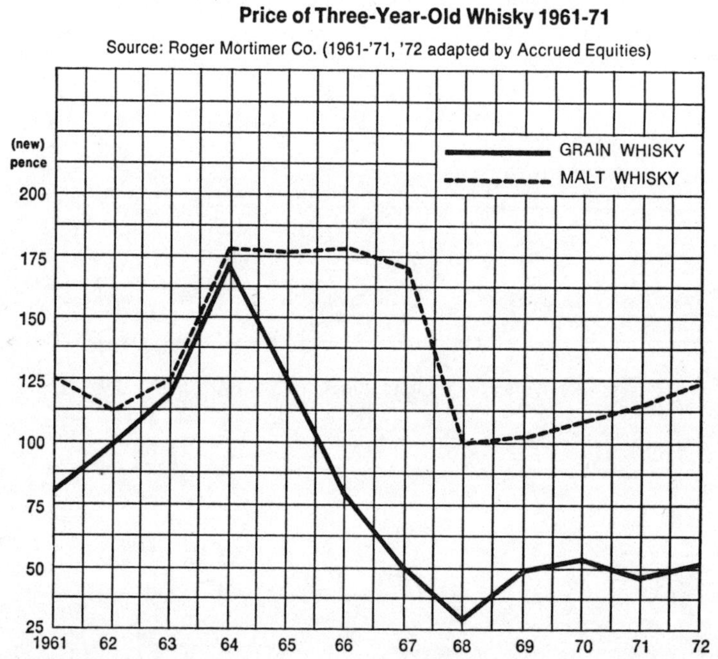

FIGURE 1: PRICE OF THREE-YEAR-OLD WHISKY 1961-71

Source: The Investing Professional, 420 Lexington Ave., NY, NY 10017, July 1973. "Scotch Whiskey, A Turnaround Investment Situation" by Maurice L. Schoenwald.

Figure I would appear to show that we may have indeed turned the corner. Buyers of 1968 grain new saw at least some price appreciation (but a net loss after expenses) by 1972, after the traditional four year holding period, which is more than 1968, for instance, brought to 1964 whiskey holders.

The typical economic cycle of commodities involves periods of scarcity giving rise to higher prices. Higher prices, in turn, encourage overproduction as producers scramble to cash in, resulting, in the end, in lower prices and cutbacks in production. This leads to another period of scarcity. Ad nauseum. The question remains—at which point of the whiskey cycle are we? There is at least a fair chance that we are at the brink of another price markup. And, again, if that is the case, whiskey could turn out to be the gold coin of 1975-1980. Speculative? Highly. Rate grain a C– for risk, based upon past disasters. Malt gets a B. Potentially profitable? An A for sure. Grain whiskey, aging 4 years, appreciated by 330 per cent between 1954-1958 and by 300 per cent between 1960-1964. The potential is there all right—if the timing is right.

THE SPECIFICS OF INVESTING

Types of Whiskey: Whiskey falls into two broad categories, grain and malt. *Grain* Scotch whiskies are neutral spirits, blended with malt to produce the blended whiskey popular in the United States. The usual blend now consists of 70 per cent grain, 30 per cent malt. There are no major qualitative differences among grains; most blenders use the various grains interchangeably. Certain premium or standard grains do cost a few pennies more per gallon than others. These include Caledonian, Cambus, Cameronbridge, Carsebridge, Port Dundas, North British and Strathclyde. Because grains are essentially of one quality, the investor need not be overly concerned regarding the particular grain he is purchasing, although it is preferable to purchase the premium grains if you can secure them at no higher a price than the others.

Malt Scotch whiskies are another matter entirely. The malt is the source of the taste in Scotch whiskey. Pure malt Scotch whiskey, becoming more popular in the United States recently, has a distinct smoky, medicinal flavor. There are approximately 100 malt distillers in Scotland, turning out malts which vary considerably in quality and price. A favorite tricky maneuver by promoters has been the passing off of second quality malts to neophyte investors at premium prices. In any malt whiskey purchase, *secure the exact selection of malt you are being offered before signing up.* Do understand, for instance, that Glenlivet represents a region, not a particular distiller, and some second grade, as well as fine, whiskey originates there. Top quality malts include Smith's Glenlivet, Glenfaeclas-Glenlivet, Glen Grant, Balmenach, Macallan-Glenlivet and Mortlach. Lower grade malts include Glenfiddich, Macduff, Ardmore, Dufftown and Tomatin, an acceptable whiskey which has become a favorite item in the second class retail business.

Malts have not been subject to the wide price fluctuations of grain; however, overproduction is always a danger. Many experts suggest that investors stick to the highest quality malts only, but the past history of pricing does not seem to support this conclusion.

Blends are whiskies already blended, including grain and malt. There is no good resale market for blends. Avoid them for investment, if not for drinking purposes.

WHAT TO BUY

Flip your own coin. Malts have been steadier performers than grain over the years, but grains have racked up the best as well as the worst individual performances. Opinion within the industry appears divided, some brokers recommending the purchase of malt, some recommending the purchase of grain. Study Tables II through VIII and arrive at your own conclusions. *Summing up:* Grains are more speculative, but all grain is, for practical purposes, of uniform quality. Malts have been steadier but you must ascertain the quality of malt you purchase. Again, avoid blends completely. I also suggest that beginning investors avoid "balanced inventories" which some dealers promote, consisting of small quantities of various malts and grains. You get one from column A and two from column B. Sort of like a Chinese dinner. Resale of whiskey in small quantities can be quite difficult.

BACK TO THE MECHANICS

During better times, it was customary for investors to purchase fresh whiskey and hold it for the 4, 8 and/or 12 year bottling periods. Investors could either sell their whiskey at these times or trade it in for greater quantities of younger whiskey, letting their new holdings age in turn (See Tax Tips, below). Recent turns of events have taken the starch out of this tactic, and the current consensus is that purchases of 4 year old and older stock is preferable, letting it age to the 8 and 12 year bottling periods. Scotch whiskey under four years of age cannot be legally exported, and under three years, it is not bottled at all. There is virtually no resale market for whiskey under 3 years of age, and little bottling of whiskey at 5, 6 and 7 years of age. You can, however, invest in 6 year old whiskey with the intent of selling it in two years when it reaches the 8 year bottling age.

INVESTMENT EXPENSES

Whiskies may be purchased either from dealers or from brokers. Dealers profit by making bulk purchases and selling parcelled out lots at whatever markup the market and their consciences will bear. Some dealers have been honest and reliable; others not. Brokers do not maintain their own inventory, but will shop around for you, usually to their regular sources of supply. This does provide the advantage of the broker having less conflict of interest regarding his recommendations; he has less need to push his own holdings. However, brokers do receive commissions usually in the area of 5 per cent at both buying and selling times. To boot, there is always a spread between the bid and asked prices, ranging upwards from 10 per cent. At times, it may be difficult to dispose of holdings at all. More usually, holdings can be sold at reasonable prices within 30 days. Keep in mind, however, that when the 10% round trip commissions and the 10% spread are considered, your whiskey has to rise in value by at least 20 per cent for you just to break even. Small investors may face an even more serious handicap. Blenders, buying in quantity, can secure whiskey for prices as much as 50 per cent below retail. Therefore, for a blender to be interested in your parcel, the bulk market for your whiskey has to stand at the level at which you are ready to sell. In other words, your retail purchase may have to rise by about 50 per cent, in many cases, before you can come out even selling to a blender. Altogether, then, a rise of 70 per cent in your whiskey might be necessary before you can profitably dispose of your holdings. Occasionally, careful shopping can reduce this handicap, but rarely below 20 per cent. And this does not include costs of insurance and storage.

Incidentally, usual purchase terms call for a deposit of approximately 10 per cent down, the balance of payments due upon final invoice.

OTHER COSTS

Insurance: The majority of investors will elect to carry "all risk" insurance on their holdings, issued by companies such as Lloyds of London. Cost, ½ of 1% of your holdings per annum. An additional policy covering "fraud and misappropriation" is more optional at ¼ of 1% per annum. Insurance coverage is usually arranged for you by the broker or dealer who sells you the whiskey.

Storage: Whiskey holdings are stored in government licensed, bonded warehouses–well supervised and controlled. Storage is also arranged by your whiskey dealer or broker at the time of purchase. Cost, about 9¢ per gallon per year. This sounds small, but storage costs alone for a gallon of 1968 Scotch grain, $1.02 per gallon new, now about $1.35, totalled 36¢ over the first 4 years, or about 35 per cent of the original price. Do be certain that you receive clear title to the whiskey you buy. Purchasing via letters of credit, payable against invoice may be a good idea, although you do usually have to put up some deposit.

Containers: Investors are also obligated temporarily for the cost of containers. These include the barrel (50 gallon capacity, $6.15), the hogshead (60 gallons, $12.30) and the butt (110 gallons, $24.00). You cannot usually specify the type of container you receive. However, though these outlays represent money tied up, you do receive a refund of container expenses when you sell your holdings.

Evaporation: Whiskey is sold in terms of original proof gallons (o.p.g.). Evaporation to the extent of 11 per cent is presumed normal during the first four years of a whiskey's aging, and allowance is made for this at disposal time. Your purchaser expects to receive 44.5 gallons of whiskey after 4 years, though you started with 50 gallons, and this evaporation does not affect the price you receive. All risk insurance does include coverage for excess evaporation, but claims against this provision are unusual.

RESULTS

Tables II-VIII show the results of investment in Scotch grain and two classes of malt since 1954. Pay particular attention to the columns showing the actual returns *after* expenses (insurance, commissions, storage), because those are the columns that tell the true story.

Price data has been secured from the October, 1972 prospectus of *Accrued Equities, Inc.*

In my research, I have found considerable variance among price tables from different sources, which is reflective of some of the problems faced by small investors. However, I have reason to believe that the prices herein employed closely approximate current and past markets.

TABLE II

Returns From Investment In One Original Proof Gallon of Grain Scotch Per 4 Year Holding Period, 1954-1968[1]

Year of Filling	Price, O-Age	Price 4 Years Later	Price Appreciation, 4 Years	Return After Expenses [2]
1954	$1.33	$5.72	+330%	+274%
1955	1.33	4.48	+237	+186
1956	1.75	4.20	+140	+101
1957	2.52	3.36	+ 33	+ 6
1958	3.22	3.43	+ 7	- 17
1959	1.54	4.13	+168	+125
1960	1 40	5.60	+300	+247
1961	1 40	3.64	+160	+114
1962	1 68	3.15	+ 88	+ 49
1963	1 75	1.26	- 28	- 59
1964	1.89	1.17	- 38	- 67
1965	1.43	1.47	+ 3	- 34
1966	1.40	1.50	+ 7	- 30
1967	.98	1.10	+ 12	- 37
1968	1.02	1.35	+ 32	- 15
Average (1954-1968)	1.64	3.04	+ 94.9%	+ 56.2%

The average purchase was made at a price of $1.64 per o.p.g. The average sale was made at $3.04 per o.p.g. Price appreciation before expenses averaged 94.9% over a four year period. However, the net gain per four year period after expenses averaged 56.2%. This is equivalent to a compound growth rate of approximately 12 per cent per year.

1. Source of all Table data: Prospectus, *Accrued Equities, Inc.* (October 27, 1972), originally from J. F. Haffenden Ltd., of London.

2. Expenses in all tables include ½ of 1% annual insurance based upon original purchase price multiplied by the number of years in the holding period; 9¢ per gallon per year storage charges; 5% purchase and 5% selling commissions. No deductions were made for the spread between bid and asked prices or for the costs of the containers. The percentage returns in column 4 are not quite statistically correct, since buying commissions are paid at the time of purchase, and insurance and storage costs are paid out during the life of the holding. To simplify calculations, all expenses are treated as though they accrued at the time of sale, and are deducted from the selling price. The errors in percentage returns resulting from these mathematical liberties are, however, insignificant. If anything, this method of calculation tends slightly to exaggerate the percentage returns from investment in whiskey.

TABLE III

Returns From Investment In One Original Proof Gallon of Grain Scotch Per 8 Year Holding Period, 1954-1964

Year of Filling	Price, O-Age	Price 8 Years Later	Price Appreciation	Return After Expenses
1954	$1.33	$7.56	+468%	+377%
1955	1.33	8.40	+532	+437
1956	1.75	10.36	+492	+412
1957	2.52	8.40	+233	+179
1958	3.22	7.56	+135	+ 92
1959	1.54	3.76	+144	+ 76
1960	1.40	2.88	+106	+ 35
1961	1.40	4.26	+204	+129
1962	1.68	4.44	+164	+ 99
1963	1.75	2.40	+ 37	- 20
1964	1.89	1.35	- 29	- 79
Averages (1954-1964)	1.80	5.58	+226	+158

The average purchase was made at a price of $1.80 per o.p.g. The average sale was made at a price of $5.58 per o.p.g. The average price appreciation over eight years amounted to 226 per cent. The average return, after expenses, over eight years amounted to 158 per cent.

It should be kept in mind that a total return of 158 per cent over eight years is equivalent to a compound growth rate of 12 per cent per year.

TABLE IV

Returns From Investment In One Original Proof Gallon of Grain Scotch Per 12 Year Holding Period, 1954-1960

Year of Filling	Price, O-Age	Price 12 Years Later	Price Appreciation	Return After Expenses
1954	$1.33	$11.34	+753%	+618%
1955	1.33	6.00	+351	+336
1956	1.75	6.00	+243	+153
1957	2.52	6.00	+138	+ 72
1958	3.22	7.00	+117	+ 62
1959	1.54	9.00	+484	+374
1960	1.40	7.80	+457	+341
Averages (1954-1960)	1.87	7.59	+363.3	+279.4

The average purchase price was $1.87 per o.p.g. The average selling price was $7.59 per o.p.g. The average price appreciation over the 12 year period amounted to 363.3 per cent. The average net return after expenses per 12 year period amounted to 279.4 per cent.

It should be kept in mind that Tables III and IV are heavily weighted by the favorable years prior to 1964. We might anticipate that the performance of the 8 year and 12 year periods will suffer, on average, as the mid-1960 fillings come of age and can be included in the above calculations.

It should further be kept in mind that the above are not compounded growth rates. A total return of 279 per cent over a twelve year period is roughly equivalent to a compound growth rate of 12 per cent per year.

TABLE V

Returns From Investment In One Original Proof Gallon Of "Good Malt" Per 4 Year Holding Period, 1954-1968

Year of Filling	Price O-Age	Price, 4 Years Later	Price Appreciation	Return 4 Years Later
1954	$1.82	$4.42	+143%	+104%
1955	1.82	2.60	+ 43	+ 8
1956	1.82	3.64	+100	+ 63
1957	1.82	3.64	+100	+ 63
1958	1.82	3.64	+100	+ 63
1959	1.82	3.64	+100	+ 63
1960	1.82	3.90	+114	+ 77
1961	1.82	3.12	+ 71	+ 36
1962	1.82	3.12	+ 71	+ 36
1963	1.82	3.12	+ 71	+ 36
1964	1.95	2.86	+ 47	+ 14
1965	1.94	2.86	+ 47	+ 14
1966	1.94	2.86	+ 47	+ 14
1967	1.95	2.85	+ 46	+ 14
1968	1.95	3.51	+ 80	+ 46
Averages (1954-1968)	1.86	3.32	+ 77%	+ 43.4%

The average price paid per o.p.g. amounted to $1.86; the average selling price amounted to $3.32 per o.p.g. The total price appreciation over four years amounted to 77 per cent. The average net return, after expenses, amounted to 43.4 per cent over a four year period. This is equivalent to an annual compound growth rate of 9 per cent.

TABLE VI

Returns From Investment In One Original Proof Gallon Of "Good Malt" Per 8 Year Holding Period, 1954-1964

Year of Filling	Price O-Age	Price, 8 Years Later	Price Appreciation	Return, After Expenses
1954	$1.82	$4.84	+166%	+104%
1955	1.82	4.84	+166	+104
1956	1.82	5.46	+200	+136
1957	1.82	5.20	+186	+123
1958	1.82	5.20	+186	+123
1959	1.82	5.20	+186	+123
1960	1.82	5.20	+186	+123
1961	1.82	5.72	+214	+150
1962	1.82	6.50	+257	+191
1963	1.82	6.50	+257	+191
1964	1.95	8.00	+310	+244
Averages (1954-1964	1.83	5.70	+210%	+147%

The average price paid for malt amounted to $1.83 per o.p.g. The average selling price amounted to $5.70. The average price appreciation over the 8 year periods amounted to 210%. The average net return, after expenses, per 8 year holding period, amounted to 147%. This is equivalent to an annual compounded growth rate of slightly under 12%.

TABLE VII

Returns From Investment In One Original Proof Gallon Of "Good Malt" Per 12 Year Holding Period, 1954-1960

Year of Filling	Price O-Age	Price, 12 Years Later	Price Appreciation	Return, After Expenses
1954	$1.82	$8.58	+371%	+277%
1955	1.82	8.58	+371	+277
1956	1.82	6.50	+257	+169
1957	1.82	6.50	+257	+169
1958	1.82	8.58	+371	+277
1959	1.82	10.40	+471	+373
1960	1.82	12.00	+559	+456
Averages (1954-1960)	1.82	8.73	+380%	+285%

The average purchase price amounted to $1.82 per o.p.g. The average selling price amounted to $8.73 per o.p.g. Prices, on average, increased by 380% over these 12 year periods. Net returns, after expenses, averaged 285% for the 12 years. This is equivalent to an annual compounded growth rate of 12 per cent.

Tables V, VI, and VII illustrate the price history of "good malt". Prime malts, prices somewhat higher, show similar results.

SUMMARY OF RESULTS

1) After expenses, investments in Scotch grain whiskey have produced compounded annual returns of approximately 12 per cent. These results have been consistent for the 4, 8 and 12 year holding periods. Based upon past performance, it appears to matter little whether investors start with new or previously aged fillings.

2) Grain has shown both the best and the worst performing periods, compared to malt. Past performance indicates that grain is the more speculative vehicle. However, on average the performance records of grain and malt have been similar.

3) Malt has been a consistent performer. No period of investment produced any losses, even after deductions for expenses. Prime and "good" malt seem interchangeable based upon past performance.

4) New malt fillings produced profits averaging the equivalent of 9 per cent, compounded annually. Longer term holding produced greater gains, in the order of 12 per cent compounded annually.

5) The above results slightly overstate the past performance of whiskey investment, because of the statistical method employed.

SUMMING UP:

Grain for the speculators, malt for the conservatives. Forget the 20 per cent returns promised by the ads. After expenses, 12 per cent seems more realistic over the long haul. However, grain has had some strong years.

CAVEAT EMPTOR

Whiskey pricing makes me long for a Scotch ticker tape. Equity Funding stung more than a few investors, but day in, day out stock players at least can keep accurate score; you are always aware of what the guy on line ahead of you plunked down for his shares of Telephone.

Helped out by a lot of free publicity (I know of only one other source which has published *net* investing results), more than a few dubious whiskey dealers have been peddling the product to intoxicated customers. In short, it's been common practice to charge what the market

TABLE VIII

Price Histories Of Scotch Grain, Prime Malt and "Good" Malt, 1954-1972

Year of	0-Age			4-Year			8-Year			12-Year		
Filling	Grain	Prime Malt	Good Malt	Grain	Prime Malt	Good Malt	Grain	Prime Malt	Good Malt	Grain	Prime Malt	Good Malt
1954	$1.33	$1.95	$1.82	$5.88	$5.72	$5.46	$9.10	$8.58	$7.80	$11.83	$9.10	$8.84
1955	1.33	1.95	1.82	5.88	5.20	4.84	9.10	8.58	7.80	11.83	9.10	8.84
1956	1.75	1.95	1.82	8.40	5.20	4.68	10.36	7.80	7.54	13.46	9.10	8.84
1957	2.52	1.95	1.82	8.40	5.20	4.68	10.36	7.80	7.54	13.46	9.10	8.84
1958	3.22	1.95	1.82	5.72	4.68	4.42	10.36	7.28	5.72	13.46	9.10	8.84
1959	1.54	1.95	1.82	4.48	3.30	2.60	9.10	5.85	4.84	11.83	10.40	9.88
1960	1.40	1.95	1.82	4.20	4.68	3.64	7.56	6.50	4.84	9.82	10.92	8.44
1961	1.40	1.95	1.82	3.36	4.16	3.64	7.56	6.50	4.84	10.10	10.92	8.44
1962	1.68	1.95	1.82	3.43	4.16	3.64	7.56	6.50	4.84	10.10	10.92	8.32
1963	1.75	1.95	1.82	4.13	4.16	3.64	8.40	6.24	4.84	11.34	10.40	8.32
1964	1.89	2.13	1.95	5.60	3.12	3.90	10.36	5.46	5.46	13.98	8.58	7.80
1965	1.43	2.13	1.94	3.64	3.12	3.12	8.40	5.46	5.20	10.98	8.58	8.58
1966	1.40	2.13	1.94	3.15	3.12	3.12	7.56	5.46	5.20	11.34	8.58	8.58
1967	.98	2.13	1.95	1.26	3.12	3.12	3.76	5.46	5.20	6.00	7.80	8.58
1968	1.02	2.13	1.95	1.17	3.12	2.86	2.88	5.20	5.20	6.00	7.02	6.50
1969	1.08	2.13	1.95	1.47	3.12	2.86	4.26	5.20	5.72	6.00	7.02	6.50
1970	1.14	2.13	1.95	1.50	3.12	2.86	4.44	7.28	6.50	7.00	9.10	8.58
1971	1.15	2.47	2.21	1.10	3.90	2.85	2.40	8.00	6.50	9.00	12.50	10.40
1972	1.30	-	2.21	1.35	-	3.51	1.35	-	8.00	7.80	-	12.00

Data for Table VIII was secured from the prospectus, *Accrued Equities, Inc.*, October 1972.
Accrued Equities derived the tables originally from J.F. Haffenden Ltd., of London.

will bear, a practice fostered by the lack of regularly published prices within the country, outside of imported trade publications. Serious investors should subscribe to at least one trade periodical, most emanating from London. These include:

Harpers Wine & Spirit Gazette
Southback House
Black Prince Road
London SE1, England

Ridley's Wine & Spirit Trade Circular
Wheatsheaf House
Carmelite Street
London ED4, England

Wine & Spirit Trade International
Gillow House
5 Winsley Street
London W1A 2HG, England

Accrued Equities Inc., 122 E 42nd St., N.Y.C. 10017, puts out an irregular market letter detailing recent prices. This is among the oldest and largest of American whiskey brokerage houses, and the first to register its offerings with the S.E.C. Copies of the informative prospectus and samples of the market letter are available to inquirers. Accrued Equities charges 5 per cent purchase and sales commissions, and, from what I hear, has a good all-around reputation. Their prices, based upon my own investigation,have fallen into the lower brackets.

As of this writing, only three brokerages are registered with the S.E.C., Accrued Equities is one. The Scotch Whiskey Investment Co., Walnut Creek, California is a second and Scotch Whiskey Equities, San Diego, California is the third. Look for ads in *Barron's.*

AMONG THE SHADY PRACTICES

The major one has already been cited—overcharging naive customers. This is often accompanied by delivering second rate malt at premium prices, and pushing whatever the company has in inventory—all the while failing to inform customers of cheaper, competitive sources for the same goods. The Securities and Exchange Commission has been attempting to secure regulatory control over the industry, which has been fought by most dealers on the grounds that they are selling a product, not a security. Recently, the S.E.C. did win an important court test.

Charges of selling unregistered securities have been brought against the Strathmore Distillery of Glasgow, Tam O'Shanter of Zug, Switzerland, and Warden Walker World Wide Investment Co., of London. Other charges have been brought against Brigadoon Scotch Distributing Co., Milbank Trading Co., and the Leith-Moor Scotch Whiskey Co.

Strathmore is a good case in point. The company has been offering new grain fillings, worth about $1.15, to unsuspecting takers at $3.00 per gallon. They have, however, been giving refunds upon request. Other companies have been asking $4 and up per o.p.g. for Tomatin, a secondary malt available elsewhere at about $2.80-$3.25.

Still another company may be withholding full title to the whiskey it sells, so that it can continue to use the fillings you've paid for as collateral.

Finally, some outfits will accept almost any size order, even for a few hundred dollars.

They are willing to undergo some complicated paperwork for a sale of a hundred gallons or so, largely because of the huge markups they are receiving. *It is difficult to sell small quantities of whiskey holdings* when the time comes. If you can't put down a minimum of $2,000, forget about whiskey, except for drinking. Accrued Equities will accept no order under $2,400–a policy good for broker and customer alike.

REMEDIES

1) *Make no purchase without comparison shopping several sources.* Secure specifications. If they offer to sell you malt, establish precisely the name of the distiller, and secure competitive quotes. Some outfits will even disclaim knowledge of what precisely they are offering–go elsewhere.

2) It will probably be safer to deal with an S.E.C. registered broker–or at the least, a state licensed dealer.

3) Pay by letter of credit through your bank, payable against your receiving invoices and clear title to your whiskey.

WHISKEY HAS BEEN A GOOD CURRENCY HEDGE

As any commodity, whiskey stands as a hedge against inflation. The spirit is generally purchased and sold in pounds sterling; however, sales can often be executed in dollars. This means that if the dollar weakens in relationship to the pound or vice versa, the investor may have the choice of currency in which to take payment.

TAX TIPS

Profits from the sale of whiskey are treated as capital gains if the whiskey is held for at least six months (highly likely). Whiskey has not been subject to the interest equalization tax, and U.S. citizens living here are not subject to British taxation on whiskey profits. Storage and insurance are considered not expenses but capital expenditures by the Treasury Department. Therefore, no tax deductions until you sell.

Most investors will be exempt from permit fees and dealer taxes. However, if you trade very actively, you may come under a liquor dealer classification. Incidentally, check with your accountant as to whether a jaunt to Scotland to examine your holdings might not be tax deductible.

TAX FREE UPGRADING

Scotch whiskey has been offering one excellent and perfectly legal tax gimmick. Suppose you hold your whiskey from O-age to 12 years and want to dispose of your holdings. If you sell and take cash, you are liable for capital gains taxes. If, instead, you trade in your whiskey for greater quantities of younger whiskey—a like for like trade—you are spared any taxation until you actually close out all or part of your position by accepting cash for your holdings. You can sell part and trade part. You will be taxed only on the portion you sell. By taking advantage of this feature, you may be able to forestall taxation until retirement, at which time your tax bracket will probably drop.

DISADVANTAGES

1) Investment in Scotch whiskey brings in no current income. In fact, it draws from current income additional funds for storage and insurance on an ongoing basis.

2) This is a long term investment only. You have to be prepared for a minimum 12-24 month holding period in order to recapture your costs.

3) Scotch is not a liquid investment. You can't drink the unblended, raw stuff and you may have to wait several weeks to consummate a sale. If you're in a hurry to get out and the market's inactive, you may have to accept a lousy bid.

4) You are competing with professional buyers in a distant market. Almost certainly, you will be dependent upon your broker for full direction.

5) There is no guarantee that consumption of whiskey will continue to increase or that pricing will be advantageous when it suits you to sell.

Against these disadvantages lie a rather consistent growth rate, especially in malt, and the opportunities for a real killing in grain. There has always been considerable interest in whiskey as a form of unusual, sophisticated investment. Currently, 5 to 10 thousand Americans are playing the game. If a 12 per cent return with some favorable tax advantages suits you, whiskey just may become your favorite ballpark.

To tell the truth though, I would rather drink the stuff myself.

Chapter 17

''It's Classy All Right, But This Just May Not Be A Vintage Year''

Investing In Wines

Potential Reward,	A-
Potential Risk,	B-
Liquidity,	B-
Tax Considerations,	B-

A case of 1967 Chateau La Tour could have been purchased for $90 in 1971 and sold for $280 one year later. By 1973, the price had fallen to $200. California's Beaulieu Vineyard's Cabernet Sauvignon Private Reserve, 1951, fetched over $700 per case at the Heublein auction in 1973, nearly triple the 1970 price. Single, yes single, bottles of wine have sold for as high as $11,000, which is, after all, quite a gulp in any language.

Wine has clearly been among the "in" investments of the seventies. Time to hop aboard? Perhaps. However, you just might want to keep the wine cellar stocked with Pepsi Colas for the time being. I, for one, would be cautious. The rise in wine prices has perhaps received too much publicity, attracted too much of a public following and become too speculative for my tastes—but then, of course, my taste for liquor doesn't run at $500 an ounce.

The case for wine rests upon the premise that the amounts of wine available are essentially fixed in quantity, and, of course, diminish in quantity as imbibers, as opposed to investors, sip away potential profits. It is, indeed, certainly true that continuing affluence here and abroad has led to rising consumption, aided and abetted by status seekers who may not know a Cote Rote from Chianti, but who do want the best of labels on their dinner table. It is also true that premium wines cannot be hurried or mass produced and that there is only so much fixed prime wine acreage in the world. It is likewise true that inflationary pressures are bound to maintain an upwards thrust on wine prices, just as they exert an inflationary thrust elsewhere.

On the other hand, how high the moon? And what would be the potential effects of a recession on the luxury liquors? Should the energy crisis continue to unfold in its worst ramifications, an ounce of oil may just end up selling for more than an ounce of La Fite. No less knowledgeable a wine expert than William Sokolin of the well known wine merchant, D. Sokolin Co., believes that a shakeout will develop sometime during 1974 *(The Investing Professional,* February 1973). The firm itself, D. Sokolin, is no longer recommending wine for investment, believing that prices have already leveled off, will continue to do so for the time being, and that resale problems may develop over the next year. Others are less pessimistic, and prices at the fifth National Auction of Rare Wines did total a record $273,000 in Atlanta this year. Of course, if you can't make a successful resale, you can, unlike whiskey, always drink the stuff. Some price reaction, incidentally, has already developed in certain areas. Wines which tripled between 1971-1972, have in many cases already given back fifty per cent of the gains made. The 1973 harvest was heavy and prices for that year have not matched previous excesses. Despite these caveats, however, wine investment has brought in good profits in the past, and, with patience, most investors should stand a better than even chance of coming out ahead in the future. A fifteen per cent return seems attainable on average, with individual windfalls running much higher.

THE BASIC STRATEGY

As with whiskey, the basic ploy involves simply the buying and waiting. Fine wines are not considered drinkable until they are aged; slow aging wines may not reach their prime for as much as a decade after bottling. In the meantime, they must be stored carefully in a cool cellar, away from light, and left undisturbed. Some wine merchants will arrange storage for you—at a price of course. If you have the facilities, you may want to store yourself, but do be prepared for some skepticism at resale time unless you are known in the field, and have established the reliability of your facilities. Storage should take place in an even temperature, preferably between 50-58 degrees. Stability of temperature is vital. If you contemplate self-storage, you may have to plan on an air-conditioned wine cellar. The area should be relatively humid. Improper storage can ruin top quality wines. Wines can also be purchased as futures, in advance of the harvest, for delivery several months later. Recently, these futures have increased in value even before the first grape was crushed.

Wines that improve with age are the best investments. Their supply diminishes over time as bottles are consumed, and their quality receives wide recognition. Bordeaux are usually slow aging wines—Chateau LaFite, Chateau La Tour, Chateau Margaux and Chateau Haut Brion among the finest. Chateau Mouton Rothschild, Cheval Blanc and Petrus are also among the highest ranking. Burgundies such as La Romanee, La Tache and Romanee Conti are highly regarded—indeed, at times you cannot locate a drinkable bottle of the Conti at any price. The prices of these wines have soared to heady heights in recent years, and may have hit the roof already.

D. Sokolin Co. does recommend true vintage ports for potential price appreciation. These include Hoopers (1960, 1963) and Craft (1960-1963). Both have recently doubled in price. Sheldon Wasserman (*The Investing Professional,* June 1973) recommends Chateau Grillet (1970), Hermitage (1969, 1970) and Condrieu (1970) as potential investment candidates. These are Cotes du Rhone Wines, which have not appreciated as rapidly as the Bordeaux and may, therefore, have more room on the upside.

Once you have made your purchase, you can sell your wine at auction, via advertisement, or to a merchant. In the last case, you will receive only wholesale prices. You do, of course, have to abide by local ordinances if you resell wine and may not be legally allowed to do so without a proper license. For this reason, many investors transact their sales overseas, selling at auction in England and Switzerland. You will be liable in that contingency for shipping charges, roughly $6-10 per case. Dealers and wine merchants will handle arrangements for you at negotiated commissions, ranging from 3-10 per cent.

BUY LARGE QUANTITIES AND BE PREPARED TO WAIT

Strangely enough, the larger the quantity of your wine parcel, the better the prices you are likely to receive. Large quantities of high quality wine enjoy the best resale market since they have the potential of becoming dealer inventory. Prices derived from overseas auction are very likely to approximate retail.

As I said before, wine investment is largely a waiting game, although occasional speculative flurries do produce rapid profits. Be prepared for holding periods measured in years rather than months.

WHAT ARE THE GOOD YEARS?

Wines are rated on a basis of 20 points. A rating of 20/20 indicates a perfect wine. 1970 is considered an exceptional year (20/20). 1961, 1962, 1966 and 1971 were all fine years. Avoid the 1968 vintage; it was poor. Even the "grand crus" vineyards faired badly in 1968, so don't be dazzled if you see a 1968 La Fite selling for swizzle wine prices.

TAXES

The only real gimmick possible is donating your holdings to some charity and trying to take a deduction on the total market value. The IRS has, however, been looking askance at such ploys. Just be prepared to pay capital gains taxes. Some investors who sell privately do not record the sale—but, of course, that is not legal.

ANOTHER ANGLE TO WINE

While D. Sokolin Co. is not currently recommending wine as a purchase for investment, they have been promoting investments in wine vineyards, within the United States mainly, and to some extent abroad. There are about 270 wineries operating in California, currently the hot spot in U.S. wine. Land prices have more than quadrupled in some areas as California wines have caught fire on the sipping scene. The California Wine Advisory Board, San Francisco, California, can make arrangements for visits to wineries.

Also, inquiries can be made to D. Sokolin Co., 178 Madison Ave., N.Y.C. 10016. This year, they sponsored a wine tasting tour of France, for afficionados.

Vineyards offer no particular tax incentive. The land itself is non-depreciable; however, development and interest costs are deductible.

TO REFINE YOUR PALATE

Newcomers to the wine scene may want to read:

The First Book of Wine by Alexis Bespaloff, World Publishing, New York, $7.95.

Encyclopedia of Wine and Spirits by Alexis Lichine, Alfred A. Knopf, New York, $15.

Wines of France by Alexis Lichine, Alfred A. Knopf, New York, $8.95.

The Fine Wines of California by Hurst Hannum and Robert S. Blumberg, Doubleday, Garden City, N.Y., $5.95.

Interested readers might also want to contact wine merchants such as Morrell, Sherry-Lehmann and Sokolin in New York City for specific advice and suggestions regarding potential purchases. These are all legitimate and highly regarded dealers.

SUMMING UP

Wine investment has reaped some sweet tasting profits in recent years, but a sour grape is due any day now. As a form of investment it's classy all right—but this just may not be a vintage year.

Chapter 18

"Collecting Can Be Profitable, If...."

Investing In Collectibles

Potential Reward,	A-C (Some collectibles have moved nicely over the years, some not at all.)
Risk,	B-
Liquidity,	C
Tax Considerations,	C

In early 1973, Norton Simon, wealthy industrialist and collector, put ten paintings from his private collection up for auction at Parke-Benet. "Vase de Tulipes" by Cezanne went for a cool $1.4 million. A Gericault, purchased by Mr. Simon for only $20,000 ten years previous, went for $160,000. A Pisarro, selling for $150,000, produced a 67 per cent profit for its owner that evening, after a five year holding period.

In 1940, Frederick Small, an Australian engineer, purchased the famous British Guiana One-Cent Postage Stamp for a price of $42,000. It was sold in 1970 to a partnership for $280,000. The purchasers now place a value of at least one-half million dollars on the stamp.

An American half-dollar was purchased for $9,500 in 1962, sold for near $20,000 in 1965 and is now offered at $75,000.

A ten cent *Batman* comic (1940) has been bringing in $150, while a first edition *Superman* draws over $300.

Not to mention the fabulous profits secured by salting away firearms, scrimshaw, antique cameras, autographs, post cards, old books, diamonds, campaign buttons, armor, bottles, Indian craft, porcelain, stock certificates, movie magazines, silverware, old clocks and, in a different time–Dutch tulips.

It certainly does sound easy, doesn't it? Certainly. If you're not last on line, that is.

There have, indeed, been fabulous profits in collectibles–for those knowledgeable or lucky enough to accumulate the right things at the right time. But have you tried selling your pop art lately? Michael Laurence, in his delightful book, *Playboy's Investment Guide* (Playboy Press, 1971), casts a somewhat jaundiced eye at collecting for cash. Commenting on the often illusory profit potential in collectibles, Mr. Laurence noted that the price increase in the British Guiana between 1940-1970 represented only a five per cent annual compounded growth of the original investment. (According to my calculator, he's wrong. I work it out to a huge 6.5 per cent growth rate *excluding* auctioneering expenses, and insurance costs over the years). The Pisarro produced a 10.3 per cent compounded appreciation for Mr. Simon, *before* expenses. The moral is simple: profits are not always what they seem.

Against the well-publicized record prices brought in for unique pieces at high quality auctions, the typical investor has to consider the odds for and against his picking those items that will appreciate, whether there will indeed be a ready market for his collection when it comes time to sell, and the value of the time required for painstakingly ferreting out finds in farmhouse attics.

The fact, plain and simple, is that while collectors of collectibles frequently do show profits, investors in collectibles frequently do not. True, collectors acquire an intimate and detailed knowledge of their specialty. Searching, hunting, bargaining and restoration are part of the game–they know what's worthwhile, enjoy the hunt, and recognize a true find when they see one. Profit is incidental to the interest, and, because of that, more likely. The investor, by contrast, typically becomes attracted to art, antiques or stamps only *after* widely publicized price gains have aroused his interest and because of that, is all too often last on line. The stock market public isn't the only group that buys in at the top.

Commenting on the 70 per cent rise in turnover shown at Christie's this year, Souren Melikian (*International Herald-Tribune,* August 11, 1973) observed that a 15 to 20 per cent appreciation in art prices may result in an increase in turnover by 50 to 60 per cent. In short, high prices bring out the sellers, selling to buyers who, in turn, hope to find ready buyers from them at higher prices next season. Somewhere, the plug gets pulled. Even Norton Simon couldn't see all his old masters at Sotheby's last June.

All this is by way of warning. If you have a special interest, hobby, avocation, love of antiquity, itch for stamps—great. Enjoy yourself, and, with some luck, you'll make money too. If, however, you're thinking of entering the collecting game as a pure investor, think again. If you still want in, be leery of joinıng any crowd stampede or fad and do apply contrary opinion. Try to anticipate rather than follow the crowd, and be certain that you do your homework.

THE BIG WINNERS—AND SOME LOSERS

It's not as easy to keep score in the collectible game as it is on the New York Stock Exchange. Figures for price appreciation generally reflect only the highest grade merchandise auctioned at the finest houses. Private sales may or may not be recorded, and certainly the bulk of exchange goes unnoticed. Nonetheless, Sotheby's of London estimates that various forms of paintings and drawings have appreciated between 700 and 2200 per cent over the past twenty odd years. This applied to internationally collected work only, not to $20 graphics sold through the mails as "investment".

In the little leagues, price appreciation for memorablia, lesser grade antiquities, comics and such, are not as well publicized nor as well documented. Popular collector comics—the scarcest—may have risen by 300-500 per cent over the past five to ten years. Nostalgia's been "in" lately. Certain early model Leicas, 1924-1925 vintage, have shown similar gains. Gold coins have been consistent winners. Recently, at least until 1973, wines have been getting a big play. A handful of stamps, particularly from the Ryukyu Islands, have moved well. We'll look at some of these more specifically later on.

Barron's have been presenting, at the beginning of each year, an assessment of the investment scene, compiled by Dr. Franz Pick, who metes out his judgments based, as usual, upon the selling prices at major auctions. The following are the winners and losers, 1970-1973, according to Dr. Pick:

1970

Winners		Losers	
Tankers	+75%	Cheaper and Medium Grade Art	
Numismatic Coins	+60%	Old Masters	no change
Art Nouveau	+40%	Antique Porcelain	- 10%
High Quality Drawings	+40%	Set Diamonds	- 25%
American Paintings	+40%	Gold Coins	- 7%
Chinese Art	+40%		
Old Weapons	+35%		
Top Quality Old Books	+30%		
French Impressionists	+30%		
Sculpture	+25%		
Silver Items	+25%		
Rare Stamps	+20%		
Antique Furniture	+20%		
Etchings	+20%		
Clocks and Watches	+15%		
Snuffboxes	+10%		

1971

Winners		Losers	
Race Horses	+50-60%	American Paintings	- 11%
Numismatic Coins	+80%	Silver Objects	- 15%
18th Century French Furniture	+40%	Firearms	- 15%
Snuffboxes	+35%	French Impressionists	- 15-20%
Etchings and Drawings	+30%	Books and Manuscripts	- 15-20%
Chinese Art	+25-30%	Set Diamonds	- 10-12%
Sculpture	+25%		
Modern Paintings	+20-25%		
Old Masters	+20-22%		
Clocks and Watches	+20%		

1972

Winners		Losers	
Numismatic Coins	+225%	French Furniture	- 5%
Firearms	+175%	Drawings	- 15%
Etchings	+ 75%	Old Masters	- 20%
Porcelain	+ 65%	Books and Manuscripts	- 30-35%
Chinese Art	+ 50%	Art Nouveau	- 30-35%
Tapestries and Carpets	+ 45%		
Antique Art	+ 40%		
Violins	+ 30-35%		
American Furniture	+ 30%		
Vintage Wine	+ 30%		
Postage Stamps	+ 30%		
French Impressionists	+ 25%		
American Paintings	+ 25%		
Modern Paintings	+ 25-30%		
Silver	+ 48%		
Gold Bullion	+ 42%		

1973

Winners		Losers	
Etchings	+400%	Firearms	- 20%
Surrealists		Violins	- 25%
Drawings and Pastels		Wines	- 25%
Stamps		French Furniture	- 46%
Clocks and Watches		American Furniture	- 50%
Porcelain		Old Masters	- 50%
Post Impressionists	+ 90%		
Books and Manuscripts	+ 95%		
Antique Art	+ 90%		
Chinese Art	+ 75%		
Gold	+ 63%		

continued on next page.

1973 (continued)	
Silver	+57%
Gold Coins	+90%
Silver Coins	+36%
Collector Automobiles	+50%
Numismatic Coins	+46%
Sculpture	+37%
Diamonds	+24%
Art Nouveau	+10%
Snuffboxes	+10%

Tables abstracted from articles by Dr. Franz Pick in *Barron's,* January 4, 1971, January 3, 1972, January 1, 1973, and December 31, 1973.

Numismatic coins stand out as the consistent performer of the seventies, thus far. Chinese art has been strong, aided and abetted, no doubt, by Mr. Nixon's detente with Mao. Diamonds have generally been weak. One might, of course, raise question as to whether a few outstanding items, brought to auction each year, are representative of a whole class of collectibles. After all, how many of us can plunk down $530,000 for a Degas, not to mention $4 million for a Titian? Or even $19,000 for a Queen Victoria gold coin—90% increases in value between 1970-1971 notwithstanding?(At that rate, the coin will be worth over $6.1 million by 1980).

These numbers, of course, must give pause. The price increases that have pertained recently are simply not sustainable. Etchings are listed as rising 75 per cent during 1972. A set of Picasso etchings sold for $225,000 during 1972. Compound that at 75 per cent and we get a value of over $19 million for the set by 1980, and nearly $325 million by 1985. Now, I can see a set of rare etchings selling for $225,000, but for *$325 million!* Not unless the dollar goes the way of the old German mark.

SOME GUIDELINES

1973 has seen some sharp increases again, in etchings and surrealistic art. These are relatively easy items to date and regarding which authenticity can be readily verified. By contrast, forgeries abound in autographs and ancient coins. Archeological objects, difficult to authenticate, have not appreciated at all commensurate with their rarity.

As a general rule, whether you are purchasing a Botticelli or a Batman, secure the very best conditioned example possible. Damaged specimens do not hold nearly the collector interest of fine conditioned items.

The real test of the collector-investor is the ability to foresee and to act upon trends generated by events outside the collector market itself. I've already noted how Nixon's exploits in China reawakened American interest in items Oriental. Could an astute collector have anticipated this? Silver bullion weakened in price during 1971. Was it coincidence that 1971 was a poor year for antique silver objects, although collectors were hardly planning to melt down antiquities to regain the silver content within. The Revolutionary Bi-Centennial is coming up in 1976, and already the American collector market is showing particular interest in anything connected to the Revolutionary Period. The affluence developing in Japan in recent years might have alerted collectors to the Japanese interest in and, more important, capability of bidding heavily for antiquities originating in, but since sold out of, their own country.

Far from Sotheby's, perhaps, but more within popular reach, nostalgia has pushed up items from the thirties greatly. Not just Superman. Old movie posters, toys, Mickey Mouse watches, gum machines, movie magazines, table radios—all have appreciated nicely, prices starting well under $100. The styles of the fifties are coming back this year. How about old records, books, baseball cards and cameras from the period—anything that evokes remembrances of childhood past? There are links between collectibles and current history—witness the sharp increase in value in McGovern-Eagleton campaign buttons. Rumor has it that the stock exchanges will soon be eliminating stock certificates; ownership of corporations will be recorded by computer. Would such a development enhance the already growing collector market for old certificates? What happened to the collectability of old tea and tobacco tins when the country went plastic?

GENERAL CAVEATS

Investments in collectibles have to be considered long term holdings, and bring in no current income while investors wait. Sometimes, a workout takes years. Therefore, it is all the more important for the collector-investor to maintain a genuine interest in his art, stamps, or what have you. Miros, Picassos and Roualts are pleasant on the wall—if they are to your taste—and in that case the wait will not hurt. After all, art investments can and do bring in intangible returns each day other than money. Postage stamps can be fascinating. Fine furniture can be a true delight in the home. But only if you approach these items with the right attitude—they are artworks and hobbies first, investments afterward.

Nor is liquidity in any way assured, except at sizeable price discount. Should you pick up a piece at auction, you know that you secured it only because you outbid the crowd, and were ready to pay more for the piece than the rest of the competing public. To whom could you sell at that point? Dealers work on a close to 100 per cent markup. Placed at auction, your sale will cost you in the area of 20 per cent in auction commissions. If you offer your piece for auction, with a minimum price, you pay a fee even if the article is not sold. A private offering is a possibility to secure better than dealer price, but you are out the costs of classifieds, and there are still no guarantees of sale.

The major secret to profit lies in the buying, although by now every small-town Vermont homeowner knows what his old spinning wheel will bring in in New York City. Still, private purchase remains the best avenue for bargain hunting, and, at the least, you and the seller will probably arrive at a price somewhere between dealer wholesale and Madison Avenue retail. Occasionally, some fine opportunities do come along. One Long Island couple does collect—but not invest in—antiques. The couple recently picked up a 16th century Italian refectory table at a private house sale for $750. Before it was even delivered, they were offered $1,000. This has been the exception—not the rule—and the table was purchased only because the family liked that particular table and wanted to live with it.

Hobby buffs may do considerable buying, selling and swapping at hobby fairs, shows and conventions. The markets for items such as old comics, photographica, buttons and post cards are less formal than the market for fine antiques. Transactions are often completed through the mail and advertising costs are low. But again, such transactions may have more appeal for the true collector, who enjoys his jaunt to the convention, and does not necessarily expect to profit.

Which raises another issue. True collectors rarely collect for profit. Sales of their collectibles are usually undertaken with an eye to reinvesting the proceeds to upgrade their collections, in which case they are paying for the price appreciation that takes place as well as profiting by it. It is the rare true collector who suddenly stops adding to his collection. In that sense, again, some of the profit is illusory—you are selling inflated goods to purchase other inflated goods. There are, on the other hand, astute hobbyists who do carefully accumulate collectibles with the plan of ultimate resale, using proceeds from this portion of their activity to finance their personal collections, which may or may not ever be put up for sale. There is one big "but", however. These people know their specialty. It will usually pay for the collector-investor to specialize, to become familiar with one area, to know it well, and to be able to rely upon himself rather than upon any dealer.

TAX CONSIDERATIONS

Collectors, for the most part, get a lousy deal from Uncle Sam. A collector is defined as someone who holds the collectible object—art, antique or otherwise—primarily for his own use and enjoyment. As such, the collector is liable for capital gains profits on collectibles sold for a gain (if he declares), but cannot deduct losses on sales, insurance and storage costs, or incidental expenses. An established investor, on the other hand, can deduct capital losses as well as various costs of ownership. It is not easy to establish an investor position with the Internal Revenue Service, but you may have a chance if you can demonstrate that your accumulation of collectibles has brought in steady profit, that you have substantial expertise and that your holdings represent a reasonable portion of your total worth. Do check this out with your accountant.

Be careful though that you do not go so far that they consider you a dealer. A dealer's major involvement is in the purchase of collectibles for the express purpose of resale to customers. He receives the deductions granted the investor, but profits are taxed at ordinary rates, no matter how long the holding period. The investor and collector receive capital gains treatment if they hold longer than six months.

Before the Tax Reform Act of 1969, various games were possible involving contributions of art objects to charities. Many of these loopholes have been closed. One good deal, currently available, involves a gift to a tax-exempt institution, say a museum, which will display and not resell the object. In that event, you get to deduct the full market value of the gift.

We'll be going on in the next chapters to discuss a number of collectible arenas in more detail. *Summing Up:* Collecting Can Be Profitable, If . . . .

Chapter 19

"What's To Say That You Won't Pick Up The Next Upside-Down Airmail That Comes Along?"

An Overview Of Collectibles

It goes without saying that even if I could write the definitive book on collectibles, I could not by any means do it within 30 pages. Therefore, treat these chapters only as an introduction—an introduction to several fascinating areas for study and investment. If something catches your interest, all the better. Pursue the matter with the resource material provided in Chapter 20 by investigating dealers, museums, and auction houses, and when you feel ready, begin serious collecting.

Nor can I cover, even briefly, all the avenues for collecting. There are literally thousands, ranging from the most obscure bottle caps, to the hobby of millions, stamp collecting. Still, do consider some of the hoards garnered by past hoarders and see if you can catch the next trend.

AMERICAN COLLECTIBLES

Until recently, American art was the stepchild to Matisse, Cezanne and Pisarro—not to mention Rembrandt, Titian and Raphael. Sotheby's, for a time, didn't even bother to construct a price index for U.S. art, since European collectors had little interest in the "colonies". However, an important auction at Parke-Benet in 1969 pinpointed the start of a new ball game in American art, confirming the reversal of the downtrend in American masters that had prevailed throughout the early fifties. In 1970, Benjamin West's *Portrait of John Eardly Wilmot* brought in a record $86,400 at Sotheby's, broken later that year when Thomas Eakin's *Cowboys in the Badlands* was knocked down at Parke-Benet for $210,000. This was matched a year later by John Singleton Copley's *Portrait of General Thomas Gage.*

All records for American masters were eclipsed in October 1972, when *Steelworkers-Noontime,* a realistic work by the heretofore relatively obscure artist, Thomas Anshutz, brought in $250,000 to Dr. Irving F. Burton, a physician-collector. A Burchfield, at the same auction, fetched $65,000 (a record for the artist), and a new world's record for an American watercolor. Paintings by such American masters as Charles Marion Russell, Gilbert Stuart, John Singleton Copley and Charles Wilson Peale now command prices into the six figures. Even these numbers paled into insignificance this year when a Jackson Pollack fetched over $2 million!

Works of 19th century American artists are still reasonably priced by collector standards, and, of course, there is a very fertile, if highly speculative, market in contemporary works and prints. In recent years, works by 19th century New York artists, painting the Hudson River and environs, have appreciated greatly. Among the group of such artists are Thomas Cole, Sanford Gifford, Worthing Whittredge and Caleb Bingham. If you happen around Tarrytown, look around. Works by lesser artists may begin to soar as the better known masters become exhausted.

Recent auctions have also seen the emergence of 20th century American art. The sale of the Edith G. Halpert collection brought in $3.7 million at Sotheby Parke-Benet, top price of $220,000 going for *Little Joe With Cow* by Yasuo Kuniyoski. Works by Georgia O'Keefe, Elie Nadelman, Lyonel Feininger, Stuart Davis, John Marin and Ben Shahn all sold well above expectation. Graphics by some of the above are available at reachable prices.

American contemporary graphics have been offered in sometimes massive editions, billed as collector investments. These are, for the most part, of dubious quality although obviously some have worked out well for investors. If you do want to try your hand in graphics, be certain to authenticate the signature and stick to limited editions by established artists.

Be aware that should you resell to a dealer, you may have to accept less than 50 per cent of retail value, and that at auction, you are liable for auctioneering costs. Employ the services of a reliable dealer to authenticate any major purchase.

American art has been underpriced in relation to European work. The price discrepancy should narrow, American pricing supported here by the coming bicentennial. This could prove to be an excellent time to get in.

Still with objects Americana, fortunes have been made by early collectors of the Queen

Anne and Chippendale furniture, but many experts believe that prices may be topping in these areas. Certainly, prices for these popular American periods have begun to match their European contemporaries. $100,000 and better are being commanded for the best pieces. Queen Anne is pre-revolutionary. Many experts are suggesting that investors move at this time into the Federal period (1780-1820), prices from which are considerably more reasonable than pre-Revolutionary work. Federal prices start at near $100 for decent quality small pieces of furniture. Empire furniture may show fine gains also in the coming years. As usual, try to purchase items in good condition only; they're the only pieces likely to appreciate. And also as usual, beware of reproductions and fakes.

Moving down the list, collectors of Americana have had a field day in any number of areas. The Civil War has its buffs. Swords, belt buckles (marked U.S. or C.S.A.), bayonets, enlistment and other papers are all in high demand. Should you encounter one, grab those old wooden canteens; they're becoming quite scarce. Political campaign buttons have been gaining in popularity too. If you should chance on some in your travels, and can secure them reasonably, stock up on political items regarding George McClellan (1864), Horace Greeley, Samuel Tilden, Eugene V. Debs and, of course, Senator Eagleton.

Old postcards are fast becoming collector chic. There are an estimated 50,000 collectors in the country now. Arthur Capper Co. put out a set of artistic cards, now quite collectible, and linen post cards (1930-1940) are bringing in profits to lucky holders. Look for nostalgia items and complete sets. (More information can be gathered from the Metropolitan Post Card Collectors Club, 140 E. 8th St., New York City).

Posters, World War I vintage, are likewise catching on, not to mention earlier examples, for instance, of the art nouveau genre. These display nicely with contemporary memorablia such as early ice boxes, games, toys and even old barber's chairs. Pre-twentieth century posters, and nostalgia items from the thirties (old coke trays, confectionary signs, etc.) have become quite popular and remain relatively inexpensive (but rising fast) on the usual antique circuits. Prices have skyrocketed in recent years. Again, condition is vital.

Old books and magazines have been drawing buyers' eyes, and dollars, at the antique and flea market shows. No, not the rare manuscripts. That's for the high priced trade. Nostalgia items, such as old editions of the Saturday Evening Post, have doubled over the past few years. Early comics have already been mentioned. But do you remember those Big Little Books, circa 1933-1949, chunky little volumes with large print and cardboard covers? Flash Gordon, Tarzan and Buck Rogers are the favorites among collectors, followed by Dick Tracy, The Phantom and Mandrake the Magician. Funny characters are by no means as popular.

Among the magazines, first issues have been rising in price. Early *Playboys* range from $100 (first issue) down. Vintage *TV Guides* and movie magazines are commanding fat premiums over their original cost. Even old *Life* magazines have been up, despite huge printing runs, although future gains are doubtful; the quantity printed was just too great. Shirley Temple is very in. *National Geographics* are out. For an interesting reason. The *Geographics* were well bound and printed and regarded as a publication to keep by their owners. Hence, no shortage ever existed since countless copies have been found in old attics. Your best bet in collecting old publications is to stick to nostalgia appeal. If you find yourself smiling as you remember when, you've probably picked a winner.

Early sound-track albums have been giving old Carusos a run for their money. These include original sound track albums of movies such as *Gone With The Wind, Spartacus, Forever Amber* and *Quo Vadis.* You can pay up to $100 a record, unless you chance upon a well-stocked musical attic or second hand record store. Incidentally, *The Capitalist Reporter* (150 Fifth Ave., New York, N.Y. 10011) regularly features articles relating to memorablia and nostalgia items.

We could go on at great length. Bottles, insulators, watches, electric trains, toys, banks—all are collectible nostalgia items, fun to own, and available to all. Ron Hollander, writing in the August 1972 issue of the *Capitalist Reporter,* suggested the following items as excellent nostalgia bets:

- Coke Signs
- Coke Trays
- Penny Arcade Machines
- Coin Operated Flip Card Peep Shows
- Beatle Albums
- Memorablia of Singers of the 50's
- Old Life Magazines
- "Peanuts" memorablia
- Patriotic Items
- Cast Iron and Tin Toys
- Zeppelin Toys
- Old Radio Giveaways (Tom Mix, Jack Armstrong, The Lone Ranger, etc.)
- Tobacco and Cookie Tins
- Movie Posters
- Memorablia of the Moon Landing

Chippendale, these items are not. Still, a Mickey Mouse watch that sold for $1.29 in 1935, now goes for $300, and Howdy Doody timepieces have jumped by 3,000 per cent over the past dozen years or so. Risks? The usual: liquidity, changing fashion, markets that peak, forgeries, etc. Nonetheless, nostalgia certainly has been a cure for inflation over the years, and you do not have to become an expert to accumulate *Famous Funnies.*

AUTOGRAPHS

The Bicentennial has added an extra flourish to the signature of John Hancock, and for that matter, almost everyone connected with the American Revolution. Letters by George Washington now sell regularly in the area of $3,000, up more than 1,000 per cent in the last decade alone, while certain other letters by our first president have commanded prices of over $25,000. Charles Hamilton, of the Charles Hamilton Galleries, Inc., expects these to double again over the next few years, (*The Professional Investor,* February, 1973). Estimates place the appreciation for fine autographs at anywhere up to 2,500 per cent over the past 10-15 years, and certainly autographs appear "in" now as a collector's item.

For an autograph to have any value, it should consist of a letter, document, or manuscript including, preferably, a legible signature. However, 450 odd pages of Albert Einstein's notes were recently auctioned for $12,500—mainly unfinished jottings. On the other hand, signatures alone have relatively little value. For example, a George Washington signature alone is worth only a few hundred dollars.

Presidential letters have always been favorite collector items, but be leery of letters attributed to recent presidents which were, in fact, signed by an Autopen, a machine that duplicates signatures in pen and ink. As a result of such devices, legitimate signatures of contemporary presidents bode to become quite valuable in the years ahead.

Scarce items? Christopher Marlowe, William The Conqueror, Chaucer, Edgar Allan Poe and William Shakespeare. Revolutionary War generals should be appreciating, as well as such scientific luminaries as Sigmund Freud and Louis Pasteur. Signed photographs of theatrical personalities—Lillian Gish, Sarah Bernhardt, Charlie Chaplin—have been bringing in between $50-$80 per specimen.

SOME WORDS OF CAUTION

Autograph collecting has traditionally been the ballpark for forgery and other misrepresentation. There are a number of well-known, reliable dealers who sell directly or at auction, and who will provide with your purchase a pedigree authenticating the history of the autograph. These dealers also issue catalogues and price lists, sometimes free, sometimes at a slight fee. Among the better known dealers are:

Charles Hamilton Galleries, Inc.
25 East 77th St.
New York, N.Y. 10021

Bruce Gimelson, Autographs
96 S. Limekiln Pike
Chalfont, Pa. 18914

Walter R. Benjamin
Autographs, Inc.
790 Madison Ave.
New York, N.Y. 10021

The first of these, Charles Hamilton, has been conducting regular auction sales at the Waldorf-Astoria Hotel in New York City.

Needless to say, price appreciation of the current order will not continue forever. For example, should those $3,500 George Washington autographs continue to double every 4 years, by the year 2005, they will be worth approximately $1 million. And that's a lot of money for a sheet of paper no matter how you look at it.

STAMPS

Stamp collecting is probably the world's most popular hobby, but unfortunately is one of the most misunderstood from an investment viewpoint. The value of the majority of stamps increases little, if at all, and barely enough to cover the cost of inflation. If you stake your son to an album and "sampler" of stamps, do not expect any price appreciation whatsoever.

Most stamps are available retail at from 60 to 75 per cent of catalogue value, for even less in many instances. Couple that to dealer markup and the very limited resale value of any but the best quality merchandise—well, you get the picture.

Still, stamp collecting can prove profitable as well as fun if you stick to a few basic rules:

1) Concentrate on stamps of known quality and popularity. Expensive stamps are likely to become more expensive; cheap stamps will stay cheap.

2) Collect only stamps in fine condition. Avoid tears, heavy postmarks and creased stamps.

3) Specialize. Become familiar with one or two particular areas. A watermark or a minute line here and there can spell the difference between a rare find and a common stamp.

4) Try to purchase wholesale. See if you can acquire whole collections rather than make retail purchases, stamp by stamp. If necessary, advertise yourself in stamp collecting periodicals.

5) Be patient. Like wines, stamps improve with age.

6) Mount your stamps carefully. Unused stamps should not be hinged. A premium is often paid for fully gummed stamps, in mint condition.

POTENTIAL WINNERS

Collector-investors generally specialize in the one area or the other–selecting stamps either by topic, country, period or historical interest. Animal stamps are popular; so are stamps dealing with space, art, ships and flowers. Recently, in the United States, considerable interest has come to center on zeppelin stamps and early air-mail editions–possibly an offshoot of the memorablia craze now sweeping the country.

All else equal, concentrate on accumulating stamps having the fewest number in the original issue. The Scott Catalogue provides this information for U.S. stamps. The smaller the amount originally issued, the more valuable the stamp, is not an infallible rule; however, as a rule of thumb, it is applicable. Printing errors, particularly in small numbers, can become almost priceless. In 1918, the United States printed a number of the famous 24¢ carmine air-mail stamps with the airplane design inverted. One collector purchased a sheet at 24 cents per stamp. These stamps are now worth $35,000 apiece!

Stamps from the Ryukyu Islands (Okinawa) have been appreciating very rapidly. Only 259 were issued between 1948-1972. The Islands have since reverted from American occupation to Japanese control. Japanese and American collectors prize these stamps, which were issued in limited numbers. The complete set should prove an excellent investment in the years to come.

Among the United States stamps, the Graf Zeppelin set, three stamps, face values 65¢, $1.30 and $2.60, issued in 1930, looks like a winner. A good mint set now sells for about $600 and has been rising in price steadily. The 1893 Columbian set is another candidate for appreciation. Incidentally, a top plate block number of six Graf Zeppelin stamps sold for $6,500 at auction recently. A cheaper find may be the 1960 10¢ air-mail, Scott #C57. Current value around $6.50 per plate block and rising rapidly.

Investors are advised to secure plate blocks or complete coils of high priced stamps as they are issued. Younger and less prosperous collectors do not generally have the finances to purchase $100 of a new $1.00 issue, so these do not find their way into collector hands in large quantities.

Therefore, complete sheets rapidly increase in value when the issue is no longer produced. As an investor, you can, in future years, offer your sheets for sale as a unit, or individually, stamp by stamp. You must, however, be willing and able to hold these stamps for some period of time. Upon a premature forced liquidation, you may have to take less than face value of the stamps.

Many European stamps sell for less in this country than in Europe and consequently are finding their way back home as European dealers shop here for resale in the local market. Vatican air-mail stamps, pre-World War II Austrians, post-war Germany stamps (1945-1955), and away from Europe, the Phillipine occupation stamps, are rising in value. Remember, concentrate on condition. If the stamp is used, it should have only a light postmark. The borders should be even all around. Avoid those attractive stamps issued by Communist bloc countries. These are often put out strictly for the cheap export collector market. Some of the cancellations are not even genuine, but placed on the stamp simply to establish legitimacy. Stamps from Poland, Hungary and Czechoslovakia frequently appear in 1,000 stamp samplers, selling for $1-5 per thousand, and worth not one penny more. In general, stamps pre-1955 will be your best bet; even better are likely to be stamps issued previous to World War II. Early air-mails have been achieving popularity on a worldwide basis, here and abroad.

THE SCOTT CATALOGUE

A must for the stamp collector is the Scott catalogue, which serves as the standard pricing guide for collectors. This catalogue is available from the Scott Publishing Co., 10102 F Street, Omaha, Nebraska 68127. The catalogue provides information regarding the identification of stamps, identifying photographs, used and unused prices, and the amount minted of U.S. stamps. United States stamps comprise one volume, the rest of the world, three. See Chapter 20 for other references.

SUMMING UP

You may make some money by a lucky find and/or by staying with high grade merchandise. The run of the mill stamp is likely to do nothing more than match the rate of inflation.

COINS

Collector coins have been among the very best of collectible investments. Sample gains:

	Price, 1958	Price, 1973	Per Cent Gain
1921 Peace Type Silver Dollar	$ 9.50	$ 75.00	+ 689.5%
1926 S Peace Type Silver Dollar	3.00	20.00	+ 566.7
1877 S Trade Dollar	14.00	200.00	+1328.6
1899 Quarter Eagle	16.50	110.00	+ 566.7
1849 Large Date Half Cent	20.00	150.00	+ 650.0

The key to collecting coins is to secure the highest quality coins you can afford. You should concentrate on uncirculated coins or very fine coins at the very least. For example, while the uncirculated 1921 Peace Type Silver Dollar advanced from $9.50 to $75.00 for a 689.5% gain, the very fine coins, same type, gained only 500% (only?). Uncirculated coins are scarcer and their supply diminishes more rapidly than circulated items.

I suggest that readers make their selections through coin brokers rather than through coin dealers. Dealers are set up to handle coins on a retail basis, and in so doing, they have to secure a markup on their goods, while also having an interest in recommending their own merchandise. Brokers operate on commission, perhaps at about 5% on buys and sells, and can often secure wholesale prices for you. This is not meant to impugn dealers as a group—some are excellent, but if a preference has to be made, I would choose working with a broker.

If you do not know any in your area, I suggest:

John Kamin
19623 Ventura Blvd.
Tarzana, California 91356

Another alternative is to sell at coin auction. At auction, you can expect to receive about 75% of current retail price.

Current Recommendations: As of this writing, the following coins appear to be good investment buys:

O-Mint $10 Liberty gold pieces (eagles) . . .$135 (extra fine), $195 (uncirculated)
D-Mint 1906 and 1907 eagles . . .$95 (extra fine), $120 (uncirculated)
1960 proof sets . . .$4.50
D-Mint 1907 half eagles . . .$80

PROFITS IN YOUR POCKET

Did you know that many "common" coins are worth over face value? Check your change daily. Any U.S. cents with the wheat stalks on the back are worth not one, but one and one-half cents to dealers. Dated prior to 1939, they are worth at least 2¢ per. Buffalo nickels, dated prior to 1930, bring in $4.50 per 40 nickel roll. Walking Liberty half-dollars, 20 to a roll, are worth $22 per roll after 1940, about $23 dated prior to 1940. Any and all U.S. silver dollars are now worth $3.70 apiece.

WHAT TO EXPECT

Collector coin prices have, again, risen steadily over the past decades. Investors can expect, based on past performance, returns in the area of at least 12-25% on common coins, as much as 50% or better on the better grade items. For example, circulated Indianhead pennies, 1891-1909, have produced annualized rates of return since 1956 ranging between 23% and 67%. While it is questionable whether these gains can be sustained in the future, it does appear likely that, barring serious recession, the price of coins has no place to go but up.

THE RED BOOK

The "Red Book", *A Guide Book of United States Coins* by R.S. Yeoman, Western Publishing Co., Inc., Racine, Wisconsin is to coins what the Scott Catalogue is to stamps. Very inexpensive (about $2.50 at coin shops) it provides the catalogue value and amounts of mintage of collector coins. The lower the mintage, the more potentially valuable the coin. In addition, the Red Book provides a good deal of information relating to the history and identification of coins.

CAVEATS

The most prevalent form of chicanery in coin dealing is the passing off of lower grade coins (e.g., fine) as higher quality (e.g., very fine) to unsophisticated investors. If you deal with a broker, be certain that he makes at least some attempt to protect your interests. Otherwise, make purchases only if they can be contingent upon your having a third party verify the condition of the coins. Incidentally, coin collections are prime objects for theft—by burglars or simply by a neighbor's child who may be attracted to money lying about.

Keep your coins in a safe place, preferably a vault. Ancient coins are for experts only; counterfeits have been rampant.

SUMMING UP

Coins are probably the best of the collectibles. You can start inexpensively, storage is no problem, the variety is sufficiently limited to allow you to develop some expertise in the area, and the price history has been better than excellent.

ANTIQUE PHOTOGRAPHICA

One up and coming group of collectibles is the whole arena of antique photographica, prints and equipment. The price market in this field is rather chaotic since many items are something of one of a kind and there is no central vehicle for recording prices of transactions for many items. Still, prices have been rising and the future outlook appears favorable. I can, however, offer no estimate of future profitability.

WHAT TO COLLECT

As usual, accumulate the best you can afford. The best of the antique cameras are the daguerreotype cameras, circa 1840-1860. Specimens run to several thousand dollars. Detective cameras, vintage 1880-1900, have been coming into collector favor as well. These can be obtained for $50 and up, although good quality items run into several hundred dollars. Old string-cocking Kodaks are becoming quite scarce and the folding model Kodaks from the 1920's have tripled in value over the past few years.

Among more recent vintage cameras, Leicas have been the camera of choice for collectors and have retained their value to a far greater degree than any other camera. Nikons, the S and S-2, are appreciating as well. *Suggestions:* The Contax II and IIA and the Kodak Retina IIIC show strong potential. Prices are in the $100 range.

Look for cameras in good working order and with the finish as unmarred as possible. Do not trade in or throw away your old camera. Sooner or later there may be a collector's market for it.

In general, cameras that embody a major technological advance are your best bets. These include the Kodak Six-20, the first fully automatic still camera (now about $300), early Leicas, and the various innovative cameras of the 19th century.

Prints of photographic masters have recently assumed collector importance. If you like to hang fine photography, consider the accumulation of prints by Frederick Evans, Matthew Brady, Julia Margaret Cameron (doubled in price over the last five years), Bellocq, Weston, Walker Evans, Henri Cartier-Bresson, Ansel Adams and Eugene Atget. Original prints of collector quality can be purchased from the New York City Museum of Modern Art's Lending Library, 53rd St. and Fifth Ave., New York, N.Y. as well as from any number of galleries throughout the country specializing in this area.

WHERE TO BUY EQUIPMENT

Olden Camera and Lens Co., 1265 Broadway, New York, N.Y. 10001 has a fine selection of antique and more modern collectible cameras ranging from $25 up.

Shutterbug Ads, P.O. Box 730, Titusville, Florida 32780, provides monthly listings of collectible equipment for sale plus articles on collecting. Subscription rates have been $5 per year.

Photographic Antiques and Literature is a quarterly catalogue of photographic prints, literature and equipment for sale. Very nicely illustrated and prices are reasonable. Send $6 to The Daguerreian Era, Pawlett, Vermont 05761, for a subscription.

Summing Up: Photographica may be a coming thing, but there's no track record to match coins as yet.

RULES FOR PURCHASING ANTIQUES AND COLLECTIBLES

To sum up the rules for accumulating any sort of antique or collectible:

1) Purchase only what you like and in areas in which you will retain interest. I love photography and have already begun to collect photographica. The work involved is personally pleasurable and the task of acquiring some expertise will not be onerous. You should concentrate in areas that *you* like. You may have to hold onto your investment for years to come. You might as well enjoy it.

2) Buy the best you can afford, even if you must accept limited quantities. If possible, purchase from a dealer who will guarantee your purchase price back in the future if you trade in for higher quality. Many dealers in coins, art and antiques will offer such a stipulation.

3) Confine your purchases to items in excellent condition. These always enjoy good resale value.

4) Any piece of any value to speak of should carry a ticket guaranteeing its origin and, in the case of better pieces, its travels over the years.

5) The authenticity of the piece should be guaranteed against a full cash refund.

6) Stick to reliable dealers. They should be members of accredited dealer organizations. The Art and Antique Dealers League of America, Inc. is one such organization.

7) Be prepared for long holding periods. You have to allow time for sufficient markup to cover the difference between wholesale and retail prices, auction commissions, etc. Not all antiques will appreciate rapidly.

8) If you are relatively new at the game, stick to pieces of known and proven worth with a history of regular price appreciation.

9) If you are purchasing graphics for investment, purchase only guaranteed signature pieces of a fixed edition. The dealer should positively guarantee authenticity.

10) Do not be dazzled by mail order promotions sent out to thousands of prospects. Graphic art is often promoted in this manner. The editions are generally much too large to have any real potential.

11) Read the trade journals, visit museums and keep track of what the art critics are saying. Familiarity with coming trends can help you get aboard early.

12) Avoid galleries that price objects of art according to size or that charge equal prices for different works by the same artist. They are exercising little discrimination in how they are stocking works.

13) Try to avoid galleries where salesmen work strictly on commission. Such arrangements encourage pressure tactics.

14) Don't be dazzled by fancy frames or by antique shops with large selections. Such trappings can unduly lead to over-valuation of the piece itself.

15) If possible, buy on approval. Many art and antique dealers allow this. See caveats in coins.

16) Comparison shop. Price spreads between shops can be great. If you are considering a major purchase, consider calling in a professional appraiser.

17) Many antique shops overmark their items to allow for decorator discounts. If you are not a decorator, you should attempt to negotiate a price break. If not, secure a decorator as your purchasing agent, after making a deal to split the discount. This is common practice.

18) Avoid buying into areas which have demonstrated recent and heavy price gains accompanied by wide publicity. Wines during 1973 are one example. After strong gains in 1971 and 1972, the price structure began to weaken with the 1973 crop. Don't ever be last on line. Apply contrary opinion.

19) Pay attention to the prevailing economic climate. A rising stock market often results in extra discretionary income for investors and more likelihood of surplus funds for items such as antiques, etc.

20) At auctions, try to spot the dealers in the crowd. They generally bid inconspicuously but the auctioneer usually knows them. Keep a sharp eye out for the quick glances between the auctioneer and his known customers. It may pay to outbid the dealers. They are planning to pay wholesale prices.

21) In putting in sealed bids, bid what you are ready to pay. Don't expect to get the item cheap.

22) In bidding from the floor, start high! Continued bidding from a low level stirs up crowd interest. A high bid can knock the competition right out of the game before crowd contagion takes hold.

23) In figuring rates of return based on past history, compute the number of years it took for a piece to move from one price level to another. Remember, in moving from $40,000 to $240,000 in 30 years, the British Guiana advanced only about 6% per year.

Go to it. What's to say that you won't pick up the next up-side-down air-mail that comes along?

Chapter 20

"Isn't It Worth A Few Hours Of Study?"

Learn Where To Put Your $10,000

I am always rather amazed at the ease with which stock brokers—or investment advisories for that matter—can get investors to lay out thousands, yes thousands of dollars, on an investment or a hot tip. Usually a phone call or two and the customer is hooked.

Why not try it another way? You've probably worked a long time for your money; no need to just give it away. There are any number of excellent books, periodicals, and advisory letters dealing with the areas of investment outlined in this book. The following is just a sampling. Do look into these arenas further; you have little to risk but a few hours here and there for some interesting reading.

After all, isn't it worth a few hours of study to learn where to put your $10,000?

REAL ESTATE

How To Get Rich In Real Estate by Robert W. Kent, Prentice Hall, Englewood Cliffs, N.J.

How To Buy Recreational Land For Profit by Francis L. Bitney, Prentice Hall, Englewood Cliffs, N.J.

Real Estate Syndicator's Manual and Guide by Martin Hussander, Prentice Hall, Englewood Cliffs, N.J.

Tax Saving Opportunities In Real Estate Deals by Daniel S. Berman and Sheldon Schwartz, Prentice Hall, Englewood Cliffs, N.J.

Double Your Money in Six Years by D. Robert Burleigh, Parker Publishing Co., West Nyack, New York.

THE STOCK MARKET

Books:

Winning Market Systems by Gerald Appel, Signalert Corporation, Great Neck, N.Y.

The Stock Trader's Almanac by Yale Hirsch, The Hirsch Organization, Old Tappan, N.J.

The Profit Magic of Stock Transaction Timing by J.M. Hurst, Prentice Hall, Englewood Cliffs, New Jersey.

Consistent Profits In The Stock Market by Curtise Dahl, Tri-State Offset Co., Cincinnati, Ohio.

A Strategy of Daily Stock Market Timing for Maximum Profit by Joseph E. Granville, Prentice Hall, Englewood Cliffs, N.J.

How To Make Money Selling Stock Options by Robert Asen and R. Scott Asen, Parker Publishing, West Nyack, N.Y.

The Stock Market Indicators by William Gordon, Investors Press, Inc., Palisades Park, N.J.

Bear Markets: How To Survive and Make Money In Them by Harry D. Schultz, Prentice Hall, Englewood Cliffs, N.J.

The Secret of Selecting Stocks for Immediate and Substantial Gains by Larry R. Williams, Conceptual Management, Carmel Valley, California.

How To Select Undervalued Stocks by Robert N. Peisner and Darryl Peisner, E. P. Dutton and Company, New York City, N.Y.

The Art of Low Risk Investing by Michael G. Zahorchak, Van Nostrand Reinhold Company, New York, N.Y.

The 14 Point Method for Beating the Market by William P. O'Connor Jr., Henry Regnery Co., Chicago, Ill.

Technical Analysis of Stock Trends by Robert D. Edwards and John Magee, John Magee, Springfield, Mass.

Stock Market Blueprints by Edward S. Jensen, Strother & Co., Portland, Oregon.

Mutual Funds Almanac, 1973 by Yale Hirsch, The Hirsch Organization, Old Tappan, N.J.

STOCK ADVISORY SERVICES

These are among my favorite stock advisory services. Addresses are listed. Many publishers will send a free sample to inquiries upon request.

The Value Line Investment Survey, 5 E. 44th St., N.Y.C. 10017. Fundamental assessments and reports on over 1,500 stocks updated quarterly.

Growth Stock Outlook, P.O. Box 9911, Chevy Chase, Md. 20015. Fundamental reports on small, rapidly growing companies.

Worden's Weekly Reports, 1915 Florenada Rd., Fort Lauderdale, Florida 33308. Automatic trading signals on monitored stocks and computerized ratings of big money flow into roughly 1,000 securities.

Trade Levels Report, Suite 400, Mutual Savings Bldg., 301 E. Colorado Blvd., Pasadena, California 91101. Computerized ranking of some 5,000 stocks, measuring their technical strength and the amount of money flow entering them.

The Consultant, 3310 N. 24th St., Phoenix, Arizona 85016. A technical trading letter for market investors.

The Professional Tape Reader, P.O. Box 96, Wall St. Station, N.Y.C. 10005. A technical trading letter.

Maxwell's Advance Stockmarket Report, Suite F, E. Badillo, Covina, California 91723. A trading service that uses bond yield data to forecast the direction of the market several weeks in advance.

The Master Indicator, P.O. Box 12706, Las Vegas, Nevada 89112. A trading service that measures large money flows into and out of the stock market.

Technical Trends, Box 228, Chappaqua, N.Y. 10514. A compendium of stock market indicators.

The Professional Investor, P.O. Box 2144, Pompano Beach, Florida 33061. A very educational service, featuring a good deal of miscellaneous information, indicator coverage and overviews of what other advisories are saying.

Indicator Digest, Palisades Park, N.J. 07650. An eight page survey of stock market, business and monetary indicators.

The Value Line Convertible Survey, 5 E. 44th St., N.Y.C. 10017. An excellent report on convertible bonds and warrants, including hedge ratios.

Mutual Funds Scoreboard, 6 Deer Trail, Old Tappan, N.J. 07675. Rankings of mutual fund performance.

The Powell Monetary Analyst, 63 Wall St., N.Y.C. 10005. Concentrates on gold, gold coins, silver and precious metal securities.

The Forecaster, 19623 Ventura Blvd., Tarzana, California 91356. Specializes in monetary matters and general economic commentary.

Systems and Forecasts, P.O. Box 1227, Old Village Station, Great Neck, N.Y. 11023. My own service. Sophisticated hedge maneuvers, convertible bonds, trading tactics, market commentary and miscellaneous information.

NUMISMATICS

Guide Book of United States Coins by R. S. Yeoman, Western Publishing Co., Racine, Wisconsin, $2.50.

A Guide to the Grading of United States Coins by Martin R. Brown and John W. Dunn,

Western Publishing Co., Racine, Wisconsin, $3.00.
Historic Gold Coins of the World by Burton Habson, Doubleday, Garden City, N.Y. 11530
How To Invest In Gold Coins by Donald J. Hoppe, Arlington House, New Rochelle, N.Y.
Encyclopedia of U.S. Coins by Mort Reed, Henry Regnery Co., Chicago, Ill. $10.00.

Publications & Newsletters:

Many of these publications will send a free sample upon request.
Coinage Magazine, 16250 Ventura Blvd., Encine, California, 91316.
Coin World, P.O. Box 150, Sidney, Ohio 45365.
Coin Investing Communique, P.O. Box 265, Carlsbad, California 92008.
World Coins, P.O. Box 150, Sidney, Ohio 45365.

PHILATELY

Basic Knowledge for the Stamp Collector by Sid Pietzch, Linn's Stamp News, Sidney, Ohio.
The Dictionary of Stamps in Color, by James A. Mackay, Mac Millan Publishing Co.,N.Y., N.Y.
United States Specialized Catalogue, Scott Publishing Co., Omaha, Nebraska.
Scott's Standard Postage Stamp Catalogue, Scott Publishing Co., Omaha, Nebraska.

PRECIOUS METALS

Gold–How and Where To Buy and Hold It by Franz Pick, Pick Publishing Corp., N.Y., N.Y.
Silver–How and Where To Buy and Hold It by Franz Pick, Pick Publishing Corp., N.Y., N.Y.
How You Can Profit From the Coming Devaluation by Harry Browne, Arlington House, New Rochelle, N.Y.

ART

Graphic Art in the 20th Century by Wolf Stubbe, Praeger, N.Y., N.Y.
How To Identify Prints, Bell & Sons, Ltd., London, England.
Encyclopedia of Modern Art Auction Prices by Michele Berard, Arco Publishing, N.Y., N.Y.
Art As An Investment by Richard H. Rush, Bonanza Books, N.Y., N.Y.

Investment Newsletters and Publications:

Art News, 750 Third Ave., N.Y., N.Y. 10017
Art Investment Report, 54 Wall St., N.Y., N.Y. 10005.
The Print Collector's Newsletter, 205 E. 78th St., N.Y., N.Y. 10021

POLITICAL CAMPAIGN BUTTONS

The Illustrated Political Button Book by Dick Bristow, Dick Bristow Publications, Box 1741, Santa Cruz, California 95060.
The 1972 Presidential Campaign in Buttons by Tom French, Political Collector Publications, Box 80816, San Diego, California 92138.

WINES

The World Atlas of Wine by Hugh Johnson, Simon and Schuster, N.Y., N.Y.
The First Book of Wine by Alexis Bespaloff, World Publishing, N.Y., N.Y.
Encyclopedia of Wine and Spirits by Alexis Lichine, Alfred A. Knopf, N.Y., N.Y.
Wines of France by Alexis Lichine, Alfred A. Knopf, N.Y., N.Y.

AUTOGRAPHS

Collecting Autographs and Manuscripts by Charles Hamilton, University of Oklahoma Press, Norman, Oklahoma.
Autographs: A Key to Collecting by Mary A. Benjamin, Walter R. Benjamin Autographs, N.Y., N.Y.

ANTIQUES

The Complete Antiques Price List by Ralph and Terry Kovel, Crown Publishers, N.Y., N.Y.
Antiques As An Investment by Richard H. Rush, Bonanza Books, N.Y., N.Y.
The New York Times Book of Antiques by Marvin D. Schwartz, Quadrangle Books, N.Y., N.Y.
The Antique Buyer's Dictionary of Names by A. W. Coysh, Praeger, N.Y., N.Y.
Collecting Antiques in America by Thomas H. Ormsbee, Deerfield Books, N.Y., N.Y.
Chinese Jade of Five Centuries by Joan M. Hastman, Charles E. Tuttle Co., Rutland, Vermont.
Jade: Stone of Heaven by Richard Gump, Doubleday, Garden City, N.Y.

SCOTCH WHISKEY

Scotch Whiskey, published annually by Roger Mortimer & Co., 241 Salisbury House, London Wall, London, E.C.†, England.
World Whiskey Market 1965-1976, published annually by Economic Associates Ltd., 34 Upper Brook St., London, W2Y 1PE, England.
Wine & Spirit Trade International Yearbook, published by "Harpers Wine & Spirit Gazette", Gitlow House, 5 Winsley St., London W1A 2HG, England.
Prospectus: Accrued Equities Inc., 122 E. 42 St., N.Y., N.Y. 10017

MISCELLANEOUS

The Capitalist Reporter, 150 Fifth Ave., N.Y., N.Y. 10011. Diverse suggestions regarding various arenas of investment.
The Investing Professional, 488 Madison Ave., N.Y., N.Y. A closed circulation publication relating to several areas of investment. Subscriptions available for $20.00 per year.
Money, Rockefeller Center, N.Y., N.Y. 10020. $15 a year. Covers many areas of investment and financial interest.
Select Information Exchange, Box 770, Wall St. Station, N.Y., N.Y. 10005. Offers a diverse sampling of investment letters at very moderate cost. Write for their catalogue.

Chapter 21

"These Ploys Won't Make You Rich, But They Ought To Put At Least A Few Extra Bills In Your Pocket."

How To Make Money Without Really Trying

This chapter was written to make sure that each and every reader gets his money's worth. To start with, I'm willing to make one concession—not everybody will find the investment of his dreams in these pages. You, for instance, may not be tempted in the slightest by whiskey, wine, land, bonds, C.D.'s, stocks, coins, antiques, or even had I chosen to write it up, investment in a German bordello (featured in *Barron's* last year, so don't snicker). But, and I'm sure you'll grant me this much, if you have purchased "How To Double. . .," you must be holding an amount of money some place—in the bank, your checkbook, maybe even in your mattress. And I do want you to see the price of this book back somehow. So, let's consider some miscellaneous ways to save and make money without really trying, any one of which should be worth the price of this book to you at some point in the very near future. (Seriously do consider some of the ideas below. More than likely you will be investing, but at least some of the time you will be holding money in the bank. You might as well make the most of it while it's there).

A COUPLE OF WAYS TO OUTPLOY YOUR STOCK BROKER

Yes, I know. This violates one concession already. We'll have to presume that you're in the stock market in one manner or another.

There is a way to maintain complete, one-hundred percent liquidity of at least half your stock market money without paying exorbitant margin costs. Many investors purchase stocks on margin in order to make use of the increased leverage involved. They do so even though funds are also maintained by them in a savings account–set aside, and properly so, foı emergencies, vacations, education and so forth. Finances are managed in this manner despite the fact that brokerages have charged up to 12%, and more at times, for margin interest costs, while investors are receiving only 5% at the bank for money that could have gone into that same margin account to reduce or eliminate those debit balances altogether.

Now, if you purchase a listed, marginable security for cash, you can always borrow an amount from the brokerage on the securities, the amount determined by current margin regulations and the current value of the securities. On January 2, 1974, the Federal Reserve Board lowered stock margin requirements to 50%. That means that you were allowed by the Fed to acquire marginable securities by depositing only 50% of the purchase price, borrowing the remainder from your broker. It also means that you can pay cash for these securities at purchase and receive, if need be, 50% of their value back in cash from your broker at some future date, your securities going on margin at that time. Suppose you had set aside $2,000 to invest and $2,000 to save. By depositing the $4,000 as a full cash purchase, you save the interest differential between what you pay in margin interest costs and what you receive from your bank account. If need be, you still have access to the $2,000 you set aside.

Handle the maneuver in the following manner. Establish a margin account. When you receive your statement, pay the $2,000 as required for a fully margined position. Simultaneously, or the next day, send in another $2,000, stipulating that it should be kept separately in your miscellaneous account, and not applied to the payment of the securities you just purchased. The fact that your money is on deposit will remove your net debit to your brokerage house. Most houses will apply the funds in your miscellaneous account as a credit against your debit, and you will incur no margin costs. At the same time, you will always have full access to those funds should you need them, so long as you make no further security purchases. You have, in effect, maintained your liquidity and saved yourself some interest at the same time. On a $5,000 margin debit, this ploy could easily save you 5% per year, or $250.

SHOP AROUND, AND NEGOTIATE

Many investors are not aware that rates charged for margin interest vary from brokerage to brokerage, and from customer to customer. Differentials can range up to 1% and more, or to $100 per year for an account that maintains an average debit balance of $10,000 over the course of a year. Unless you have a passion for your registered rep, either shop around—or threaten to. You may, in the one case, find a house that charges less, and/or in the second case, secure a preferential rate, lower rates given by brokerage houses to active or large accounts.

In many houses, your rep can plead for lower rates for you as an alternative to losing the account. Your bargaining power may be greater if you can act in concert with a group of investors, either offering to place or to withdraw accounts unless you receive preferential rates.

Do not take margin costs lying down. Brokers have been hungry for customers; you can and should have some say in the matter.

HOW TO RECEIVE INTEREST ON CASH BALANCES LEFT IN BROKERAGE ACCOUNTS

Well, not exactly, to be precise, but close.

Brokerage houses generally pay either no or very niggardly interest on cash balances left in the account, though they charge by the day for money you owe to them. The best policy is to never keep cash at your brokerage. If you operate a cash account, demand to have your surplus sent to you as soon as possible, and pay, when you make a purchase, on the last day permissable by law. Even at 5%, a month's interest in your savings account means more than $40 to you per $10,000; there's no reason whatsoever to let your broker have tnat money.

Suppose, however, that you prefer to keep your money at the broker—let's assume that you are an in and out or occasional trader. Consider this possibility. Put your money in Treasury notes, and deposit the notes in your account. The notes will return better interest than a savings account. If you do require buying power for a trade, you can margin those notes for up to 95% of their value, therefore having almost 100% buying power for a trade on money that is drawing interest for you the rest of the time. When you close out the trade, you still are receiving interest on the notes, and you pay margin costs only for the time that you owe against those notes.

Do try to project the proportion of time you will be invested against the proportion of time you expect to be in cash. This technique pays only if you are normally in cash for a good deal of time; otherwise margin interest costs can eat up the gain, and then some.

As an alternative, consider moving into Treasury notes whenever you develop a cash surplus. If you can buy ir quantity, commissions are very low—less than $2.50 per note at many houses—and you can draw interest on your money while awaiting your next investment opportunity.

DON'T GIVE AMERICAN EXPRESS YOUR MONEY! YOU CAN GET FREE TRAVELER'S CHECKS

Traveler's checks are another rip-off. You're whacked two ways. First off, you pay generally at least $1 per hundred, or 1%. Second, since you usually buy in advance, you lose interest on your cash, which you lay quiescent by buying traveler's checks even before you actually spend the money. A European trip for four can easily cost $4,000 nowadays—that's $40 blown to American Express, not to mention lost interest.

Consider, instead, the traveler's checks issued by Barclay's Bank of England, branches in New York City, Chicago and California. You pay no charges at all on these checks and they are accepted throughout the world. Only drawback: you have to secure them in person at Barclay's, no mail orders accepted.

HOW TO EARN INTEREST ON YOUR VACATION MONEY, EVEN AFTER YOU'VE SPENT IT

Even better than Barclay's are your Master Charge or American Express cards—not to mention those other credit cards you tote around.

Get into the habit of charging your vacation as you go along, wherever and whenever possible. I'm writing this chapter just after a trip to Disney World, and I found that the restaurants at the hotels, and the hotels themselves, were more than happy to honor credit cards. That means I don't get billed for perhaps another couple of weeks with another few weeks on top of that to make interest-free payment (more about this below). In the meantime, that means fewer traveler's checks, less cash to lose, and my money drawing interest for me all that time until I have to pay.

All told, on this trip alone, I'll draw 5% savings interest for about five extra weeks *after I have spent the $1,500 trip cost.* That's another $7.50 in my pocket, rather than someone else's.

You can do even better on European or other overseas jaunts. It can take *months* before you are even billed, and the amounts can be that much greater. Suppose you are able to charge $2,000 on credit cards throughout your trip. More convenience, less risk, less numbers to keep track of, and let's figure conservatively three months delay before you have to pay. At 5%, that's another $25 in your pocket—free and clear—more than the cost of this book already. It's certainly a simple enough habit to acquire.

By the way, just in case you do insist upon American Express traveler's checks and your bank offers a springtime special, say $500 in traveler's checks for only a $2 cost. Let's suppose you consider buying on April 1 for an August 1 trip. Well, you save $3 on the checks, but you lose four months interest on your $500, or at 5%, $8.33. Does it pay to lose $8.33 to save $3? Need I say more? You can see why the bank makes the offer. Someone's going to have free use of your money for four months, and they'll be earning the return you should be receiving.

HOW TO RECEIVE INTEREST ON MONEY YOU'VE BORROWED

While we're on the subject of credit cards, don't overlook the hidden benefits of making as many purchases as possible on your credit card rather than for cash. You probably already have, or can readily secure, a myriad assortment, including oil company credit cards, Master Charge, American Express, BankAmericard and Diner's Club. Between the lot of them, you hardly ever have to pay cash. Let's suppose that you typically spend $200 per week on expenses that could otherwise be charged on one or the other of these credit cards. First off, there is a gap of time, again, between your purchase and the time you are billed, and after that, you have usually about 25 days to pay without interest expense. Why not put the cash in a day of deposit to day of withdrawal interest paying bank account instead? When the time comes to pay up, withdraw the money and pay. In the meantime, you've collected interest on money you have borrowed and already spent.

IF YOU REALLY WANT TO PLAY THE CREDIT CARD GAME FOR KEEPS

Try this maneuver. First, accumulate an arsenal of credit cards. It is possible, you know, for you to own an assortment of Master Charge cards or an assortment of BankAmericards. Just pick up different cards from different banks (each bank issues its own). Each of your cards will have its own billing date. When you make a purchase, you will not be billed until the billing date and you have 25 days thereafter to pay, interest free. Use, each week, the card which provides *the furthest billing date,* setting aside in a day of deposit to day of withdrawal account, the funds you have "spent." In this manner, you should be able to set aside nearly eight weeks worth of money before you ever have to make a payment. At $200 per week, that's $1,600. On the ninth week, you use the money normally earmarked by you for cash payments to pay the first bill due, and you continue to do the same in subsequent weeks. In effect, you will have established a permanent $1,600 loan which can be carried indefinitely, interest free, while you *collect* interest on the money—in this case better than $80 the first year alone, interest that will continue to compound over the years. That's an infinite return on your money, since that's money you've already spent.

Remember, whether you want to play for keeps or want to just play around, use credit cards whenever possible. By paying a number of bills with one check, you'll be saving on checking costs and picking up extra interest as well.

SOME TAX DEDUCTIONS YOU MAY OR MAY NOT HAVE CONSIDERED

Do you own stocks? If so, have you deducted the cost of your telephone calls to your brokers, the cost of mailing payments, checking costs, subscriptions to financial publications such as *Forbes* and *Barron's,* travel expenses to the brokerage and the costs of any advisory services to which you may subscribe. This book is probably tax deductible. They are all legitimate. Do check it out with your accountant.

HOW TO INCREASE YOUR BANK INTEREST RETURN BY NEARLY 11%

A number of systems have made the rounds lately for increasing your return from savings institutions. Some of these involve complicated maneuvers such as taking your money out of one bank on Friday afternoon (after they've closed the books) and depositing it that evening in another bank (to pick up duplicate interest over the weekends). All much too time consuming for the return, even presuming that the banks don't throw you out eventually, bankbook and all. There are, however, two ploys that may well be worth the trouble.

First, do not keep any sizeable surplus in your checking account, with one exception. A regular checking account (minimum balance required) may prove worthwhile if the savings on checking costs for you are greater than the interest you would receive by keeping the funds in an interest bearing account. But beyond that minimum, get into the habit of depositing your income in a day of deposit to day of withdrawal account. Pay all your bills once each month. At that time, transfer your funds from the savings to the checking account. This process won't result in any time expenditure to speak of, but as a result, you'll be drawing interest each month on money that would otherwise remain unproductive.

A second technique involves the use of two savings accounts, one account with grace days and one day of deposit to day of withdrawal account. Many banks offer grace days, usually per quarter, occasionally per month. This means that if you deposit money on the tenth of the first month of each quarter, it earns interest from the first of the quarter. A day of deposit to day of withdrawal account means that your money earns interest for each and every day it is left on deposit.

With a little effort, you can parlay these variations into an extra 11% interest on your money. Open one of each type of account. Start with your day of deposit to day of withdrawal account, for example, on January 1. On January 10, transfer the money to an acconnt with grace days. Interest will be credited from the first of the month, for the same period of time that you received interest on that same money from the previous account. From January 1 to January 10, you received double interest. At the end of the quarter, return the money to the day of deposit to day of withdrawal account. On April 10, again transfer the funds over.

All told, you will pick up 40 extra days interest per year that way. On a $10,000 account, that can be worth about an extra $55 per annum or 11% extra interest to you, or about $13.75 per transaction. Odds are, you can accomplish the maneuver in just a few minutes. Is it worth the trouble? That's up to you. Would you walk across the street if I offered you $13.75? I would.

ONE TIME IT PAYS TO BORROW FROM A BANK

Suppose you have accumulated $3,000 in your savings account for an automobile, and suppose that you want to buy the car on March 1. Should you withdraw the money from the bank? If you have a day of deposit to day of withdrawal account, yes. If, however, your bank pays interest quarterly, it will probably pay you to take a passbook loan for a month instead. A passbook loan is a bank loan secured by your funds on deposit, the best collateral possible. Since the bank is lending you your own money, interest rates are low, 7 percent typical. If you withdraw the money, you have the whole quarterly interest (at 5% per annum, on a $3,000 amount this would amount to $37.50 for the quarter). In borrowing the $3,000 for one month you will be paying $17.50 in interest–net profit, $20.

WHEN THE SUM OF THE PARTS IS GREATER THAN THE WHOLE

Although the practice has been curtailed recently, many banks still offer free gifts to depositors when new branches are opened, but do be aware of provisos that make you keep the funds on deposit for fourteen months or more. Gifts are generally offered in differing value ranges, depending upon the size of deposit.

Banks are allowed by regulation to spend $10 on a gift for a $5,000 account, $5 for a gift for a $500 account and $2.50 for a gift for a $50 account. Retail value of these gifts is about double the bank's cost, or about $20, $10, and $5 respectively. Don't be misled into making the larger deposits. You can secure better returns by putting the money into two year savings certificates, and you are tying it up anyway.

Your best deal is secured by opening as many $50 accounts as you can–spread among various family members–sometimes even two or more in the same name but with different bankbooks. Each $50 account brings in a gift worth $5 plus 5% in interest. Over a fourteen month period, the total return in value and cash comes to about $7.92 per $50 or nearly a 14% return on your money, which isn't too bad at all.

GENERAL HINTS

It's worth shopping around. Put your money into banks that offer the highest rates of interest. These may vary. All else being equal, pick a bank that compounds daily instead of quarterly, that pays interest at the most frequent intervals, and that offers the best deal in terms of grace periods, at the beginning and at the end of quarters. Some banks around the country now offer free checking and at least one, the Citizens Bank and Trust Company of Park Ridge (Chicago, Illinois) pays interest on checking deposits (by combining the checking and savings accounts–checks are free). When borrowing, compare the true interest rates charged by different banks. You do have a choice. Many banks now offer Keogh plan depositing (see Chapter 1) and long-term accounts yielding near 8%. But again, remember that 8% is peanuts compared to some of the investments we've outlined, so do review the contents of this book once again. Your passbook may not seem so attractive after all.

HOW TO BUILD IN A DISCOUNT AT DEPARTMENT STORES

Many shoppers do not take full advantage of the fact that some department stores charge interest on unpaid bills while some do not, even if charges are paid late. Now, I am not suggesting that anyone rip-off department stores—but, human nature being what it is, we are all late in paying sometime. Why not shop in stores that charge no interest? There will be many occasions each year when that 1½% per month will stay in your pocket rather than theirs.

By charging your purchases at no interest stores, and keeping your money in the bank, you again get to secure some extra interest until it's time to pay.

Incidentally, many stores offer two types of charge accounts, one which costs you interest (with an option for monthly payments) and one, interest free, which requires payment in full within thirty days. Pick the latter. The odds are that nothing will happen but a series of polite letters if you pay within ninety days—and it's all interest free. The money you earn by keeping your cash in the bank as long as possible is a discount you have created for yourself.

WHEN IT CAN REALLY PAY TO TAKE A STRAIGHT LIFE POLICY

A straight or whole life insurance policy actually consists of two parts—the portion which involves insurance itself, and the other portion, which is money you are paying to the insurance company to invest for you. Returns are niggardly, usually about 5% per year. An alternative is simply purchasing term insurance, investing the premium differential yourself. It's easy enough to beat a 5% return—just set up a long-term savings account.

However, let's suppose that you are in a high tax bracket, say 50%. To keep 5%, you have to make 10%. The growth in the cash values of your policy, meantime, are *tax-free,* in effect, a 10% return to you. To see if whole life pays for you, figure how much you would have to make in *pre-tax* dollars to achieve a 5%, after tax, return. The deal just might prove worthwhile after all.

Well, there it is. These ploys won't make you rich—that's for the rest of the book—but they certainly ought to put at least a few extra bills in your pocket.

STOCK MARKET BOOKS AVAILABLE FROM WINDSOR BOOKS

Described below are other investment books which are available from the publisher to help further your investment capabilities. Please remit payment of check or money order with your order to:

Windsor Books
Box 280
Brightwaters, N. Y., 11718

Your order will be filled the same day it is received–however, allow approximately 2-3 weeks for postal delivery.

How I Find Stocks That Double In A Year — by Michael R. Scott

The author describes, in detail, his method for selecting and timing stocks that double in price in a year. Scott's system covers all the areas necessary for rapid capital appreciation. He shows how to select potential doublers, how to time their purchase and several different techniques to decide when to sell out. Scott's system does not require active trading–it seeks out those profit-laden situations that his system indicates are likely to double, triple or quadruple money over a two or three year period.

Not a cheap book, but if you learn to apply the author's techniques, it may be worth many, many times its cost.

Sample Chapter Titles: •How Smart Money Operates •How to Screen the Charts •How to Select the Strongest Stocks • Selecting Issues with Low Capitalization •Timing–With the Scott Method •How to Recognize a Potential Winner • How to Recognize the Buying Stages •The Scott Pricing Formula: 100% Growth Per Year •A Formula for Selling •Timing the Purchase: Two Approaches •Daily Volume as a Guide to Buying •How to Select Low Priced Issues •The Profit Secret of Reverse Splits •Two Approaches to Volume Analysis •How to Detect a Fizzle •Pricing Formula as a Guide to Selling •How to Find Optimum Selling Points

220 pages, Hardcover, $19.95

Jesse Livermore's Methods of Trading in Stocks — by R. D. Wyckoff

Jesse L. Livermore is universally recognized by stock market sophisticates as one of the most fabulous market operators of all time. He started trading securities at fourteen, made his first thousand when still a mere boy, and in the next forty years took several fortunes out of the market.

Mr. Livermore, like most big individual operators, was secretive in all his market activities, and usually maintained absolute silence when questioned about his operations. But he did allow noted publisher, Richard D. Wyckoff, a series of exclusive interviews at a time when Mr. Livermore was the single most formidable factor in the market, and when his reputation was at its zenith.

Now for the first time all the trading wisdom of the fantastic Jesse Livermore obtained in these interviews is available for you in this book.

Sample Chapter Titles: •The Secretive Operator •Solid Investments During Weak Markets •One Sure Way to Succeed in the Market • Livermore's Essentials to Success • He Concentrates On Essentials • How He Interprets the News •How Livermore Reads the Tape •How He Judges the Turning Points •How He Plays the Intermediate Swings •How He Makes His Commitments • Lessons From Successful Operators • How He Limits His Risk • How He Keeps His Capital Turning Over • The Kind of Stocks in Which to Trade •Livermore's Method of Pyramiding

Flexible Cover, $3.00

Stock Market Perspective — by Mark Douglas

Now for the first time this noted Wall Street insider takes you behind the scenes, shows you through the eyes of a professional the ten important economic factors to consider when planning investments . . . how to assimilate and evaluate new trends . . . which factors determine long-term trends, which short-term trends.

You learn how to assess the technical condition of the market . . . what effect short selling has on individual securities . . . the value of charts, and why, in the long run, the chart follower will go broke . . . why studying the tape is often deceptive and dangerous to the uninitiated . . . how to evaluate tips . . . much, much more from the viewpoint of an insider looking out to open your eyes and develop a winning perspective.

Sample Chapter Titles: •The Background–Economic Trends •The Foreground–Securities •The Vogue in Securities •Intangible Factors •Technical Position of the Market •Strength and Weakness in Distribution •Floating Supply •The Short Interest •The Pitfalls of Market Reasoning •When is a "Tip" Good •Obtaining Winning Perspective.

Flexible Cover, $2.00

100 Rules On How To Trade Profitably — by George Seamans

George Seamans' 100 rules are primarily geared for the active intermediate term trader–trades typically several months in duration. This type of trading looks for profits in the 20-40% range on each trade. It requires more work, but for those adept in its methods, it probably represents the fastest means available to multiply capital in the Stock Market. Seamans has been selected by Wall St. professionals as "one of the 21 greatest Wall St. minds of the 20th century." His 100 rules are all stated with explanation of when and how they are applied . . . and, where applicable, the exceptions to the rules are also discussed. These rules represent the essence of trading wisdom not only of Seamans, but all the master stock market operators of the past 100 years. This is truly a classic.

Flexible Cover, $3.00

The Stock Digest Price Rate Test Method to Stock Market Success

by Robert L. Robertson

A unique, virtually mechanical, method of trading in stocks that has enabled the author to win on three out of every four trades in the Stock Market.

The author has discovered that every stock has its own private bear and bull cycle, often entirely independent of what "The Market" is doing. Mr. Robertson's Stock Digest Price Rate Test is a unique timing technique that applied the Law of Cyclic Averages directly to *individual* stocks. It tells you at any given point in time exactly where in its cycle each stock is. It prevents you from buying any stock that does not have its big risk behind it and its big up-move ahead of it.

Because timing is so important a part of this novel system, profits can be built faster than with any other technique we know of–and with a great deal more safety. And, the timing is automatic . . . no difficult decisions, that can hang you up, need be made.

When the technique works–which is most of the time–profits multiply fast. You can often increase your investment by two, three, four times or more in a short period. On those few occasions when the method doesn't work, its built-in "radar" warns you to get out of a position with no, or little loss.

Sample Chapter Titles: • A New Method to Make Money • Conservative Speculation • How to Avoid Unnecessary Risks • The Phenomena of Cycles • The Law of Cyclic Averages • The Stock Digest Price Rate Test • Opportunity–To Make Money • The Cyclic Phenomenal Divergence of Money-Making Mavericks • Phenomenal Price and Volume Divergence • Money Making Mavericks • Chart Example of How to Use Volatility to Make Money • Cats and Dogs Can Be the Most Profitable • Low Priced Stocks • Medium Priced Stocks • High Priced Stocks and Big Blue Chips • The Baby Blue Chips–Stock Market Sleepers • How "Buy" Rated Stocks are Automatically Timed • Technique of Making Money • Accumulating Profitable Stocks • Where and How to Find Buy Rated Stocks • Baby Blue Chips Are Your Best Money Makers • How To Pick a Potential Winner • How Volume Can Help You to Profits • Use Charts to Make Money • How to Spot a "Sleeper" • Distribution–How To Sell.

255 pages, Hardcover, $12.50

Psyche, Sex And Stocks: The Psychodynamic Key To Beating The Market

by Stanley Block, M. D. and Samuel Correnti, Ph. D.

This book, written by a psychiatrist and a clinical psychologist, may be just what you have been waiting for all your life to turn you into a "big" winner in the stock market.

Step by step, in clear, easy-to-understand case histories–one of them most likely will fit you to a "T"–it shows you how to harness those hidden forces that have caused you to cut your profits and take losses when, instead, you should have been letting your fortune build.

The early chapters of this book constitute the major building blocks with which you can develop a more effective, efficient money-making style in order to do "your own real thing" on Wall Street. The second part of the book shows you with case histories how to change your "bad luck" to "good luck." Once you see the dynamics of these simple strategies and devices in action, you're on your way to your own winning investment style. These guidelines, when followed, will absolutely lead you to increased success in the stock market.

This is not just another "how-to-get-rich-quick" book . . . this is the book you have been waiting for. It unlocks the secret to your own personal stock market fortune.

Sample Chapter Titles: • Hidden Forces Behavior and Stock Profits • Harnessing Hidden Forces Can Turn You Into a Winner • Getting At the Roots Of Your Money Tree • Who Determines To Buy Or Sell–You Or Your Moods? • Moods Hold Many Secrets To Your Mind • Sex and Success On Wall Street • Sexual Conflicts • Sexuality Is In the Market To Stay • The Market As An Outlet For Repressed Sexual Conflicts • The Womb of Wall Street and Women's Liberation • Exorcising the Hex by Mastering Your Own Sexual Conflicts • How Does Your Aggression Affect Your Market Style? • Bringing Together Personality and Those Hidden Forces • Reading and Understanding Your Personality "Profile" • Personality As a Key To Investment Behavior • Begin to Catalogue Your Personality • Can "Failures" Succeed In the Market? • The Swinging Non-Conformist • Developing Free Functioning Market Behavior • Childhood Experiences Shape the Investor • Acquired Guilt Feelings Tie You Down • Doing It Yourself: Conscious Tools For Change • Starting To Mold a More Potent Investment Style • Seeing the "Old" Stock Market With New Eyes • Another Tool For Investment Health–De-Identification • Conflict Disclosure–Is a Necessary Tool • Are You Selling Your Stock Or Your Wife? • Freeing Yourself From Day-To-Day Traps • Doing Your Thing On Wall Street • Tooling Up For The Street • Stock Market Killings • The Cunning and Calculating Investor • The Pessimistic and Easily Discouraged Investor • The Bragging and Boisterous Investor • Moody and Unhappy Personality Types Can Be Winners • Pitfalls For "Happy-Go-Lucky" Investor • How Women Can Find Happiness and Success On Wall Street • Cashing-In On Your Mental Assets • Taking a Page from the Gambler's Notebook • Remember Your Environment • Harnessing Time • Developing Your Own Investment Style • Are You a Short Seller? • Is the Over-The-Counter Market For You? • All the Nuances You Need To Consider • Who Should Stay Out of the Market?

247 pages, Hardcover, $9.95